2 ⁰⁰

THE POLITICAL TRADITION OF THE WEST

LONDON : GEOFFREY CUMBERLEGE

OXFORD UNIVERSITY PRESS

THE
POLITICAL TRADITION
OF THE WEST

A Study in the Development
of Modern Liberalism

BY

FREDERICK WATKINS

HARVARD UNIVERSITY PRESS

Cambridge, Massachusetts

1948

TO

CARL J. FRIEDRICH

Contents

Introduction

At the present time most people are aware that liberalism is in the throes of a major crisis. Unfortunately, the full significance of the crisis is less adequately understood. If liberalism were simply an offshoot of laissez-faire capitalism, as some would have us believe, there would be nothing especially disturbing about the possibility that it might prove incapable of coping with the conditions of an increasingly monopolistic world. The only problem would be to relegate it, as rapidly and as painlessly as possible, to the graveyard of outworn political conceptions. But modern liberalism is not in reality the property of a single social group, nor are its adherents confined to the supporters of any one economic system. It is the modern embodiment of all the characteristic traditions of Western politics. If liberalism fails to survive, it will mean the end of the Western political tradition. This lends a more than passing interest to the contemporary crisis.

In view of the narrowly partisan uses to which the term is often put, there might seem to be some difficulty in identifying liberalism with the general problem of Western civilization. In its normal contemporary meaning, however, the word "liberal" embraces all those who believe in the ideals and institutions of constitutional democracy. Social democrats, laissez-faire industrialists, Christian democrats, and other liberal groups, while differing widely in their social and economic objectives, are united in their acceptance of certain political principles. Modern liberalism believes that freedom under law is the proper condition of man, and that the maintenance of that freedom depends on the subordination of government officials to the dictates of independently organized agencies of public opinion. In one form or another, these beliefs have always been the characteristic assumptions of Western politics. Totalitarianism, with its emphasis on self-determining and uncontrolled political authority, is radically opposed to the liberal conception of government. At a time, therefore, when totalitarianism stands as the only alternative to constitutional democracy, the acceptance or rejection of modern liberalism involves nothing less than the acceptance or rejection of the Western political tradition.

Ever since the days of ancient Greece and Rome the concept of freedom under law has been the distinguishing feature of political life in the West. In many highly civilized societies men have tried to achieve social order by ethical rather than by legal means. Through precept and example they have endeavored to create individuals with a highly trained sense of ethical obligation, on the assumption that individuals thus trained could be trusted to rule their fellows on the basis of enlightened discretion, with a minimum of reference to fixed legal rules. This mode of thought stands poles apart from the normal Western habit, which has been to emphasize jurisprudence rather than ethics as the core of politics. The object of most Western thinkers has been to establish a society in which every individual, with a minimum of dependence on the discretionary authority of his rulers, would enjoy the privilege and responsibility of determining his own conduct within a previously defined framework of legal rights and duties. Since law, with its Procrustean generalizations, is at best a clumsy instrument of social action, the result of this emphasis on jurisprudence has been to deprive the West of many of the ethical refinements of other civilizations. Precisely because of its rigidity, on the other hand, the existence of a stable legal order has had the compensating advantage of making life comparatively secure and calculable. Most of the characteristic achievements of the Western world, including its miracles of industrial and bureaucratic organization, are the product of a centuries-long attempt to rationalize human conduct in terms of an effective rule of law. This is the specifically Western contribution to the history of mankind.

Modern liberalism is the secular form of Western civilization. If law is to serve as a reliable check on the acts of public officials, it is necessary that there should be some external agency strong enough to hold those officials to the performance of their legal duties. During the Middle Ages the concept of the rule of law found its primary sanction in the institutions of the Christian religion. Obedience to the law was a duty ordained by God, and enforced by the moral authority of a universal church which claimed the right to hold all secular rulers within the limits of their divinely appointed function. With the advent of the Renaissance and Reformation, however, religious sanctions became increasingly ineffective as a basis for political and social action. The breakdown of religious unity and the rise of secularization deprived the church of the moral authority which had previously enabled it to restrain the discretion of secular rulers. The ensuing growth of state absolutism threatened for a time to destroy the traditional

conception of freedom under law in favor of royal absolutism. In the long run, however, the Western tradition
proved strong enough to outlive the religious sanctions on
which it originally rested. During the centuries which followed the rise of absolute monarchy, the Western world
slowly succeeded in reëstablishing its old habits of
thought and action on purely secular foundations. Natural
law theories arose to unite religiously divided or indifferent men in support of universal norms which, like the
divinely sanctioned laws of an earlier age, would serve
to limit the discretion of otherwise absolute rulers.
Through the growth of parliamentary institutions, and
through the awakening of successive social classes to a
sense of political responsibility, the Western world moved
toward the creation of organized communities of citizens
which, like the organized church-community of medieval
times, acquired moral authority sufficient to control the
operations of many modern states. The history of the
various movements which contributed to this result is
the history of modern liberalism. Through the development of parliamentary democracy as a secular substitute
for the declining political authority of the church, the
concept of freedom under law was able once again to
assume its traditional place as the guiding principle of
Western civilization.

The contemporary crisis is a repetition, on the secular
plane, of the crisis which accompanied the collapse of
Christian unity in the course of the sixteenth century.
When the men of the Renaissance and Reformation lost
confidence in the institutions of the universal church,
royal absolutism threatened for a time to become the
dominant form of Western government. The rise of total-

itarian movements in our own time marks the beginning of a similar withdrawal of confidence from the institutions of constitutional democracy, and points to the possibility of a comparable absolutist reaction. Will parliamentary institutions prove more successful than the medieval church in retaining the allegiance of the Western world? Or will they likewise fail to maintain a generally effective basis for the concept of freedom under law? These are the questions which must lie uppermost in the mind of anyone who is concerned with the problems of contemporary politics.

The importance of the issue points to the need for a careful reassessment of the historic position of modern liberalism. Although the past does not determine the future absolutely, it does much to define and to limit the possibilities of future action. In order to make the most of their remaining opportunities, the supporters of constitutional government should acquaint themselves with the strengths and weaknesses of their inherited system of thought. Insofar as modern liberalism has already succeeded in finding ideal and institutional equivalents for the deeply rooted traditions of Western politics, it is in a strong position to resist the pressure of hostile forces. Insofar as it has failed to do so, it betrays weaknesses which, unless promptly remedied, may be fatal to the existence of Western civilization. The defense and extension of modern liberalism calls, therefore, for a thorough awareness of the traditions on which it has been built, and for a realistic appraisal of those factors in recent historical development which have inhibited its efforts to adapt those traditions to modern conditions. Although constitutional democracy is a comparatively recent phenomenon, its present significance can only be understood in the light of its place in the general history of the Western world. To analyze the problem of modern liberalism from this standpoint is the purpose of the following study.

The Political Tradition
of the West

1

The Origins
of Western Legalism

In its emphasis on the conception of freedom under law, the modern world stands in a direct line of inheritance from ancient Greece and Rome. This is, indeed, the vital point of contact between ancient and modern times, and gives the modern world its genuine claim to be the exponent of an unbroken classical tradition. It is true that nothing in many respects could be farther removed from the present day than the conditions of life in classical antiquity. This makes it all the more important for us to understand the circumstances which attended the birth of Western legalism. In the classical period the Greeks themselves felt that the unique experience of life in the city state had set them apart from other peoples, opening an almost unbridgeable gulf between Greek and barbarian. The difficulties of understanding and communication which beset contemporary Westerners in their contact with other cultures indicate that this peculiarity of the Western mind has never been overcome. No analysis of the problems of contemporary liberalism would be complete without a consideration of the conditions which, at the dawn of its history, did so much to set Western civilization upon its distinctive course of development.

In most parts of the world, the emergence of great civilizations has been effected by bureaucratic means. If a people is to advance beyond the limits of a rather simple culture, it must be able to command material resources sufficient to insure that some at least of its members shall enjoy a degree of wealth and leisure above the level of mere subsistence. If it is to avoid the sterility of narrow provincialism, it must also have military resources sufficient to enable it to participate in the main currents of contemporary life without losing its capacity for self-determination. These requirements can usually be met in no other way than by the establishment of large military empires supported by an efficient bureaucratic machine. By subjecting large numbers of local communities to the rule of a single military authority, and by drawing on the resources of the subject population for the support of a privileged ruling group, imperial conquerors have often succeeded in creating the material conditions for advanced cultural achievement. Thus the advance of civilization has normally been at the expense of local communities, and the problem of government has been to develop a military and bureaucratic organization capable of insuring the maximum exploitation of local resources. The history of China, Egypt, and many other famous centers of civilization bears witness to the efficacy of these means.

The peculiarity of the Greeks and Romans lies in that they were able to achieve a high degree of civilization on a communal rather than on a bureaucratic basis. During the formative period of classical history, city states were the typical form of political organization. Because of the unusual geographic and other features of the Mediterranean world, small and tightly integrated societies were able, under the conditions of military and administrative technique then prevailing, to maintain their local independence and at the same time to participate in the great historic events of the time. It is true that the culture of the city states, like those of the neighboring Asiatic empires, rested in large measure on the exploitation of subject populations. Slavery was everywhere an important factor, and some of the more powerful states, most notably Sparta, were also able to draw upon the resources of nonservile but unenfranchised dependent communities. In comparison, however, with the vast areas and populations controlled by the Asiatic empires, these subject groups were remarkably small, and could be managed without resort to elaborate administrative procedures. By ancient and by modern standards alike, the material basis thus provided for the development of cultural activities was rather narrow. In material luxury none of the city states could bear comparison with the neighboring imperial cultures. But if the wealth of these small communities did not permit the building of pyramids, it sufficed to provide the citizen body with a considerable amount of leisure, and to encourage a high level of cultural achievement.

Because of the peculiar nature of its political development, the ancient world was faced from the beginning with unusual political problems. Whereas organizations like the Asiatic empires had had to concern themselves with questions of large-scale military and bureaucratic organization, the city states were under no similar compulsion. The administrative needs of small communities are relatively simple, and can be met by correspondingly simple means. At the height of its power the city state of Athens, for example, was able to get along with administrative procedures of a rudimentary sort. Public business was so organized that most important functions fell within the competence of ordinary citizens, without the aid of a professional civil service. From the beginning the decisive questions of Greek life tended, therefore, to be political rather than administrative in character. Since the city state was a community of citizens, the maintenance of an effective communal spirit was a matter of supreme importance. If the citizen body maintained its inner loyalty and cohesion, all was well. If it became divided against itself through the conflict of private or class interests, nothing could save it from disaster. To secure a basis for harmonious group action was therefore the crucial problem of ancient politics.

In their attempts to solve this problem, the statesmen of antiquity were unanimous in the belief that law was the only force capable of uniting the city-state community. This was not an original discovery, but a continuation of earlier traditions. Like most primitive peoples, the inhabitants of the ancient world had lived originally in small tribal or local communities governed in accordance with immemorial custom. As usual in such contexts, political power was largely judicial in character. Authority rested in the hands of village or tribal elders who were thought to be especially qualified to apply the traditional rules of social behavior. Unquestioning respect for the customary law was the bond of union between members of the community, and the source of all legitimate power. In most parts of the world, primitive legalism waned with the progress of civilization. Large territorial empires, which seek to unite many different communities with widely varying customs, can hardly hope to establish their authority on a common traditional basis. In the earlier stages of imperial expansion organized power, in the form of efficient military and civilian bureaucracies, must therefore take the place of law as a bond of union among men. No such necessity existed in the case of the city state. Although somewhat larger than the tribal and village communities it replaced, the new political unit differed from its predecessors in degree rather than in kind. With a population so small and homogeneous, there could still be hope of securing unity by legal rather than by bureaucratic means. To expand the concept of law to meet the needs of the city-state community became the guiding preoccupation of classical politics. In this way important elements of primitive legalism were preserved to serve as a basis for the development of Western politics.

In its relation to the problem of law the city state was in a different position, on the other hand, from that of a truly primitive community. Under the relatively static conditions prevailing in most primitive societies, unquestioning adherence to custom may provide an adequate answer to the needs of social life. But the ancient Greeks were an extremely dynamic and progressive people. The creation of the city state itself constituted a break with the tradition of earlier tribal and local groups. Through their vigorous participation in colonization, through their widespread trading interests, and through various other contacts with the changing currents of Mediterranean life, the more important city states were subject to influences which called for constant readjustments of domestic and foreign policy. Interest groups soon discovered that the control of state policy was a matter of life or death. Bitter factional cleavages and open class warfare emerged as a perpetually threatening factor in Greek political life. In the earlier stages of class conflict the attempt could still be made to resolve it by appealing to traditional law. When the lower classes in Athens, for example, lost confidence in the impartiality of aristocratic magistrates judging in accordance with unwritten custom, it was possible to allay their discontent for a time by reducing custom to the form of a written code, known as the Draconian Law. In the long run, however, people who found themselves oppressed by changing social conditions could not be content to abide by the usages of an earlier age. Conscious effort had constantly to be made to devise new institutions to meet new needs. Thus the city state was forced to abandon the primitive view of law as an unquestioned traditional force, and to look upon it as a problem of creative statesmanship, to be solved by the deliberate efforts of men.

The result was to set a pattern decisive not only for ancient Greece, but for the future of Western civilization. Unlike the Chinese and other highly civilized peoples, whose political thought always tended to be ethical rather than legal in character, the Greeks had from the beginning to devote most of their political energies to the creation and enforcement of law. Leaders like Solon, who in the Far East would have been content to mould society by ethical precept and example, found their highest form of usefulness as legislators, restoring harmony to faction-ridden cities by appropriate constitutional innovations. The idea that moral and intellectual leadership is incomplete until it has been embodied in law was thereby fixed in the Greek tradition, achieving its most lasting expression in the political writings of Plato and Aristotle. This idea still continues as a distinguishing feature of the Western world.

Preoccupation with the problem of law expressed itself not only in the careers of outstanding thinkers but also in the lives of ordinary men. In the Greek democracies the making and enforcement of law was a responsibility of the entire citizen body. The citizens of Periclean Athens spent a startlingly large proportion of their time in the work of legislative assemblies, or as members of citizen juries. To some extent even the competition of political parties assumed judicial form. In the attempt to undermine the position of opposition leaders, prosecutions for alleged violations of law became a well-established procedure. For an ambitious newcomer the effective management of such a prosecution was one of the surest roads to political advancement. Few societies have ever gone so far in orienting the lives of its citizens toward legislative and judicial institutions.

The specific institutions of the Greek city state were short-lived, and have no modern parallel. Their importance lies in that they gave the Western world a new political ideal, the ideal of civic freedom. In the course of history most societies have thought that the good life was to be attained by making men the obedient subjects of wise and enlightened rulers. Although the responsibility of the individual for the conduct of his own affairs might be considerable, it was to be exercised only within limits set by the incalculable discretion of higher powers. Nothing could be farther from the attitude of the ancient Greeks. Because of their belief in law as the essential bond of union among men, it was impossible for them to be content with the exercise of purely discretionary authority. The rights and duties of public officials and of private citizens alike were defined by legal provisions which tended, with the passage of time and the improvement of legislative technique, to become increasingly specific. The result was to give men an unusual range of personal freedom and responsibility. Within the known and calculable limits set by law, all citizens were at liberty to seek their own version of the good life, without having to reckon with the discretion of personal rulers. It is true that the scope of legal regulation was comparatively wide. It is also true that, in a society as compact and closely integrated as the ancient city state, informal social pressures sufficed to impose a large measure of conformity. In comparison with the situation of most other peoples, however, the civic freedom of the ancient Greeks was a remarkable achievement. The funeral speech of Pericles is an eloquent expression of the pride which they themselves took in this particular accomplishment. Although the picture of Athenian democracy there presented is no doubt idealized, the ideal itself has been a source of lasting inspiration.

The influence of Greek legalism, far from being confined to the field of politics, affected the general character of Western thought. People whose experience of the intellectual process has been confined within the framework of a single culture are apt to assume that the ways of thinking characteristic of that culture are part of the immutable order of nature. When various civilizations are compared, however, it becomes apparent that styles of thought are hardly less variable than styles of architecture or dress. In their contacts with the Far East, Europeans have been constantly baffled by the necessity of dealing with men whose conduct seemed by Western standards to be hopelessly vague and illogical. The initial reaction was to conclude that Asiatics were people of inferior intelligence. More intimate acquaintance with the achievements of the Oriental civilizations soon demonstrated the absurdity of this view. The real difficulty lay in the fact that the foundations of Western culture were conditioned by the experiences of the ancient city state, while the Far Eastern cultures originated under the conditions of bureaucratic imperialism. Because of the widely different setting in which they arose, intellectual developments in these two areas followed widely divergent paths. Present difficulties of communication between East and West are a result of these divergencies of historic experience.

The characteristic feature of Far Eastern thought is a tendency to avoid sharp logical distinctions, and to emphasize the underlying identity of apparently irreconcilable phenomena. In this it reflects the normal needs of a society held together by ethical rather than by legal bonds. In any sphere of life, such as the field of contemporary labor relations, where the range of accepted legal principles is insufficient to provide a basis for judicial action, the only method of resolving social conflict, without the use of force, is to resort to a process of arbitration and compromise. Under the conditions of bureaucratic and military technique prevailing in early times, the widely extended empires of the Far East generally lacked the power to assert thoroughgoing judicial authority over their subject populations. They had therefore to confine coercive action within a narrow range of particularly vital questions, and to rely on arbitration as the general means of achieving social harmony. By inculcating men with common respect for certain broad ethical principles, like those of the Confucians, they tried to create a basis on which morally respected leaders could eliminate potential conflicts by the use of arbitral methods. Since the art of the arbitrator consists in minimizing rather than emphasizing the differences among men, the best intellectual talents of the Far East were accordingly directed to the avoidance of conceptual clarity. Every experienced orator knows that the best way of evoking unanimous response from a heterogeneous audience is to refer to vague concepts, such as Americanism, which have the advantage of being so unclearly defined that every hearer can approve of them in his own particular way. The fact that exact definition tends to divide rather than to unite men was well known to the sages of the Orient. Experience taught them that the most effective way of accomplishing their mission was to embody their thought in gnomic sayings and allusive anecdotes. All the resources of philosophy converged on the task of showing that the differences to which unenlightened men cling are actually embraced within a higher unity. Thus the distinctive experience of bureaucratic imperialism gave rise to a distinctive pattern of thought which still exerts profound influence over a large part of the human race.

Western thought, on the other hand, has always been litigious in character. Ever since the time of the ancient Greeks it has been dominated by the feeling that logic is the basic weapon for the discovery of truth. To classify reality in terms of a system of clearly defined categories is the essence of the logical process. It is also the basis of all judicial action. The task of the judge, as distinguished from the arbitrator, is to decide whether a given set of facts does or does not fall within the scope of a definite legal principle with definite legal consequences. To achieve the highest possible degree of clarity in the definition of concepts, and the utmost subtlety in the distinguishing of actual cases, is the objective of juristic thought. Because of their intense preoccupation with legal problems, citizens of the ancient city states grew so familiar with this way of thinking that it became second nature to them. In the Socratic dialogues an essentially litigious process of defining categories and distinguishing cases is relied upon as a means to the discovery of philosophic truth. To a modern reader the dangers and weaknesses of the Socratic method are often painfully apparent. By forcing his interlocutor to choose between successive pairs of falsely defined alternatives, the lawyer-like ingenuity of the philosopher often succeeds in evoking the inevitable, "By Zeus, Socrates, you are right!" in support of the most unlikely propositions. Just as the besetting sin of the arbitrator is to stifle real differences in the name of a fictitious unity, the temptation of the jurist is to violate common sense by hair-splitting and unrealistic distinctions. In its amazing triumphs of systematic analysis, and also in its tendency to disruptive logical extremism, the history of Western thought bears witness to its legalistic origins.

The development of the natural sciences, which in recent times has become the most striking feature of Western civilization, is also a direct inheritance from the legalism of classical antiquity. For the ancient Greeks, as for most primitive people, it was natural to look upon the gods as friends and protectors of the communities in which they were worshipped. When the maintenance of law came to be regarded as indispensable to the life of the city state, divine sanction for the welfare of the community took the form of a belief that the gods approved of lawful and disapproved of unlawful action. From this it was only a step to the assumption that the order of the material universe, for which the gods were also responsible, was likewise governed by law rather than by caprice. Greek philosophers accordingly began to look for underlying laws which would explain the observed phenomena of nature. Since the methods of scientific investigation were as yet relatively undeveloped, many of the hypotheses advanced by these early natural scientists were more or less fantastic. The results achieved in many fields were, however, sufficient to show that the basic scientific conception of an observable lawful order was capable of serving as a useful basis for inquiry. Although this point of view was largely submerged in the Middle Ages, it came forward with the revival of Greek studies in the period of the Renaissance to provide the starting point for modern scientific development.

From the political standpoint the most important consequence of the rise of natural science lay in its relation to the development of natural-law concepts. One of the most interesting phases of intellectual history is the way in which hypotheses originally developed in one field of experience are often applied with even greater success to another field, and then return with enhanced prestige to exert fresh influence in the field of their origin. The history of law provides a characteristic example of this recurrent phenomenon. When law first emerged as the primary preoccupation of the city state, the sanctions which supported it were largely religious in character. Oracles and other direct manifestations of the divine will helped to justify the work of great legislators, and obedience to the law appeared as a religious duty. As the older forms of religious belief began to fade with the advance of civilization, the effectiveness of religious sanctions suffered a corresponding decline. Before this decline had proceeded very far, however, the independent prestige of natural science had become so great that it was possible to use it to give the legalistic conception of politics a new and more compelling sanction. In the later stages of Greek intellectual life a considerable amount of energy was devoted to the task of developing a scientific form of jurisprudence. Just as the Greek physicians had made substantial progress in the science of medicine by classifying the various types of human constitution, and defining the laws to be observed in maintaining the health of each, political scientists like Plato and Aristotle proceeded to subject the various types of political constitution to a similar process of classification and analysis. Their purpose was to defend the laws of the city state not merely as religious obligations but as natural conditions which could be violated only at the expense of the health of the community. The methods of natural science were used to provide new sanctions for the maintenance of that lawful order among men from which the natural sciences themselves had derived their original inspiration.

In spite of its striking achievements, however, the Greek experiment in freedom under law was finally unsuccessful. To a large extent this failure was due to the inability of the city state to provide a basis for effective international

order. Law to the ancient Greeks was a strictly civic affair,
a privilege and an obligation limited to the citizens of a
particular community. Even in those cases where a new
colony was founded by members of a single city state, it
was seldom possible within the framework of existing legal
conceptions to provide for the retention of any sort of
common citizenship. In order to maintain joint defense in
the face of barbarian pressure, and to prevent the Greek
world from dissolving into a chaos of mutually warring
states, it was necessary, on the other hand, to discover
forms of leadership transcending state bounds. Through
the efforts of Athens, Sparta, and other powerful cities, a
considerable measure of unity was achieved from time to
time. Because of their unwillingness to extend civic rights
beyond the limits of their own borders, these cities were
able to maintain their hegemony only by the use of
naked power, reducing subject communities to a status of
legal inferiority. In a society long accustomed to regarding
freedom under law as the right of all free men, this type of
dominance could only lead to widespread dissatisfaction
and rebellion. In the absence of any persuasive principle
of legitimacy, the power of no single city was sufficient in
the long run to compel lasting obedience. Thus the history
of ancient Greece resolved itself into a futile conflict of
rival imperialisms. This conflict did not end until the moral
and physical energies of the Greek people had been exhausted.

Even within the limits of the city state, moreover, the
problem of law was never wholly solved. The purpose of
the great legislators was to eliminate class conflict by
devising institutions which would satisfy the minimum
interests of all members of the community. In socially

conservative states like Sparta, political stability was achieved on this basis. Because of their rapidly changing needs, however, the more progressive communities were seldom able to give lasting assent to any given constitutional arrangement. In a society where the entire citizen body was actively engaged in the conduct of government, it was difficult to maintain a clear distinction between legislative and constitutional authority. Public opinion could hardly impose constitutional limits on the conduct of government in a situation where the public itself was directly and continuously engaged in the management of public affairs. When a given interest group gained control over the machinery of the state, there was nothing to prevent it from asserting its power at the expense of its rivals. In the face of uninhibited class legislation, control over the legislature became a matter of life or death for all social classes. The result was an interminable series of civil wars, in which successive groups of citizens wore themselves out in an attempt to impose their interests on the rest of the population. In domestic as well as in foreign affairs, the conditions of Greek life made it difficult to maintain or develop legal standards acceptable to the community as a whole. The ensuing conflict could only end with the collapse of Greek civilization.

The failure of the ancient Greeks to develop a professional legal caste was a secondary but important factor in this process of decay. In societies where trained specialists play a major part in the making and enforcement of law, professional standards may serve even in the midst of change to insure a certain measure of traditional continuity in the development of legal institutions. The unspecialized character of Greek political life deprived it of this resource. In the deliberations of popular assemblies, legislative proposals were introduced and discussed by ordinary citizens, without the benefit of informed advice as to their conformity or lack of conformity with the existing body of law. In the courts citizen juries decided questions of law and fact without the guidance of professionally qualified judges. The resulting obstacles to the maintenance of an effective rule of law are clearly visible in the surviving forensic speeches of Demosthenes and other Attic orators. In the absence of a presiding officer qualified to hold proceedings within the bounds of law or evidence, trials all too easily degenerated into oratorical contests, with victory as the prize for him who showed the most unscrupulous skill in distorting facts and arousing emotions. The rule of law, if it is to be maintained in practice as well as in theory, calls for a high degree of skill and sophistication in the use of legislative and judicial techniques. By its failure to create professional opportunities for the acquiring of such techniques, the Greek city state was precluded from realizing its own ideal of freedom under law.

By the end of the fifth century, the disappointments consequent upon these various weaknesses were already undermining the prestige of Greek legalism. In some cases, disillusionment found expression in an attitude of moral cynicism. When the law, once revered as the foundation of all public morality, appeared as a mere instrument of class warfare, it was natural for many to conclude that power rather than morality was the real basis of politics. The influence of the less reputable Sophists was largely due to the fact that they, as professional teachers of rhetoric and other persuasive arts, were able to promise their pupils increased power and influence by giving them skill in the use and abuse of legal processes. For people like Plato, on the other hand, disillusionment with the current state of affairs led to different but hardly less damaging conclusions. Convinced that the good life could only be achieved on an ethical basis, they devoted themselves to the discovery of universal moral standards unsullied by the imperfections of existing institutions. Although they initially had some hope of using their insight to reform and invigorate the life of the city state, their dream of political influence was uniformly disappointed. The result, in the later stages of political disintegration, was to lead the more advanced thinkers to adopt an attitude of increasing aloofness from the problems of practical politics. Abandoning earlier confidence in the possibility of translating ethics into law, they came to look upon morality as a personal problem, to be achieved by enlightened individuals and private groups in more or less voluntary isolation from the general life of society. Through their efforts no less than through the moral cynicism of others, belief in the essential connection between law and ethics was seriously threatened. One of the most characteristic modes of Western thought was thereby brought in question.

The final bankruptcy of the Greek city state was signalized by the triumph of Macedon. Although the conquest of the East and the establishment of great Hellenistic kingdoms by Alexander and his successors provided new fields for the expansion of Greek culture, the older forms of political life were doomed to extinction. Large bureaucratic empires, whose methods of government owed much to their Asiatic predecessors, became the decisive centers of world power, reducing most of the surviving city states to political insignificance. In the fusion of Eastern and Western elements which marked the Hellenistic age, much that was typically Greek was able to survive. Something of the earlier spirit of Greek legalism remained as a factor in the new synthesis, and might in the long run have proved strong enough to impose a distinctive character on the new imperialism. On the whole it cannot be said, however, that conditions were particularly favorable to the maintenance of legal concepts. The Macedonians, who had assumed political leadership in the Hellenistic world, were still, at the time of their rise to power, a relatively primitive people living under the conditions of tribal monarchy. Since their traditional sense of law had never, like that of the more advanced Greek peoples, been sharpened by the experience of life under city-state conditions, they were in a relatively poor position to serve as interpreters of Greek legalism. Because of the weakness and declining prestige of their own legal institutions, the Greeks themselves were hardly able to insist that the ideal of a legalistically ordered society should be applied to the government of uncomprehending oriental populations. Under these circumstances it is hardly likely that the Western concept of law would long have been able to survive the triumph of Hellenistic monarchy.

This situation was soon remedied by the emergence of Rome as the decisive factor in Mediterranean politics. Although the Romans were an alien people living at the periphery of the Greek world, their experience was akin to that of the Greeks rather than to that of the Macedonians in that their form of political organization had long been that of a typical city state. Their attitude toward the problem of law, having been formed under conditions similar to those prevailing in Greece, was also much the same. In the development of their legal institutions they had been remarkably successful, moreover, in avoiding many of the weaknesses which had undermined the spirit of legalism among the Greeks. The superiority of the Romans in the field of law was responsible in no small measure for their ability to overcome Macedonian and other rivals for mastery of the Mediterranean world. It also made it possible for them, once the Roman Empire had been established, to establish an unusually effective rule of law among the subject populations. Although the Greeks deserve honor as pioneers, it was by the genius and enterprise of the Romans that Western legalism was finally placed on a firm and lasting foundation.

Although Rome was a city state, her attitude toward the problem of citizenship was quite different from that of the Greek communities. When increasing power and population made it possible for her to establish colonies in nearby or distant regions, the colonists did not, like Greeks in a similar situation, have to abandon their original citizenship and assume an independent status. They remained an integral part of the Roman people, belonging to one or another of the various tribes in which all citizens were enrolled, and enjoying all the rights of citizenship. The Roman conception of citizenship was such that full membership in the Roman state might even be extended on occasion to allied cities of non-Roman blood. It is true that, in the absence of representative institutions, active rights of citizenship could only be exercised through personal attendance at the capital, which meant that those living at a distance were practically disenfranchised. But if the colonists were seldom able to assume positive political functions, they continued to live under the laws of Rome. This meant that the legal institutions of a single city state, instead of being confined after the Greek fashion to narrow territorial limits, became a bond of union between the inhabitants of widely scattered communities. In this way the problem of expanding the legal authority of a single city state, a problem so disastrously baffling to the Greeks, was solved to the mutual satisfaction of all concerned. The ultimate success of Rome in overcoming her competitors for the mastery of the Mediterranean world was due not only to the superiority of her military technique, but also to the enlightenment of her colonial policy, which gave her an incomparably large and loyal population to draw upon for the recruitment of her legions. Through this policy the creation of a universal rule of law was for the first time brought within the range of practical possibilities.

In comparison with most of the Greek city states, Rome was also remarkably successful in avoiding the worst extremes of civil conflict. Throughout the decisive period of Roman history, when the foundations of empire were being laid, political authority rested in the hands of a small and compact aristocracy of senatorial families. This ruling group differed from the corresponding social classes of most city states in that its power was based on an unusual talent for effective compromise. When the unity of the community was threatened in the early days by conflicts between patricians and plebeians, the situation was not allowed, as in so many Greek communities, to reach the point of a war of extinction between the contending factions. Instead, the attempt was made to devise a balanced constitutional structure whereby the vital interests of both parties would be effectively guaranteed. Although the patricians did not immediately surrender their preponderant position in the state, they provided for the creation of a new office, the tribunate, which safeguarded the interests of the plebeians by giving them the right to veto all official acts. Through timely recognition of the fact that a free community can exist only if it satisfies the needs of all, and not merely those of a dominant faction, Roman statesmanship laid the basis for a new social harmony which finally led to the disappearance of earlier class lines. It is true that, in the later years of the Republic, there arose new class divisions which could not be overcome. The ensuing civil warfare brought the collapse of republican institutions. These developments did not take place, however, until after the international predominance of Rome had been securely established. In the period of republican greatness, competent outside observers like Polybius were uniformly impressed by the fact that balanced constitutional arrangements had given the Romans a decisive advantage in their struggle for mastery of the Mediterranean world. Modern constitutional theory owes much to the memory of these early experiments in the art of government.

Because of its long-established aristocratic character, the Republic was able to go much farther than any Greek community in the direction of creating a distinct legal profession. Under the conditions of Roman political life, thorough acquaintance with the law was necessary for the performance of official functions. This was especially true of the praetorship, a judicial office through which all aspiring candidates had to pass before going on to serve in the

highest official positions. Since an official career was their
natural ambition, capable members of the senatorial class
were impelled to devote a more than average amount of
time to legal studies. The offer of free legal advice to a
group of grateful clients soon came to be recognized,
moreover, as one of the best ways of building up a following among the electorate, without whose support even the
most distinguished aristocrat could not be named to office.
In the course of time the need for competent legal instruction and counsel produced a class of specialists known as
jurisconsults, men with a reputation for unusual skill and
learning in legal matters. Their prestige became so great
that it was not long before conscientious praetors were
going to them for advice on difficult cases, and coöpting
them as semi-official associates. Thus an increasingly respected body of professional opinion became available to
instruct the ignorance and restrain the abuses of less fully
trained officials. Although the legal profession did not
reach its highest point of formal organization until well
into the imperial period, when its importance was recognized by the founding of law schools and by other marks
of official favor, it was already strong enough in the later
days of the Republic to lend a distinctive character to the
development of Roman institutions.

The influence of trained jurists made it possible for the
Roman law to reach a quite remarkable degree of technical perfection. As members of the advisory councils appointed by judicial magistrates, leaders of the profession
were able to play a direct though unofficial part in the
development of legal institutions. It was they who were
largely responsible for the drafting of the praetorian edict,
a document whereby each new praetor upon entering of-

fice informed the public of the principles and procedures
he intended to apply to the settlement of various types of
cases during his administration. Since the practice of Roman legislation was to leave officials with a considerable
range of freedom in such matters, this provided an excellent opportunity for practical experiment in the use of
methods suggested by professional experience. Although
each praetor was formally free to adopt principles of his
own choosing, there was a natural tendency for the more
successful practices of earlier praetors to be continued by
their successors. Through the accumulation of such prec-
edents a substantial part of the Roman law was gradually
built up. Since this law embodied the cumulative judgment of many generations of experienced jurists, its legal
concepts were characterized by increasing precision and
refinement. A further impulse to expansion and systemati-
zation was found in the writings of juristic scholars, a
branch of literature unknown to the Greeks but highly
developed in the later days of the Roman Republic and
thereafter. The work of systematic codification completed
in the time of Justinian, which gave the Roman law its final
and most influential form, was the fruit of several centuries
of juristic specialization. By its ability to meet the needs
alike of ancient and of modern times, the resulting legal
system proved to be the most successful ever devised.
Most of the credit for this achievement rests with the profession which did so much to guide it in all but the earliest
stages of its evolution.

When Rome became master of the Mediterranean
world, a whole new field lay open to the talents of her
jurists. Although Roman citizenship had been granted to
all Italians by the end of the Republic, the process of ex-

tending similar privileges to other parts of the Empire was comparatively slow, being brought to substantial completion only in the reign of Caracalla. Under existing conceptions it would have been unthinkable to leave the subject peoples without legal rights in their relations with one another or with the Romans. The need for an effective rule of law was recognized and met in characteristically competent fashion. In the later Republican period, when political and economic contacts with other peoples first became a matter of concern, a special judicial officer, known as the peregrine praetor, was assigned to the task of handling cases to which foreigners were a party. Through the usual instrument of the praetorian edict, he and his advisors proceeded to develop a body of law to regulate legal relations between men of different nationalities. This was done in part by taking over elements of the existing Roman law, adapting and simplifying them to meet the needs of people accustomed to different legal traditions, and in part by the application of principles which seemed, in the light of contemporary experience, to be common to the legal thought of all civilized peoples. The Stoics and other later Greek philosophers had previously come to the conclusion that a common sense of justice, based on the common and rationally discoverable needs of human nature itself, was the force underlying all particular systems of legislation. Through the Stoic doctrine of natural law the prestige of Greek science and philosophy mobilized in support of the Roman search for an effective *jus gentium*. Thus the speculative genius of Greek philosophers united with the technical skill of Roman jurists to insure the rapid development of new and generally acceptable legal institutions.

With the final extension of Roman citizenship to all free subjects of the Empire, the ancient conception of freedom under law reached its highest point of development. Although the Greeks had been the first to formulate the ideal of a society of individuals united by legal institutions, they had never been able to make that ideal effective beyond the narrow physical boundaries of a single city state. By turning the natural community of city dwellers into a fictitious community of citizens, the Romans overcame these physical limitations, and made it possible to apply city-state ideas on a universal scale. The result was an imperial system markedly different from anything previously known. To an even greater extent than in the earlier classical period, the subject was regarded as a legally responsible individual, with a substantial range of freedom in the management of his own affairs. In the place of that combination of physical force and moral persuasion used by most imperial authorities for the maintenance of their rule, the Romans looked to law as the essential instrument of social harmony. Although ethical and religious convictions might be a matter of great private importance, the state was not generally disposed to interfere with them as long as they did not encourage men to violate their legal obligations. To a greater extent than ever before it was possible for the inhabitants of a large part of the civilized world to plan their lives with the assurance that the precise range of their guaranteed rights and duties could be calculated in advance. The unexampled prosperity of the early Empire, to which the men of later times looked back as to a golden age, is evidence of the fruitfulness of this conception.

Even in its final manifestation, however, the classical

tradition contained the seeds of dissolution. Although Roman law succeeded to a remarkable degree in placing the relations between private individuals on a legal basis, it proved incapable of imposing a similar pattern upon the activities of government. The administrative needs of a large empire called for the creation of an elaborate bureaucratic apparatus. As the bureaucracy became an increasingly important factor in the life of society, the problem of placing it under legal restraint was ever more vital to the maintenance of an effective rule of law. This problem could not be solved under the conditions which prevailed in the Roman Empire. When the republican system, which once held the activities of magistrates within strict legal limits, proved inadequate to the responsibilities of imperial rule, salvation could be found only by placing unlimited powers in the hands of an emperor. Although the Roman people continued, as in their relations with the earlier magistrates, to be regarded in theory as the source of imperial authority, there were no longer any legitimate channels through which the popular will could show itself in practice. This meant that there was no legal means of holding the emperor and his servants within the bounds of law. Moral sanctions only were available, and in a society which had long been legal rather than ethical in its orientation, moral sanctions were comparatively weak. Under the more tyrannical emperors, grotesque excesses, which in the more successful Asiatic empires might have encountered substantial moral resistance, were indulged in with impunity. Even under the more enlightened rulers, the civil and military bureaucracies tended to go their uncontrolled and uncontrollable way, sucking the Empire dry with their exactions and in-

efficiencies. The collapse of Rome in the face of barbarian
pressure was due in large measure to the internal decay
consequent upon this situation. By this striking event the
failure of the ancient world was finally made manifest.

The bankruptcy of Rome was the product of causes
essentially similar to those which had previously led to the
ruin of Greece. Both societies failed because they could
not find a way to control official action through the operation of organized public opinion. In the Greek democracies government was so much a part of the daily life of all
citizens that public opinion tended to exhaust itself in the
struggle of parties for the direct exercise of public office.
An all-consuming preoccupation with competitive power-
politics made it increasingly difficult to remind men of the
need to subject power itself to legal limitations. Under
the Roman Empire diametrically opposite conditions led
to similar results. Ordinary citizens were so hopelessly remote from the centers of political responsibility that it was
impossible for them to maintain any sort of sustained and
personal interest in public matters. This also left the government free to act without restraint. The maintenance of
an effective balance between these two extremes was beyond the capacity of any ancient people. Because of this
fact, their efforts to create a society based on law were
ultimately unavailing.

But with all its limitations, the classical experiment had
a decisive effect on the course of Western history. During
the long centuries of chaos and impoverishment that followed the collapse of Rome, men never forgot the golden
age of peace and prosperity when the whole civilized
world had submitted to a common rule of law. Even in the
darkest days the hope of reviving these ancient glories

never quite disappeared. When the modern world finally rose upon the ruins of the old it still remained wedded to the legalistic conceptions of the ancient city state. Through the use of new ideas and institutions modern man has tried to solve the ancient problem of establishing freedom under law. The fact that we continue to conceive of society in these terms in a tribute to the enduring influence of classical antiquity upon the Western world.

2

The Rise
of the Christian Church

The event which provided the basis for an effective rule of law, and thus established the definitive form of Western civilization, was the rise of the Christian church. In the ancient world it went without saying that religious and political functions should be united in a single organization. The proper performance of religious rites was one of the chief duties of state officials, and even though private groups were allowed to carry out religious observances of their own, it was always on the assumption that they would do nothing to impair the efficacy of the official cult. The fact that similar conditions have also been characteristic of the Far East and other great centers of civilization would seem to show that this is the simplest and most natural basis for the exercise of political authority. So far as the Western world is concerned, however, this normal pattern disappeared with the advent of Christianity. Unlike other religious sects, the Christians insisted on maintaining a sharp distinction between the things belonging to Caesar and the things belonging to God. Although recognizing the authority of the state in temporal matters, they believed that their own church organization alone had the right to regulate spiritual affairs. Their refusal to participate in official rites made them, alone among religious sects of the time, the object of relentless persecution.

When the failure of that persecution forced the acceptance of Christianity as the official religion of the Roman Empire, the bankruptcy of classical politics was finally made known. From that time onward church and state stood side by side as separate authorities, each claiming the right to regulate a portion of the total life of man. Thus the earlier view of society as a single homogeneous structure was replaced by the radically new ideal of a twofold organization of society. With the possible exception of the concept of law itself, the concept of social dualism has done more than anything else to determine the specific character of Western civilization. No phase of Western politics can be understood without some knowledge of the forces which led to this development.

The peculiarity of the Christian view of life, which lies at the basis of the dualistic concept of society, is due, like the Western idea of law, to the adaptation, within the framework of an advanced civilization, of ways of thought normally confined to primitive peoples. In all parts of the world tribal and local communities have tried to control the mysterious forces of nature by the introduction of appropriate magic rites. Like primitive law, from which it is hardly distinguishable, primitive religion is the product of experience within a small social group, and serves to divide men from, rather than to unite them with, the members of neighboring communities. Thus the emergence of large-scale forms of political organization has normally been accompanied, in the history of religion no less than in the history of law, by a period of radical readjustment. Just as the need for a more comprehensive political authority has generally led to the substitution of bureaucracy for law, the need for a more comprehensive religious consciousness has usually meant the abandonment of primitive religious conceptions. In the case of Christianity, however, the line of development was different. We have seen that the political genius of the Greeks and Romans consisted in their ability to universalize the principles of primitive legalism to meet the needs of a great empire. The religious genius of the Jewish people, which found its most influential expression in Christianity, had similar consequences. By universalizing the principles of primitive religion, the Jews likewise succeeded in incorporating certain important aspects of primitive thought in the religious life of the modern world. This gives them the right to stand beside the Greeks and Romans as the cofounders of Western civilization.

The characteristic feature of primitive religion, as contrasted with the more sophisticated phases of religious thought, lies in its preoccupation with the needs of a specific historical community. The gods of a single tribe or village will have no worshippers if that tribe or village ceases to exist. Since the lives of most primitive peoples are precarious, the essence of religion lies for them in the discovery of supernatural means to insure the preservation of the group. By sacrifices, by the observance of tabus, and by various other procedures, the attempt is made to propitiate the mysterious forces of nature and thus to secure them as friendly champions against other less friendly forces. Magic rituals seek to mitigate the effects of drought and disease. To safeguard the continuity of the race the manifold aspects of family life undergo elaborate regulations. To prevent the group from losing its identity contact with outsiders is prohibited, or canalized within carefully prescribed forms. Although the most widely varying methods have been devised in various times and places for the accomplishment of these ends, a single purpose appears behind the bewildering multiplicity of primitive religious usages. That purpose is to preserve the historic existence of a specific community in the face of all the human and natural forces which might threaten it with extinction.

Valuable as this form of religious consciousness may be for the satisfaction of primitive needs, it is insufficient to support the requirements of the larger forms of political and social organization. No high degree of civilization can exist without the coöperative efforts of a considerable number of men. Such efforts are hardly possible as long as the smallest social groups remain devoted to their own exclusive usages, and recognize no common bond between themselves and their neighbors. Thus the advance of civilization has normally involved a thoroughgoing religious revolution. The only way to achieve religious unity over a considerable area is to persuade men to reject their local gods, or at least to subordinate them to the majesty of a universal god. Monotheism in one form or another has therefore been the foundation of most great cultures.

It is possible, however, to approach monotheism from different directions. Dissimilarities of the various world civilizations correspond in large measure to the different paths followed in their respective attempts to transcend the limitations of primitive religious experience.

In the case of India which, particularly through the agency of Buddhism, has exerted a major influence on the advanced religious thought of most Far Eastern countries, the road to monotheism was found by rejecting the foundations of primitive religion, and replacing them with a radically different view of life. Whereas the purpose of primitive religion was to maintain the physical welfare and historic existence of a specific individual or group, the mission of Buddha and other Indian thinkers was to deny that human history had any meaning whatsoever. The observable events of the material world, which so preoccupy the primitive mind, are nothing more than phases of a great and perpetually recurring cycle, through which all things must pass, and in which all things return. Since every historical event, in all its apparent individuality, has already occurred an infinite number of times in the past, and will occur again an infinite number of times in the future, all forms of historic existence are basically insignificant. The real nature of the universe can be grasped, and the true basis of human happiness be reached, only by breaking through the circle of perpetual recurrence in a life of mystic contemplation. Will and desire, even the desire for organic survival, are the sources of human suffering, and must be overcome by those who would follow the way to the blissful self-annihilation of nirvana. While recognizing that mortal man is a union of body and spirit, the Buddhists teach that the life of the body is at best irrelevant, and at worst a hindrance to the only meaningful form of life, the life of the spirit. In this way the divisive effects of primitive religion are overcome by inviting men to believe that their interest in the specific forms of individual existence are essentially meaningless.

Under the political and social conditions prevailing in the Far East, the message of doctrines like Buddhism was most attractive. This is not to say, of course, that the life of mystic contemplation was ever adopted in a pure form by any considerable number of people. Society could hardly have continued to exist if this had been the case.

But if Buddhism, in common with all advanced religious systems, envisaged a goal beyond the capacities of ordinary men, the goal itself was an object of widespread aspiration. By teaching that all particular beliefs and interests are insignificant in comparison with the universal truth to which all should aspire, it aided rulers in their attempts to establish moral leadership through negotiation and compromise. By showing that the desire for self-assertion is the source of human misery, it helped to reconcile subjects with the inescapable fact that, under the rule of a remote and uncontrollable bureaucratic machine, they could no longer hope to do much in the way of directing their earthly destinies. Thus the resignation inculcated by Buddha and by other Far Eastern mystics was admirably suited to the needs of empires which united men of widely differing traditions and beliefs.

The fact that mysticism is not a peculiarly oriental phenomenon, but a normal human reaction to the conditions of bureaucratic imperialism, is to be learned from the later period of classical antiquity. In the days when individual city states were strong enough to control their own affairs, most men were so fully absorbed in the duties of citizenship that it hardly occurred to them to question the reality or importance of specific individual action. As the practical value of citizenship declined, however, mounting disappointment and frustration soon encouraged the more reflective Greek thinkers to adopt an increasingly mystical point of view. Although Plato himself never wholly despaired of achieving political influence, his distaste for the actual political conditions of his time was already strong enough to convince him that the contemplation of ideal truth was the basis of human happiness, and that a genuine philosopher would turn with reluctance from the life of contemplation to mingle with the affairs of men. He was even attracted by the idea, so basic to the anti-historical position of mysticism, that history is a cycle of perpetual recurrence. In the writings of Plato's later followers these mystical elements were further developed. As the city state dissolved in the bureaucratic empire of Rome, the helplessness of ordinary men led, in much the same way as in the Far East, to a rejection of the visible world in favor of other-worldly compensations. Some found satisfaction within the tradition of Greek philosophy by trying to share the mystical experiences of Plotinus and other Neoplatonists. Others turned to the various mystery religions of the East, which promised their adherents eternal bliss in the after-life. Everywhere the tendency was to deny the importance of worldly affairs, and to emphasize the purely spiritual nature of man. As the political life of the West moved in the oriental direction of bureaucratic imperialism, a correspondingly oriental mysticism seemed for a time to offer the only means of satisfying the religious needs of the Western world.

The prospect of ultimate orientalization was overcome by the triumph of Christianity. It is true that this faith also included elements of mystical withdrawal. Like the mystery religions with which it was competing, it comforted the despair of humanity by denying the final importance of worldly success, and by holding forth the promise of life everlasting. No religion which failed to offer these things would have corresponded with the needs of the time. In the case of Christianity, however, mystical elements were superimposed upon and limited by the basically unmystical traditions of Judaism, of which Christianity itself was an offshoot. To a greater extent than any other people, the Jews were concerned with the spiritual significance of historic existence. Unlike the Indians, who had sought salvation by a one-sided emphasis on the spiritual at the expense of the physical nature of man, they believed that the specific events of history are themselves an indispensable part of God's universal purpose, and that the spiritual duty of man is not to escape from the world of historic accident but to conduct his life on earth in such a way as to further the divine plan. Although Christianity involved a radical modification of the original Judaic position, it never lost faith in the necessity and importance of historic individuality. This was the fact above all others which forced Western civilization, in the face of all difficulties, to move in a direction quite different from that taken by the peoples of the Far East.

The peculiar religious genius of the Jews lay in their ability to combine normally incompatible primitive and universal elements in a single religious system. In its essence early Judaism, like other primitive religions, was a set of rules designed to secure the existence of a particular people against the danger of dissolution. The efficacy of its complex dietary and other regulations in maintaining an effective group consciousness is shown by the fact that, after many centuries of dispersion, large numbers of Jews throughout the world have continued to maintain their separate identity. Unlike most peoples, however, the ancient Hebrews succeeded at a comparatively early period in uniting primitive exclusivism with a passionate aspiration toward universality. Possibly as a result of contact with Egyptian monotheism, they reached the conclusion that their own god was not simply one tribal god among many, but the one true God, and that the law imposed upon their tribe by God was the one true law to be followed by all peoples. Unlike the religious thinkers of India, who sought universal brotherhood through the mutual abandonment of all particular beliefs and interests, they sought to unite men through the universal extension of a specific religious system. In this way they hoped to gain the advantages of monotheism without compromising the practices of their own exclusive faith.

The result of this unusual form of monotheism was to give the Jews an extraordinarily heightened sense of the meaning of history. Under the conditions of primitive society, it is natural to believe that all the events of daily life are a reflection of success or failure in the performance of religious duties. Because of their consciousness as bearers of a universal message, the Jews felt the compulsion of this belief with unique intensity. If their kingdom prospered, it was a sign that God was pleased with the chosen people who had covenanted to reveal His law to all the nations. If their kingdom faltered, it was a sign that they had been unfaithful to the law which they had received in trust for all mankind. Thus the fluctuations of Jewish history acquired supreme importance as a revelation of the controlling spiritual purpose of the universe. As the theme of praise or lamentation for all the prophets, this was the most constant and deeply felt element of Jewish religious experience.

The peculiar tragedy of the Jews lay in the fact that the verdict of history, to which they ascribed such importance, was almost uniformly hostile. This tragedy was inevitable, for nothing could have been less suited than the original Jewish type of monotheism to solve the problem of religious universality. The Mosaic law, with its rigid and minute regulation of all phases of daily life, proved generally repulsive to men brought up in alien traditions. For that reason, efforts to proselytize other peoples, in spite of some successes, were on the whole quite ineffective. Since the Jewish kingdom was at best a small and inconsequential contender among the powers of the Near East, the prospects of spreading the law by imperial conquest were even more remote. Weakness and isolation served, indeed, to safeguard the purity of the law against the contaminating influences which would have come with wider contacts and responsibilities, but this purity was bought at the expense of universal aspirations. As modified and incorporated in the doctrines of Christianity and Islam, the religious conceptions of the Jews were destined to have a profound influence on the course of history. In their original form they could bring the chosen people little more than despair.

Christianity overcame the weakness of Judaism, and thus laid the basis for future triumphs, by reacting against the extreme legalism and historicism of the parent faith. Rejecting all the more detailed provisions of Mosaic law, it appealed to the hope and conscience of all men by maintaining that the observance of a few relatively simple rituals, particularly baptism, and the acceptance of a few broadly conceived moral precepts, most conveniently summarized in the two great commandments, were a sufficient basis for salvation. At the same time it broke the tragic dilemma of Judaism by divorcing the history of the spirit from the history of the rise and fall of kingdoms. By proclaiming that His kingdom was not of this earth, and by maintaining a sharp distinction between the things owed respectively to Caesar and to God, Christ sought to release men from the fetters of history, and to show that there is nothing intrinsically political about the drama of salvation. For many Jews, whose religious thought under the impact of historic failure had long been moving in a similar direction, the Christian message came as a promise of liberation. For non-Jewish inhabitants of the Roman Empire, who were increasingly discontented with the existing state of political society, the message was no less welcome. The result was a rapid process of conversion, which soon brought the God of Israel far more believers than the Judaic law had ever been able to muster.

Rejection of the specifically Judaic interpretation of history did not mean, however, that Christianity followed the mystical religions of the Far East in denying the spiritual reality or importance of the visible world. In this respect the concept of the Messiah was the vital link between the spiritual aspirations of the new religion and the historical preoccupations of the parent faith. For many centuries the prophets of Israel had been looking forward to the coming of a divine ruler who would establish the kingdom of the Jews in a position of everlasting predominance among the nations. The birth of Christ was widely regarded as a fulfillment of these prophecies. Although He disappointed the hopes of many Jews by disclaiming all desire for temporal kingship, His followers never wavered in the conviction that He was indeed the divine person of whom the prophets had spoken. Instead of coming to save the Jews only, the Son of God had appeared on earth for the purpose of saving all mankind.

For the Christians, who held the Messianic conception that the will of God had been revealed once and for all in the unique historic event of the incarnation, acceptance of the mystical position that the visible world is a meaningless scene of perpetual recurrence was no less unthinkable than it would have been for the Jews. The Judaic conception of the supreme spiritual significance of Jewish national history was simply transformed into a belief in the supreme spiritual significance of the universal story of human salvation.

The peculiarity of Christianity lay in its dramatic conception of history. This above all is what distinguished it from the mystical religions of the Far East. In most primitive religions the successive seasons of the agricultural year, the fertility of successive animal generations, and other recurring cycles of nature, have been associated with the birth and resurrection of a god. The mystical conception that all life is an endlessly repeated cycle of death and regeneration is a generalization from this most primitive form of religious experience. The various mystery religions which flourished under the Roman Empire rested on the idea that the recurring death and resurrection of a god, originally regarded as a means of perpetuating the fertility of nature, could also bring initiates the blessings of eternal life. Christianity made use of the same idea, but reinterpreted it in a wholly new direction. According to the Christian view of the universe, life is not a meaningless cycle of recurrence, but a unique and meaningful drama, with a beginning, a middle, and an end. The world was created at a definite moment in the past and will come to an end at a definite moment in the future. At a specific date between these two extremes God appeared on earth, and gave His life once and for all as a sacrifice for the redemption of mankind. From the standpoint of Christianity, therefore, all human history is embraced within a single dramatic sequence of birth, death, and resurrection. The world is a stage where men are given their one and only chance to participate in the drama of salvation. The result was to release humanity from the oppression of perpetual recurrence, and to give it a sense of the unique meaningfulness of individual existence.

Because of their dramatic conception of the nature and destiny of man the Christians, like the Jews before them, had to assume a position of painful responsibility with regard to the problem of history. The life of every individual, like that of the human race, is a short and precious period of time bounded by the irrevocable facts of birth and death. When the drama is brought to its close at the moment of the last judgment, each must render an account of his days on earth, and will be sentenced accordingly to an eternity of bliss or torment. Every individual faces the necessity of making the best possible use of his all-too-brief appearance upon the stage of history, since that appearance constitutes his unique opportunity for salvation. Thus the responsibility of the Jews to bear witness to God's law through their national history was transferred to the life-history of each individual Christian. Every moment of existence had to be transformed and spiritualized by obedience to the divine law of love. For the Christians no less than for the religious thinkers of the Far East, the world of physical necessity and desire appeared as an inevitable source of suffering and temptation. The Christian road to salvation consisted, however, not in renounc-

ing life, but in using it as an occasion for responsible conduct. The idea that suicide is one of the deadliest of sins,
an idea foreign to most religious systems, is an expression
of this particular view of the sanctity of human life. To
accept the gift of animal existence, and to spiritualize it by
a supreme act of religious will, was for the Christians the
ultimate meaning of history. In this way an atmosphere
of dramatic urgency was introduced into the life even of
the humblest among men.

From the beginning the Christian conception of human
nature, with its almost unbearable tension between this-
worldly and other-worldly forces, has been subject to attack from two opposing directions. Most people find it
natural to believe either in the absolute importance of
supernatural values or in the absolute importance of terrestrial existence. The dualistic position of Christianity
has the appearance of a daring paradox, and a paradox is
something against which men naturally rebel. By concentrating on the value of historical existence some Christians have tended, on the one hand, to relapse into a
vaguely ethical materialism, regarding religion as a system
of prudential precepts for the maximization of human
well-being, with no more than a perfunctory reference to
the life hereafter. The temptation to let spiritual interests
disappear in the pursuit of temporal advantage could not
be entirely avoided even in the earlier days of the church,
and has remained a recurring problem ever since. By concentrating on the value of the life hereafter some Christians have tended, on the other hand, to embrace mystical
doctrines which minimize the significance of terrestrial
existence. Absolute withdrawal from the concerns of human life, most strikingly expressed in the practice of

celibacy and of contemplative monasticism, has always appealed to ardent spirits as a means of preparing for the Kingdom of Heaven, and has been repeatedly advocated by mystical extremists as the duty of all true believers. To maintain an effective balance between mystical and historical forces, and thus to preserve the paradoxical view that temporal existence is necessary to spiritual salvation, has always been a difficult problem. The peculiar restlessness and dynamic tension which serves to distinguish Christianity among the great religious systems of the world is a reflection of the difficulties inherent in the Christian view of the dual nature of man.

In order to defend themselves against the rival attractions of mysticism and of materialism the Christians needed a powerful symbol to impress their dualistic conception on the minds of men. The cross provided them with such a symbol. Although many religions had preached the death of a savior-god, it had never occurred to them to emphasize the physical horror of his death, or to adopt an instrument of torture as the distinguishing sign of their faith. For the Christians, however, the significance of the death of God lay in the fact that He who died was not only a God but also a man. By living the life of an ordinary person, and by submitting to all the sufferings to which flesh is heir, God had brought men the message that the pain and humiliation of human existence are things not to be avoided but to be embraced as instruments of the highest spiritual purpose. In order that the divine significance of human suffering might be fully appreciated it was necessary to emphasize the more unpleasant aspects of Christ's life on earth. His poverty and humility were accordingly stressed in accounts of the Christian story, and there were some who even ventured to suggest that He must have been physically hideous, since only thus could He have known the worst evils of the flesh. All else paled into insignificance, however, beside the episode of the crucifixion. In the agony of that day, when Christ not only suffered the worst physical torments of death, but also experienced the spiritual desolation of feeling that God had forsaken Him, the union of the divine and of the human was consummated for all time. To recapture the unique poignancy of that moment, and to make it forever vivid in the minds of men, became a supreme preoccupation of the Christian religion. Artists vied with one another, particularly in the West, to depict the scene in all its horror. The appalling altarpiece of Grünewald, with its livid vision of the crucifixion of an apparently syphilitic Christ, represents the culmination of long centuries of effort to shock men into an acceptance of the Christian view of suffering. To visitors from other culture areas the violence of Christian iconography, with its unparalleled emphasis on scenes of physical torture, is unbearably ugly. Its justification lies in the fact that without such compelling symbols it would never have been possible to shock people into a vivid awareness of the nature of the Christian message.

If the symbol of the cross was to retain its essentially Christian significance it was necessary, however, that the Man who died should be recognized as the one true God. This necessity soon led to the development of an ever more elaborate theology, the crucial point of which lay in the definition and defense of the doctrine of the Trinity. To a civilization dominated by the forms of Greek logic, with its rigid system of mutually exclusive categories, the idea that anyone could be at one and the same time entirely divine and entirely human, or that anything simultaneously and in the same sense could be both three and one, was bound to appear as a paradoxical assault upon the foundations of human reason. Innumerable attempts were made to resolve these logical difficulties by denying either the complete humanity or the complete divinity of Christ. Although the Christians admitted that the doctrine of the Trinity was in the last analysis a mystery, inaccessible to human reason without the aid of revelation, they could not afford to rest their case on grounds of faith alone. A long line of gifted theologians accordingly arose to clarify and defend the Christian position with all the resources of a passionate and subtle dialectic. The extreme, frequently hairsplitting refinement of their reasoning, and the violence of the persecutions they loosed upon those found guilty of the most minute deviations from the orthodox position, have done much to discredit them in the eyes of later and less theologically minded generations. In this case, however, as in so many others, violence was a function of insecurity. The Christian conception of human nature involved a delicate and precarious balance between this-worldly and other-worldly elements. With the slightest exaggeration of either, the whole conception would have fallen to the ground. The skill and ruthlessness with which the early theologians fought against apparently minor deviations succeeded in preserving the balance. This guaranteed the survival of Christianity as a distinctive religion and prepared the way for a correspondingly distinctive development of Western civilization.

Interest in theological orthodoxy soon led to the creation of an elaborate church organization. In the earliest period, when most believers felt that the end of the world was near at hand, the Christian community had been content to exist in small and unassuming congregations loosely associated on the basis of their common faith. A more rigorous form of organization would hardly have been consistent with the simple law of love which primitive Christianity, as a reaction against the legalistic formalism of Judaism, had proclaimed as the necessary and sufficient basis for human life. With the advent of doctrinal controversies, however, a new spirit of legalism began to appear. If the purity of the Christian message could be maintained only by the closest attention to complex theological issues, it followed that there must be some form of organized authority to decide between rival theologians and to protect believers against the dangers of heresy. This need was quickly met. By the reign of Constantine the Great a special class of professional priests had already come into existence, and was available, under the watchful eye of bishops, to guide the spiritual welfare of the faithful. The bishops themselves came together from time to time to participate in regional or universal councils whose decisions were the authoritative source of doctrine. The Christian church, with laws and usages of its own, and with its own particular principles of organization, had taken its place upon the stage of history.

This epoch-making event gave rise to a dualistic form of society, and necessitated a radical reassessment of the scope and nature of politics. Under the monistic conditions of classical antiquity, when the state was the sole agency capable of large-scale social action, participation in the life of the state appeared as the highest duty of public-spirited men. All this was changed with the rise

of the Christian church. A separate ecclesiastical organization now challenged the state monopoly of public functions, and offered an alternative outlet for social aspirations. With regard to the value and importance of the
state there was room for a legitimate difference of opinion
among Christians. Although Augustine might seem to
dismiss it as nothing more than a robber band, the general
view was that political authority should be respected as
a useful and necessary agency designed for the salutary
chastisement of men. All were agreed, however, that the
church was the primary instrument of salvation, and that
other interests should be subordinated to its all-important
mission. In this way the age-old primacy of politics was
suddenly reversed, and the state was reduced to the position of a secondary agency subject to the moral authority
of another organization.

In the eastern half of the Mediterranean world, the
dualistic implications of Christianity were never fully
realized in politics. When Constantine recognized the
new faith as the official religion of the Empire, the church
had not yet had time to acquire effective organization.
In comparison with the highly centralized bureaucratic
monarchy of the later Empire, the ecclesiastical hierarchy
was still weak and decentralized. Since the patriarchs of
several great cities enjoyed a position of equal prestige
and authority, it was impossible for any single person to
speak in the name of a united Christendom. Questions of
general importance could only be settled in universal
councils, where all the patriarchs and bishops joined in
the formulation of Christian doctrine. The difficulty of
achieving swift and decisive action under such circumstances made it easier for the state to intervene in eccle-

siastical affairs than for the church to exert corresponding pressure on the state. In the long run it was not hard, therefore, to transform the church into a reasonably effective instrument of state policy. Although the union of temporal and spiritual authority could never again be as complete as in the days when the emperor himself was worshipped as a god, the rulers of Byzantium, from Constantine onward, were able in large measure to assert themselves as divinely appointed guardians of the spiritual as well as of the temporal interests of mankind. Under these conditions a completely dualistic conception of society could not emerge. The result was to prevent the Byzantine world from sharing in one of the formative experiences of Western civilization. From the social and political, no less than from the religious standpoint, the line of demarcation between the Eastern and the Western church still stands as a barrier to complete freedom of intercourse between Eastern and Western worlds.

With the collapse of the Roman Empire in the West, the Western branch of Christendom found itself in a novel position. The barbarian monarchies which established themselves in this area were weak and primitive organizations, lacking the prestige and self-confidence of ancient legitimacy, and incapable of operating the machinery of complex bureaucracy. The outstanding prestige and authority of Rome among the cities of the West made it possible, on the other hand, for the Western church to achieve a fair measure of centralized direction under the leadership of the Roman bishop. All this involved a complete reversal of the old balance between church and state. Whereas the Byzantine Empire offered the spectacle of a weak and divided ecclesiastical organization faced by a strongly centralized state, the church of Rome was a relatively centralized ecclesiastical organization faced by weak and divided temporal authority. Under these conditions there was every opportunity for society to develop along the lines of Christian dualism, with relatively little danger of intervention on the part of the state.

The breakdown of political authority made it necessary for the Western church to take an active part in the conduct of government. Even in the East, where a numerous and disciplined bureaucracy was still available, the state often found it convenient to entrust deacons and other ecclesiastical officers with public responsibilities, particularly in such matters as the administration of poor relief. In the West a similar tendency showed itself on a more extensive scale. The barbarian rulers who governed in this region were too primitive and rural in their outlook to understand the administrative problems proper to a complex urban society. As the sole remaining representative of the dying Roman order, the church was the only organization which still retained anything of the administrative capacity and experience needed to prevent the world from falling into chaos. Bishops and other ecclesiastical authorities were accordingly forced to step into the breach and assume most of the responsibilities of municipal government. Since the barbarians had come with the idea of appropriating rather than of destroying Roman civilization, they were only too glad to have someone else do the work for which they knew themselves to be so ill-qualified. In this way a large share of the authority of the Roman state fell by default into the hands of the church. While remaining formally the subjects and tributaries of barbarian overlords, substantial territories, including most of the surviving cities, assumed in effect the status of ecclesiastical principalities. In some cases, most notably in the city of Rome itself, even the theory of subordination was abandoned, and the ecclesiastical ruler was able to gain recognition as a full territorial sovereign. In the early and formative stage of its development, therefore, the Western church exercised a wide range of temporal responsibilities. The peculiarities of Western Christianity are in large measure a result of this experience.

One of the more important consequences of this state of affairs was a tendency to minimize the mystical and contemplative elements of religious life. In the Eastern Empire, where the influence of Greek and oriental mysticism was particularly strong, and where the state still stood as an adequate agency of social action, the idea of seeking salvation by absolute withdrawal from earthly responsibilities never ceased to exert a powerful appeal. The hermit became a typical representative of Eastern Christianity. The relative weakness or absence of comparable conditions in the West led to a different line of development. Though hermits and mystics were by no means unknown in this region, primary emphasis was laid on the necessity of spiritualizing rather than of renouncing the realm of ordinary human experience. It is true that the more extreme consequences of this position never gained full acceptance. Calvinist Protestantism, with its horror of monasticism and its emphasis on the spiritual significance of all human vocations, stands as a late and uncharacteristically radical expression of the Western point of view. But even though the West was generally willing to ascribe some spiritual value to the life of contemplative with-drawal, it tried from the beginning to hold this form of religious experience within comparatively narrow limits. The life of the solitary hermit, without being prohibited, was regarded with some suspicion. Although individuals with a particular religious gift might be encouraged to retire from the troubles and temptations of the world to the favoring environment of a monastery, this fact was seldom taken as a justification for abstention from socially useful labor. "Work and pray," the motto of the first great monastic order of the West, is a well-known expression of the spirit of Western monasticism. With the rise of the mendicant and preaching orders in the later Middle Ages, the principle that religion should spiritualize rather than withdraw from the concerns of daily life was even more emphatically expressed. No feature of Western Christianity has been more persistent or distinctive.

For a time it seemed as though the assumption of tem-poral responsibilities might lead to a complete seculariza-tion of the church. The problems and experiences of eccle-siastical rulers were not essentially different from those of contemporary secular princes. This led to a gradual merg-ing of their respective points of view. As the feudal system took shape in the course of the Dark Ages, there was a strong tendency for churchmen to be assimilated within the new governmental structure on the same terms as other local authorities. Bishops as well as barons had to take military measures for the defense of their territories, and some of them even won fame for martial exploits on the field of battle. In a society where inheritance was the normal basis of political authority, the churchmen often tried to perpetuate their authority by making ecclesiastical dignities hereditary within their own families. All this tended to deprive the church of its distinctive character, subjecting it to the normal play of contemporary political forces. Even the papacy became the object of secular ambitions. During the Dark Ages papal elections were largely dominated by the rivalries of the Roman nobility. Prominent families even strove, with occasional temporary success, to establish a hereditary right of succession to the papal office. Under the chaotic conditions which followed the breakdown of the Roman Empire, the ever-difficult and precarious balance between this-worldly and other-worldly interests leaned strongly in the direction of the former. This constituted a serious threat to the maintenance of an effective Christian dualism.

In the later Middle Ages, however, the inherent vitality of the Christian position was demonstrated by the re-emergence of the church as a distinct and independent organization. On the initiative of a powerful line of German kings, whose interest lay in the creation of a Holy Roman Empire, and with the aid of a remarkable group of churchmen, many of whom were associated with the religious revival at Cluny, the ecclesiastical structure of the West underwent drastic reform. The assimilation of churchmen within the ranks of the hereditary nobility was arrested by a determined enforcement of clerical celibacy, and by relentless attacks upon the practice of nepotism. The disintegrating ecclesiastical hierarchy gained fresh unity and discipline through renewed insistence on the supreme authority of the pope. Local churchmen, long accustomed to independence, came under the direction of a centralized bureaucracy armed with inquisitorial powers. The recruitment of this bureaucracy was facilitated by the establishment of the University of Bologna, where a revival of Roman law studies furnished the church an incomparable force of well-trained legal minds. In its later stages the process of centralization was also seconded by the rise of the mendicant orders. As a newly created group of enthusiastic and able churchmen, uncontaminated by involvement in feudal society, the Franciscans and Dominicans owed allegiance to the pope alone. Armed with extensive delegations of papal authority, they above all others could be entrusted with the task of enforcing the will of Rome against the feudalizing and particularistic tendencies of the local clergy. As preaching orders they were also in a position to assume the leadership of a popular religious revival. The reality and extent of that revival was demonstrated in the wave of crusading enthusiasm which occupied the attention of men for several generations, and found lasting commemoration in a series of great cathedrals. By the end of the Middle Ages the independent position of the church had once again been placed on firm foundations. The danger that secularization would destroy the principle of Christian dualism had been temporarily averted.

The revival of the church was so successful, indeed, that the balance of spiritual and temporal forces seemed for a time to be in danger of being upset from the opposite direction. In an age when the greatest temporal sovereigns were able to assert only the most limited and precarious control over their feudal subordinates, the pope was already master of the first great bureaucracy of modern times. Because of its professional recruitment and hierarchical discipline, the ecclesiastical organization was more effective than any existing form of secular administration. From the standpoint of ideological warfare, moreover, the activity of the preaching orders, backed by the prestige of spiritual authority in an age of vigorous faith, gave the papacy a propaganda agency more potent than anything available to the secular authorities. Ideological and administrative factors coincided, therefore, to place the church in a position of unusual advantage with reference to the state. Under the leadership of several able and ambitious popes, of whom Gregory VII was the most notable, this advantage was exploited to the full. The right of the church to control the state in all matters which it felt to be of spiritual importance was asserted in the most uncompromising terms, particularly against the Empire, and was supported by frequent resort to the weapons of excommunication and interdiction. Direct territorial claims of the papacy were substantially enlarged. England and other outlying areas were coerced or persuaded to recognize the pope as their feudal overlord. Thus the church, which had recently been in danger of absorption by the secular order of feudalism now seemed in turn to be on the point of absorbing the secular order within the framework of an absolute theocracy.

This papal threat to the dualistic organization of society was rapidly averted. In the face of increasing pressure, secular rulers began to rally their forces. By a deliberate imitation of the methods so recently used to overcome feudal disintegration within the church they set to work overcoming the feudal disintegration of the state. The concept of an absolute sovereign authority, which the popes had used to override the vested local rights of bishops and abbots, was gradually transferred to the secular world, and used to justify temporal rulers in attacking the vested local rights of feudal lords and chartered cities. The revival of Roman law, with its constant reference to the conditions of an earlier bureaucratic absolutism, helped to support these centralizing tendencies, with the result that secular rulers were soon rivaling the church in their eagerness to establish universities for the encouragement of legal studies. These universities became a major agency for the recruitment of a new class of trained and loyal state servants, who proceeded as delegates of the royal authority to place all other secular authorities under the direction of a centralized bureaucratic machine. In view of the fact that feudalism was more strongly entrenched in the temporal than in the spiritual realm, the bureaucratization of the state was a slower and more troublesome process than the corresponding bureaucratization of the church. The theory and practice of state sovereignty, as contrasted with the ecclesiastical sovereignty of the pope, cannot be said to have been fully established before the sixteenth century, when it found classic formulation in the writings of Bodin. The Holy Roman Empire, exhausted by its long struggles with the papacy, and handicapped by the excessive extent of its territorial claims, never did manage to achieve effective sovereignty and gradually lapsed into insignificance. By the end of the Middle Ages, however, the rulers of certain relatively small and compact kingdoms, like France and England, had already progressed far enough along the road of bureaucratic centralization to be able to offer effective resistance to the more extreme claims of the church. Less than a century after the days of Gregory VII and Urban IV the struggle between France and the papacy concluded with the enforced transference of the

papal court from Rome to Avignon. With this revolutionary event the possibility of a Europe organized according
to the principles of theocratic absolutism disappeared
for all time.

By the end of the Middle Ages, therefore, a dualistic
conception of human society, closely parallel to the dualistic Christian view of human nature, had become the
normal basis of political life in the West. With the negligi-
ble exception of infidels and heretics, every human being
belonged from the time of his birth to two great societies,
each with its own particular range of public responsibilities. The function of the state was to maintain the external conditions of orderly social existence through the
use of coercive power. By providing for the military defense and police regulation of society it sought to preserve
the Christian way of life against all forms of violent interruption. In their capacity as subjects all men were bound
to lend obedience and service in support of these objectives. Important as the activities of the state might be,
however, they were concerned with the execution rather
than with the formulation of policy. To decide upon the
ultimate purposes of human existence, and to direct the
activity of the state toward the accomplishment of those
purposes, was the proper social function of the church. In
their capacity as believers all men were bound to aid the
church in the performance of this function. Everyone had
to do his part toward maintaining an effective moral
pressure on the state. In extreme cases, when temporal
rulers persisted in disregarding the moral instruction of
the church, conscientious Christians, might even have to
renounce their allegiance as subjects and assume the
revolutionary responsibility of founding a new political

order. The people of the Middle Ages believed, in other words, that the state is not a moral end in itself, but an executive agency to be directed and controlled by the organized conscience of society. The idea of making so sharp a distinction between society and government, and of ascribing superior moral authority to social as contrasted with political forms of organization, was unknown in classical antiquity. Its emergence marks the establishment of Western civilization.

The principle of Christian dualism did not, however, impair the legalistic heritage of antiquity. Actually it helped to confirm and strengthen the classical tradition as an element of modern life. Even in the most chaotic period of the Dark Ages, the ancient ideal of a society enjoying freedom under law was never wholly lost. The Roman law itself, in a more or less corrupt form, persisted not only in the form of canon law but also, in many parts of Europe, as the prevailing local custom. With the revival of legal learning it became increasingly influential in the activity of ecclesiastical and secular courts. Even in those fields where Roman law ceased to operate, moreover, respect for the idea of law itself was not essentially diminished. Like most primitive peoples, the barbarian conquerors of Rome had a strong feeling for the sanctity of their own tribal customs, and long continued to apply them in all their primitive rigor. Feudalism, insofar as it laid emphasis on the contractual element in political obligation, was also a powerful factor in the maintenance of a legalistic point of view. At the height of the Middle Ages, therefore, the legalistic tradition of classical antiquity, far from having disappeared, had been reinforced by a fresh infusion of primitive legalism, and was in a position to establish itself more firmly than ever as a feature of Western life.

In ancient times, as we have seen, the absence of an independent arbiter between the individual and the state made it impossible to subject governmental action to effective legal restraints. The establishment of a dualistic form of society removed this difficulty. As the recognized guardian of all moral interests, the church through its own courts exerted immediate jurisdiction over a wide range of legal questions, including such matters as wills and contracts, and was able to enforce that jurisdiction over all, including temporal rulers. As supreme interpreter of the moral law, it also had the authority to superintend and control the secular administration of justice. If a temporal ruler used his position to violate the law of the church, or broke his official oath to render equal justice in accordance with the law of his kingdom, it was the duty of true Christians to protest against and if necessary to overthrow his tyranny. Where governments had once been free to disregard their legal obligations, the organized conscience of society now stood ready to bring the entire range of human action, governmental as well as private, within the rule of law. Christian dualism served, therefore, to reinforce classical legalism. Through the union of these two traditions the unattainable ideal of ancient society finally approached fulfillment.

By the end of the Middle Ages the essential form of Western civilization was firmly established. The ideal of a government ruling within the framework of law, and subject to the moral direction of society, has never since failed to exert a powerful hold on the peoples of the West. Like the Christian conception of human nature, from which it ultimately derives, it is a dangerous and difficult ideal, based on an ever-precarious balance of dualistic forces. Since this balance is dynamic rather than static, it can only be preserved by the most strenuous and unrelenting effort. Christ said that He came bringing not peace but the sword. The peculiar violence and instability of Western history bear witness to the truth of this prediction. During the Middle Ages the dualism of church and state led to practically incessant warfare. In later times, a parallel dualism of society and government has led to parallel disturbances. But if dualism has its obvious costs, it also has its compensations. Out of the tensions of an almost impossible ethic, content neither to accept nor to reject but striving to transform historic reality, Western man has found the energy to make great strides toward the conquest of his physical environment. Stimulated by the nearly hopeless task of achieving order within a dualistic society, he has created forms of government unique in their dynamic capacity to meet changing needs. For better or for worse, the course of Western civilization has been set by the medieval ideal of legalistic dualism. This is the ideal in terms of which it is necessary to judge the achievements of the Western world.

3

The Crisis
of Secularization

The sixteenth and seventeenth centuries mark a turning point in the history of Western civilization. Up to that time the dualism of Western society had rested on the institutions of church and state. In a world where a major part of the energies of men had found expression in religion, it had been possible for the church to compete with secular organizations on terms of substantial equality. With the Renaissance and Reformation the foundations of this traditional dualism were finally destroyed. Increasing numbers of people turned their attention to secular rather than to religious interests, while those who remained faithful to Christianity were weakened by sectarian cleavages. Where the medieval church had stood, therefore, as the spokesman for all men in their capacity as Christians, the churches of later times were able to speak in the name of a limited part of the population only. This left the state, which still claimed the allegiance of all men in their capacity as subjects, as the principal representative of society as a whole. Under these circumstances there could be no hope of relying on the church as an independent check on the power of secular authorities. The progressive secularization of Western civilization made it necessary to reconstruct the bases of social dualism. Ever since the sixteenth century this work of reconstruction has been the primary problem of Western politics.

The first step in the secularization of the West came with the revival of classical learning at the time of the Renaissance. During the Middle Ages artistic and scholarly activities had been a virtual monopoly of the church, and had served to enhance the prestige of ecclesiastical at the expense of secular authorities. Through the efforts of men like St. Thomas Aquinas, a considerable body of ancient literature, in spite of its secular and pagan origins, had been safely incorporated within the Christian tradition. After the fall of Constantinople, however, refugee Greek scholars suddenly appeared on the scene, and brought new treasures of classical learning to the attention of the West. They were welcomed not only by cultivated churchmen but by the laity as well. As a result of the urban development and commercial prosperity of the later Middle Ages, a rich and ambitious middle class had begun to appear in many parts of Europe. Unlike the illiterate feudal lords of earlier days, many of them were highly educated men eager to embrace any opportunity for social and intellectual advancement. Great banking families like the Medici were able and willing to patronize the new learning in rivalry with the church. Ambitious princes also found it desirable to attract distinguished visitors to their courts. For the first time since classical antiquity, therefore, the church ceased to monopolize the fields of art and scholarship. Much of the best work of the Renaissance was done by secular scholars and artists under the encouragement of secular patrons. Widespread admiration for these works inspired men with a new sense of the dignity and inportance of secular life. This sudden shift in the balance of spiritual and temporal interests marks the Renaissance as the true forerunner of the modern age.

The secularizing tendency of the Renaissance was able for a time to proceed virtually without opposition from the ecclesiastical hierarchy. When earlier waves of classical learning had come to Europe the church had been vigorous enough to dominate the movement and adapt it to its own ends. During the Renaissance, however, the spiritual energies of the papacy were at an unusually low ebb. After the long humiliation of the Babylonian captivity, from which it had but recently emerged, the church was sadly conscious of the danger of intervening, even in spiritual matters, in any part of Europe where territorial monarchies, like that of France, were firmly established. The defeat of the Empire had served, on the other hand, to transform Italy into a sort of political vacuum. As one of the larger and more stable political units in a land of fantastically small and disunited tyrannies, the papal state was in a position to put substantial diplomatic and military pressure on its weaker neighbors. This combination of circumstances made it natural for Renaissance popes to concentrate on the temporal power of the papacy, and to work for territorial aggrandizement at the expense of wider spiritual duties. Since their problems and preoccupations, in their capacity as secular rulers, were much the same as those of their secular rivals, it was inevitable that they should become more or less assimilated to the prevailing secular spirit. When a man like Leo X proceeded to patronize some of the greatest artists and scholars of the time, his motives were not essentially different from those of his Medici relatives in Florence. No special effort was made, as in earlier periods, to adapt and reinterpret the new learning from a Christian point of view.

The traditions of Christianity were still too strong, however, to be broken by the impact of Renaissance humanism. It is true that, in the case of certain representatives of the period, the spirit of the Renaissance was almost wholly pagan. But for all their eagerness to exploit the resources of classical art and literature, most of the leading figures of the time continued to draw much of their inspiration from Christianity. It is significant that even in Florence, when the new creative urge was at its height, the eloquence of Savonarola was capable of producing a violent if temporary religious reaction, inspiring the citizens and artists of that Renaissance city to consign their pagan paintings and other worldly treasures to the flames of a public bonfire. Beyond the limits of Italy, where the new learning was slower in taking root, resistance to humanistic paganism was even stronger. Insofar as the achievements of the Renaissance might serve the glory of God, or enhance the innocent decorum and pleasure of life, they were generally acceptable. Insofar as they tended, on the other hand, to distract or alienate men from the performance of their religious duties, they awakened quick hostility. True to the normal Christian habit of oscillating between extremes, the sixteenth century reacted against Renaissance secularism with a fresh outburst of other-worldly enthusiasm. The Protestant Reformation and the Catholic Counter Reformation were the expression of that reaction.

Ordinarily the revival of other-worldly preoccupations would have served, as in preceding crises of Western history, to restore the church to its traditional position as

the equal partner and independent critic of the state. A
few centuries earlier, when the rise of the mendicant
orders led to a comparable outburst of popular religious
enthusiasm, the papacy had managed, after some initial
hesitation, to incorporate the movement within the body
of the church. The fresh religious energy thus generated
was largely responsible for the vigor of Christian civilization in the twelfth and thirteenth centuries. The Protestant Reformation, as the name itself suggests, hoped to
inaugurate a comparable period of purification and re-
newal within the Christian church. After the fashion of
St. Francis and other successful reformers, Luther and his
associates regarded themselves not as rebels against but
as representatives of the established religious tradition.
Although they tended, in their efforts to recapture the
original purity of Christian doctrine, to lay great emphasis on the Bible and on the writings of the early fathers, they had no initial desire to repudiate the basic assumptions of medieval Christianity. Their complaint lay
not against the idea of a Catholic church, but against
the accumulated abuses and corruptions which were for
the time being preventing that church from fulfilling its
proper spiritual functions. Their purpose was to restore
the church to its ancient position as the leading force in a
united Christian commonwealth.

The actual effect of the Reformation proved, however,
to be exactly contrary to the reformers' original intentions.
Because of their preoccupation with the problems of
secular statecraft, the Renaissance popes were slow to
understand the significance of the spiritual crisis impending in the North. To satisfy the minimum demands of the
reformers it would have been necessary for the papacy to

sacrifice many profitable abuses, and to exert itself with the utmost energy for the purification of ecclesiastical and above all of monastic institutions. The Counter Reformation subsequently demonstrated that the church of Rome was still capable of making a powerful reformatory effort. This demonstration, however, did not take place in time to preserve the unity of the church. Convinced by repeated discouragements that they would never be able to make an impression on the secularized Renaissance hierarchy, the Protestants finally decided to break away from Rome. By setting up a reformed ecclesiastical organization of their own they hoped that they would ultimately be able to bring men back to the true faith, reëstablishing the universal church on a newly perfected basis. These hopes proved illusory. Although the Protestants managed to establish themselves in many regions, the unexpected vigor of the Catholic Counter Reformation, led by the crusading enthusiasm of the recently organized Jesuits, prevented a considerable part of the Western world from joining the Protestant movement. In the absence of effective central leadership, moreover, the reformers themselves were soon divided by irreconcilable schisms. Although the original purpose had been to reëstablish the authority of a universal church, the actual result was to weaken ecclesiastical influence by splitting the Christian world into a number of permanently warring factions. This led to a number of unexpected changes in the theory and practice of politics.

In the earlier stages of the Reformation these changes were not especially noticeable. On the problem of social dualism the theoretical position of the leading reformers was similar to that of the medieval church. In this respect there was, to be sure, a certain measure of disagreement between the two main branches of Protestantism. The Lutherans, with their bias toward the mystical aspects of religion, were inclined to upset the Christian balance of this-worldly and other-worldly factors in favor of the latter. To a greater extent than most representatives of Western Christianity, Luther and his followers regarded secular affairs as intrinsically evil, and emphasized cultivation of the inner life as the proper conduct of Christians. The Calvinists, on the other hand, in their preoccupation with the accidents of historic existence, tended to upset the Christian balance in the opposite direction. With their fierce concentration on the duty of acting for the fulfillment of God's kingdom on earth, they approached the spirit of ancient Judaism for which, as shown by their abundant references to Old Testament texts and by their predilection for Hebraic names, they felt a conscious affinity. Their sense of direct responsibility for the spiritualization of history made them much more prone than the Lutherans, or even than the Roman Catholics, to intervene in the conduct of temporal affairs. Where circumstances permitted, as in Calvinist Geneva or in Puritan New England, their preferences clearly lay in the direction of theocratic government. But with all their deviations from the central Christian position, the main bodies of Protestantism never abandoned the old conception of a society based on the dualism of church and state. No matter what institutional relationships might be adopted, Lutherans and Calvinists alike believed that the church was a corporate entity distinct from the state. In its capacity as defender of the all-important spiritual interests of mankind, the church for them, as for medieval

Christians, was the supreme embodiment of moral authority. When church interests were threatened by the state even the Lutherans recognized the duty of protest and, in extreme cases, of resistance. The Calvinists, at least in their later developments, were even more aggressive in censuring political authority. With all its changes of emphasis, therefore, the doctrinal structure of Protestantism envisaged no substantial alteration of the dualistic traditions of Western Christianity.

The actual circumstances under which the Reformation took place were such, however, as to render the church increasingly dependent on the state. Although the message of the reformers made no impression on the authorities of Rome, it found immediate favor with a number of secular princes. Vested ecclesiastical privileges had been one of the more perplexing obstacles faced by Western rulers in their attempts to rationalize the administrative structure of their states. The Reformation, with its promise of radical changes in the organization of the church, was welcomed by many secular princes as an occasion for the elimination of inconvenient ecclesiastical privileges. This was especially true in regions like England or Germany, where the Roman authorities, through the sale of indulgences and other means, had been particularly ruthless in exploiting the resources of the local population. From the beginning, therefore, the reformers found some of their strongest supporters among the territorial princes. When the church condemned the movement as heresy and tried to stamp it out, the protection of men like the Elector of Saxony was all that saved it from extinction. In order to avoid the danger of being persecuted, and in order to enjoy the opportunity of persecuting their opponents, the reformers had no choice but to rely on the military power of friendly rulers. As the struggle with Rome increased in bitterness they had to depend more heavily on the favor of secular authorities, and to make greater concessions in return for that favor. Theoretically they might still recognize the necessity of directing the moral authority of the church against abuses of state power; actually they could not afford to push resistance to the point of alienating their princely protectors. The result was to make the church comparatively ineffective as a counterbalance to the pretensions of secular authority.

Similar circumstances operated at the same time to weaken the position of the Catholic church. In their struggle with the Protestants the adherents of Rome did, to be sure, enjoy a number of real advantages. In the absence of any well-established organs of legitimate authority, the newly formed Protestant churches had difficulty in imposing unity of doctrine or discipline upon their own supporters. Among the Catholics, on the other hand, the disciplinary and doctrinal authority of the papacy was virtually unchallenged. This made it possible for the church of Rome, to a greater extent than its rivals, to mobilize its remaining forces with maximum efficiency. At a time, however, when several different religions were competing for the favor of secular princes, the power even of a revitalized papacy was insufficient to guarantee the survival of Catholicism. The inhabitants of most countries were by this time so divided and confused in their religious sentiments that no single authority could hope to secure the support of a united Christendom. If a secular ruler decided to adopt Protestantism and extirpate the

Catholics, the military power at his disposal, supported by Protestant elements of the population, was generally sufficient to accomplish the desired result in the face even of the strongest protests from Rome. If another ruler decided to adopt Catholicism and extirpate the Protestants, the chances were that he also would be successful. Thus the church of Rome was hardly less dependent than the Protestant churches upon the favor of secular authorities, and like them had to make concessions in order to secure that favor. Although the reduction of church power never went quite so far in Catholic as in Protestant countries, the tendency in both cases was essentially the same.

The immediate consequence of this uneasy relationship between religion and politics was to upset the traditional bases of political order. In regions where a particular religion was favored by the prince, the adherents of that religion had every interest in preaching the duty of absolute obedience to the state. The Anglicans and Lutherans, who found their chief strength in the support of certain temporal rulers, went particularly far in this direction. In most regions there were, on the other hand, substantial numbers of people who could not share the official religion, and who were in consequence liable to persecution. For them the problem of politics was to find a way to overthrow the existing order and to set up a prince of their own persuasion. During the Middle Ages most political theorists had agreed that tyrannical kings, including those who jeopardized the eternal salvation of their subjects by supporting heresy, might legitimately be resisted and even, in extreme cases, put to death by authority of other magistrates of the realm. During the period of religious warfare, these ideas were congenial to the more radical supporters of those faiths which happened, at any given time and place, to be suffering persecution. This was especially true of the Jesuits and of the Calvinists, the most militant exponents respectively of the Catholic and of the Protestant position. Both groups played a leading part in the development of a new school of political theorists known as the Monarchomachs. In their attempts to overcome the power of hostile rulers, these writers made more or less drastic assertions of the proposition that the right to overthrow tyrannical kings was vested in the people. Although their words have a somewhat modern ring, and were later to play some part in the development of modern democratic thought, the people to whom the Monarchomachs referred were not the unorganized masses of the population, but territorial magnates, local parliaments, and other public authorities, among whom the adherents of persecuted faiths were often well-represented. Essentially these theorists were doing little more than to restate the medieval doctrine of tyranny. During the Middle Ages, however, secular rulers had been subject to the discipline of a single church only, and had been safe from the charge of heresy as long as they satisfied its requirements. During the period of the Reformation and Counter Reformation this was no longer true. In countries where the inhabitants were divided between two or more rival churches, the ruler was bound to appear as a heretic in the eyes of many of his subjects. To repeat medieval theories under these conditions was nothing less than an invitation to perpetual disorder.

The invitation was accepted. For more than a hundred

years Western Europe was torn by religious warfare unexampled in its ferocity. In many countries dissenting
religious groups succeeded in arousing their supporters
to bloody revolution against the established government.
Foreign princes of like persuasion frequently intervened
on behalf of their embattled coreligionists. In the heat of
passion the rules of civilized warfare fell by the wayside.
Assassination and massacre became the accepted weapons of religious controversy. In comparison with the all-
consuming importance of placing state authority in the
hands of true believers, no sacrifice seemed too great to
those who felt that their salvation depended on the triumph of their own religious group. Under the cloak of
religious enthusiasm secular greed and ambition also
enjoyed full play. The result was a period of bloody and
lawless chaos. This chaos reached its culmination in the
disaster of the Thirty Years' War, which exterminated
approximately half the population of Central Europe,
and brought ruin to many ancient centers of European
culture. The balance of religious forces was so nearly
even that no single group, however great its exertions,
was able to gain the mastery of a reunited Christendom.
The ensuing stalemate jeopardized the existence of Western civilization.

These circumstances finally led to a complete revulsion
against the traditional view of the relations of church and
state. As the horrors of religious warfare grew more shocking, increasing numbers of people began to look upon all
forms of religious fanaticism as an unbearable evil, and
to yearn for the establishment of state absolutism as the
only means of restoring social order. The belief that religious differences should be compromised for the sake of

political harmony was the distinguishing characteristic
of an influential group of French writers known as the
Politiques. Similar convictions were shared by many
responsible citizens of other nations which had experienced the evils of the times. If established churches could
be persuaded to serve as subsidized and subordinate
instruments of state policy, without upsetting the peace
by sectarian controversies or crusading enthusiasms, they
might still be accepted as a useful bulwark of the established order. If dissenting churches would be content to
exist as private confessional organizations, serving the
needs of their own communicants without insisting on
the right to dictate public policy, they too might be allowed to go their self-appointed ways. Under no conditions, however, should disputatious churchmen be allowed to bring death and destruction by interfering with
the sovereignty of the state. After more than a century of
disaster the political prestige of the church was bankrupt,
leaving behind it a permanent legacy of distrust and hatred. The extraordinary virulence of the anticlericalism
shown by many leaders of the eighteenth-century Enlightenment, and their extreme emphasis on the virtues
of religious tolerance, are a tribute to the depth and
persistence of the impression which the wars of religion
had left upon the minds of men. The memory of that period gave rise to some of the most bitterly conditioned
responses of modern times. After such an experience,
there could never again be any serious question of allowing the church to stand beside the state as an equal partner in the government of Western society.

The triumph of the new spirit was signalized by the
Treaty of Westphalia, which brought the period of re-

ligious warfare to a close by confirming the principle of state sovereignty. The right of secular princes to determine the official religion of their own territories was officially reaffirmed. In the interests of social harmony this right was exercised in an increasingly tolerant spirit, and dissenting religious groups were for the most part permitted to exist as long as they did not seem to threaten the maintenance of public order. Although established churches continued to exercise important public functions, the authority of the prince was now sufficient to prevent them from taking an independent line of action. In Protestant countries the prince himself usually became the official head of the established church, and played a large part in the direction of ecclesiastical affairs. The existence of the papacy made it impossible for Catholic princes to assume a comparable position, but their control of the religious hierarchy was hardly less complete. On the basis of various agreements extorted from the enfeebled Holy See, they acquired far-reaching powers with regard to ecclesiastical appointments and other vital matters of church government. Even the most sincerely Catholic sovereigns had no compunction about using their bargaining position to extract concessions of this sort. Although the clergy might still have considerable influence on the conduct of devout rulers, both Protestant and Catholic, that influence was largely personal in character, and could no longer be enforced by effective social sanctions.

The period of religious warfare was accompanied and followed by an outburst of creative activity in secular affairs. Although Western civilization in the later Middle Ages had already begun, in matters like the invention of the clock and of double-entry bookkeeping, to show something of its inherent gift for technological accomplishment, preoccupation with cathedral building and other religious affairs had diverted many of its energies to other-worldly matters. In the course of the sixteenth and seventeenth centuries, however, those energies turned increasingly to secular objectives. The crusading enthusiasm of Spain and Portugal, developed by centuries of conflict with the recently defeated Moors, found expression in a sudden wave of conquest and exploration which brought the resources of new continents within the grasp of the West, thus laying the foundations for modern imperialism. The Protestant Reformation, by its rejection of monasticism and by its insistence on the religious importance of secular callings, restored thousands of monks and nuns to the world, and endowed them with a passionate determination to work for the greater glory of God by mastering the problems of secular existence. In the period following the wars of religion this preoccupation became much more strongly marked. When the church lost its leading position in society it also lost much of its power to attract the services of able and ambitious men. As religious enthusiasm gave way to mounting indifference, secular careers provided the best outlet for the release of tensions and energies accumulated through centuries of Christian experience. The result was to reinforce the spirit of Renaissance humanism, and to prepare the ground for spectacular achievements in the fields of science and technology. During the Middle Ages Western civilization had been relatively mean and impoverished, unable to bear comparison with the material wealth of other contemporary centers of world culture. By the end of the seven-

teenth century it had already begun to show those peculiar qualities of energy and resourcefulness through which,
without any particular sign of meekness, it was soon to
inherit the earth.

The spirit of secular enterprise found early expression
in the creation of rationalized state bureaucracies. During
the period of religious warfare, when the survival of embattled religious groups depended on the offensive and
defensive power of princely supporters, the problem of
achieving maximum efficiency in the use of military and
other resources became a matter of the highest importance. Much of the religious energy of the time was accordingly devoted to improving military technique and
to rationalizing the financial and administrative procedures needed to supply the sinews of war. With their
passionate determination to insure the triumph of God's
kingdom on earth the Calvinists were particularly successful in this direction, establishing a standard of governmental efficiency which other states could neglect only at
their peril. When the wars of religion came to an end, the
exhaustion of Western society made it necessary that the
resources of the state be applied with no less energy and
determination to the work of reconstruction. Conscientious princes tried to restore and increase the prosperity
of their ravaged territories by doing everything in their
power to encourage commerce and industry. Interest in
these matters led to the development of a new administrative and economic science, associated with the names
mercantilism and cameralism, which sought to direct the
activities of state officials along rational lines for the
accomplishment of the desired objectives. Ambitious and
able men, attracted by the resulting opportunities, were

drawn into the administrative service of princes. By the end of the seventeenth century, therefore, a secure foundation had been laid for the development of those efficient and well-disciplined bureaucracies which constitute the peculiar strength of modern government.

But with all the brilliance of its immediate achievements, the rising power of the state threatened in the long run to destroy the foundations of Western civilization. Now that the church was no longer in a position to check the activity of temporal authorities, the Western world was once again faced with the ancient problem of maintaining an effective rule of law in the face of an all-powerful state bureaucracy. Influential political theorists like Bodin might insist that the authority even of sovereign princes was subject to legal limitation in terms of a traditional constitution. Legal principles have little value, however, unless they are enforced in practice, and it was difficult, under the conditions of contemporary society, to see who would be able to make effective resistance to the unconstitutional action of kings. Respect for constitutional traditions did not prevent the Roman Empire from developing into a full-fledged bureaucratic absolutism. The probability of a similar development was implicit in the political situation of seventeenth-century Europe. Because of their interest in administrative efficiency, energetic monarchs were constantly tempted to violate the inconvenient and frequently anachronistic rights of their subjects. Greed and ambition might also drive them in the same direction. By reference to the absolutist texts of Roman law, which gave practically unlimited scope to the prerogative of princes, it was easy to find legal justification for anything the state might care to do. The result was a rapid growth of royal absolutism which promised for a time to eliminate the rule of law as one of the constituent elements of Western civilization.

To many people this development was not unwelcome. After more than a century of catastrophic disorder the policy of peace at any price was undeniably attractive, and the only way of securing peace seemed to be to make the state so powerful that no dissident group would ever again be strong enough to challenge it. The anarchical condition of Renaissance Italy, reduced to eternal warfare by the strife of republican factions and by the rivalry of petty tyrants, had previously led Machiavelli to adopt a pagan view of politics. Convinced that the creation and maintenance of an effective political order was the highest possible goal of human existence, he was ready to sacrifice any principle of law or morality which seemed to stand in the way of accomplishing that purpose. The protracted agony of civil warfare in England brought Hobbes more than a century later to similar conclusions. In his view, only a sovereign state vested with absolute and unconditional authority could hope to maintain the minimum conditions of orderly human existence. In their outspoken rejection of the idea that political action should be subject to moral and legal restraints, Hobbes and Machiavelli were at variance with the traditional view of Western politics. Since most of their contemporaries were unprepared in theory to make so radical a break with the past, both writers were more generally condemned than praised for their efforts. Many of those who abjured them in theory were prepared, however, to follow them in practice. Embarrassing and unwise as it might be to state the matter publicly, fear and exhaustion had brought most of

Europe to the point where it was willing to accept practically anything from the state in exchange for a bearable
minimum of peace and order. This psychological fact was
the basis of seventeenth-century absolutism.

The tradition of Western dualism was too deeply entrenched, however, to die without a struggle. Although
people tacitly or openly agreed that the church could no
longer be relied upon to guarantee the rule of law, the
possibility still remained that a new and purely secular
form of dualism might be found to replace the old order.
The power of the medieval church had rested on its ability to mobilize the moral consensus of the community
against the military and administrative powers of the
state. Was the community able, on the basis of secular
rather than of religious leadership, to reach an effective
consensus with regard to the conduct of public affairs?
Could that consensus be organized, without reference
to the ecclesiastical hierarchy, in such a way as to control
the conduct of government? These were the questions
raised by the course of seventeenth-century political development. In the form of a distinction between the institutions of church and state Western civilization had
traditionally operated in terms of social dualism. To
preserve that dualism on the basis of purely secular institutions was the problem of modern politics.

In their efforts to solve this problem, the political theorists of the seventeenth century began to lay great emphasis on the concept of natural law. The idea that all
men, in their capacity as rational beings, are capable of
reaching common agreement concerning the methods
and objectives of social life was already well-established
in the tradition of Western politics. Developed in ancient

times, it had been incorporated, along with the more specific doctrines of revealed religion, as an important part of the teachings of the medieval church. When sectarian differences made it impossible to secure substantial agreement with regard to the content of religious revelation, natural law was left as the only available bond of social unity. Responsible political theorists had therefore to rely on it ever more heavily as a means of restraining the abuses of government. In order to mitigate the growing ruthlessness and barbarity of interstate warfare, men like Grotius evolved theories of international law which, being based on the unifying rational consensus of the secular world community rather than on the divisive tenets of revealed religion, could be accepted as equally binding upon the adherents of all religious persuasions. Constitutional theorists like Pufendorf used comparable methods in an attempt to define the internal limits of state action with reference to the rights of subjects. In this way it was hoped that the power of modern governments, though released from the restraints of organized religion, might still be held within bounds by the moral consensus of society.

Emphasis on the law of nature was not in itself sufficient, however, to insure the maintenance of Western dualism. In ancient times the development of similar doctrines, while exerting a good deal of influence on the conduct of conscientious emperors like Marcus Aurelius, had not been able to check the growth of bureaucratic absolutism. The situation of seventeenth-century Europe was much the same. Centuries of common Christian faith had helped to produce a substantial measure of agreement concerning the moral limits of political behavior. The resulting consensus was strong enough to affect the conduct of government. The marked improvement in standards of civilized warfare which took place after the end of the Thirty Years' War is proof that contemporary political theorists had not been wholly deceived in their reliance on the authority of natural law. But if the moral consensus of the community was to become effective, it was necessary that the community itself, as distinct from the government, should be able to act through legitimately constituted organs. During the Middle Ages the institutions of the church had given the moral community a basis for organized action. Now that the church had ceased to be available, a comparable secular organization was needed to enable society to mobilize its moral forces against the power of bureaucratic governments.

Fortunately the first steps toward the creation of such an organization had already been taken in the later Middle Ages. Medieval kings, like their modern successors, were constantly troubled by the need for additional revenues. Since the primitive administrative resources of medieval states would have been hopelessly strained by any attempt to collect taxes directly, the only way of meeting this need was to place responsibility on the shoulders of men rich or influential enough to be able in their own right to collect money from the property-owning groups of the community. This led to the custom of periodically assembling representatives of the feudal nobility, the church, the chartered cities, and other prosperous classes, and forcing them to consent in the name of those classes to the imposition of special financial levies. As the normal operation of the state became increasingly dependent on these periodic grants, representative assemblies soon found themselves in a position to extort substantial concessions in return for the promised payments. It is true that the power of medieval parliaments was hardly comparable to that of their modern successors; primary responsibility for the management of public affairs still rested in the hands of the royal administration, and even the weakest rulers were not disposed to accept representative bodies as equal partners in the conduct of government. But with all their limitations, the representative institutions of the Middle Ages were vigorous enough to give currency to the conception that the community as a whole has rights and interests apart from those of the state, and that those rights and interests should be defended by a separate form of political organization.

When subsequent religious differences brought men in conflict with their sovereigns, dissenting groups naturally hit upon the idea of using the traditional rights of parliaments as a basis for organized opposition. The political theory of the Monarchomachs was largely devoted to the task of vindicating those rights. As the power of the church declined, parliamentary institutions became increasingly important as an alternative means of expressing the organized will of the community against the pretensions of princes. The authority of parliaments was the only secular parallel to the authority of the medieval church. By strengthening that authority there might still be hope of maintaining the dualistic traditions of Western society.

Although comparable efforts were made in many Western countries, the most spectacular success in this direction took place in England. During the sixteenth century, English parliamentary institutions had been reduced to a low estate by the rise of Tudor absolutism. They were never formally abolished, however, and began in the subsequent Stuart period to assume a more active role. Under the leadership of vigorous members of the landowning gentry, parliament emerged as an effective organ of protest against the expansion of royal prerogatives. When protest alone proved insufficient it set up an army and a civil administration of its own, and engaged in open conflict with the forces of the king. Decisive military victories made it possible for a time to eliminate the king entirely, and to establish a republican commonwealth. Although the difficulty of finding an acceptable form of parliamentary executive soon led to the restoration of monarchy, the power of the English kingship never recovered from this blow. As the price of regaining his throne, Charles II had to accept parliament as a more or less equal partner in the conduct of government. When his successor tried to revive the traditional position of the monarchy a bloodless revolution quickly transferred the throne to a new ruler, at the price of still further concessions. The legitimate power of the king, who remained at the head of the administrative apparatus of the state, was now checked and balanced by the legitimate power of parliament, which was recognized as possessing ultimate authority in the fields of legislation and finance. Two successful revolutions had demonstrated the feasibility of using parliamentary institutions as a means of mobilizing the secular community against assertions of the royal prerogative. From that time onward there was no substantial danger that the dualistic organization of English society would be threatened from the direction of royal absolutism.

The experience of England did much to encourage the development of a new school of political thought. In England itself, this school found expression in the writings of John Locke. According to his classic exposition of the Whig position, communities are formed for the purpose of securing the natural rights of men. Royal executives are created by the will of the community and vested with such powers only as are necessary to the attainment of community purposes. Even after the establishment of royal authority, parliamentary institutions still exist as an independent agency of community action. The exercise of legislative and financial power remains directly in their hands, serving to counterbalance the executive powers of the monarchy. Whenever the interests of society are threatened by the abuse of royal authority, parliaments have a natural and inalienable right to resist and, if necessary, to replace the erring administration. In other words, the traditional right of the medieval church, as representative of the highest moral interests of the Christian community, to check and, in extreme cases, to dissolve the authority of secular governments, was here reasserted in a purely secular form. As representative of the highest moral interests of the civic community, parliament was urged to take over the political functions formerly exercised by ecclesiastical authorities. The idea that freedom depends on the separation of powers within a balanced constitution is simply a new version of the traditional Western view of freedom as a product of the distinction between church and state. Amplified and developed in the writings of Montesquieu, the doctrine gained currency not only in England but also on the continent of Europe. It provided the only available alternative to the monistic trend of seventeenth-century politics.

Under the conditions prevailing in seventeenth-century Europe, however, there was seldom any real possibility of using parliamentary institutions to counterbalance royal absolutism. The authority of a parliament, like that of the medieval church, depends on its ability to mobilize the moral force of a united community. With a few unimportant exceptions, the parliaments of continental Europe were less well equipped than the English parliament to meet this condition. During the Middle Ages few countries were as centralized as England. Their representative institutions therefore tended to be provincial rather than general in character. During the modern period, when the central agencies of royal power grew increasingly effective, local parliaments became anachronistic. As representatives of declining provincial communities, they were in no position to offer concerted resistance to the pretensions of ambitious princes. Even in countries like France, moreover, where general as well as provincial parliaments were available, the class structure of those institutions was ill-adapted to the creation of social unity. The tradition of medieval England was unique in this respect. When representatives of the church and of the chartered cities assembled for the first English parliaments they did not try to organize themselves as separate estates, but merged with the greater or lesser landowners in what came to be known respectively as the House of Lords and the House of Commons. Since their interests were not wholly at variance, the two houses found it relatively easy to present a united front in the contest with royal authority. On the continent of Europe, on the other hand, parliaments were regularly organized in three or more separate estates, each representing the interests of a distinct social group. To reach an effective working agreement between the several estates was no easy matter. Under such conditions the king had a better claim than parliament to represent the interests of society as a whole, and the strengthening of royal authority was generally welcome as a defense against the greed of special interests. In countries lacking the natural defense of England's insular position, the fact that a strong royal army was needed for protection against the evils of foreign invasion also served as a powerful argument in favor of absolute monarchy. During the sixteenth and seventeenth centuries these factors combined to produce a radical decline of parliamentary institutions on the continent of Europe. Sporadic admiration for the English constitution could not prevent monarchical absolutism from becoming the most widely popular form of contemporary government.

Even in England, moreover, the balance of power between king and parliament was rapidly upset. The English parliament, though rather more broadly based than its continental parallels, was primarily representative of the landed gentry. When revolutionary successes demonstrated the possibility of overcoming the monarchy, this social group lost no time in securing an effective monopoly of power. Many functions of local government, which elsewhere were performed or supervised by agents of the royal administration, fell directly in the hands of landowning justices of the peace. Control over the central administrative apparatus of the state, originally recognized as a proper royal prerogative, soon shifted to cabinets responsible to parliament rather than to the king. Against the pretensions of a legislature which jealously guarded the power of the purse, and was even willing to change the rules of royal succession, royal authority was incapable of making effective resistance. Under these conditions the separation and balance of powers envisaged in the theories of Locke and Montesquieu became illusory. In practice, the form of government moved steadily toward parliamentary absolutism, exercised by a small and compact oligarchy in the interests of a limited class of the population. Within the structure of the existing constitution other social groups were able to find no legitimate means of limiting the power of this oligarchy. In England, no less than on the continent, political monism became the order of the day.

As far as the sixteenth and seventeenth centuries are concerned, therefore, the collapse of medieval dualism left a gap which could not be replaced. Under the leadership of a disciplined and united church, which occasionally called on true believers to resist the pretensions of tyrannical sovereigns, men of the Middle Ages had grown familiar with the idea that everyone must be prepared to assume a certain measure of political responsibility for the welfare of his immortal soul. The idea of assuming similar responsibility for the defense of secular interests was less familiar and widespread. Though feudal lords and chartered cities might rise against the king in defense of their vested rights, the mass of the population had been led to believe that government in its secular aspects was an exclusive concern of the ruling classes, and that the duty of simple people was to suffer in silence. This point of view continued until comparatively recent times to dominate the political thought of the West. Under these circumstances there could be no question of mobilizing the entire force of secular society as a counterbalance to the power of monarchical or oligarchical governments. A period of political absolutism was an inevitable concomitant of the crisis of secularization.

In the course of the eighteenth and nineteenth centuries, however, the vitality of Western dualism was strikingly reaffirmed. Successive classes of the population in all Western countries awakened to a sense of political responsibility. Parliamentary institutions were revitalized by their efforts, and became increasingly effective as a counterbalance to the expanding powers of modern bureaucracy. New conceptions of secular morality arose to replace the political teachings of the medieval church. In this way the dualism of Western society, originally based on the Christian dualism of church and state, re-emerged on the basis of the secular dualism of society and government. The process was slow and painful, with many disappointing setbacks, but the ultimate effect was to overcome the crisis of secularization, restoring and amplifying the traditional characteristics of Western civilization. The ideas and institutions through which these results were accomplished constitute modern liberalism.

4

The Problem
of the General Will

The main issue of modern politics is the problem of
community. In periods when the condition of society is
relatively static, people tend to accept the existing social
order as an immutable fact of nature. Successive generations perform their traditional functions in the life of the
community without stopping to ask how communities
themselves are brought into existence. Even in the sixteenth and seventeenth centuries, when the foundations
of government were being severely questioned, the existence of a community capable of performing complex and
sophisticated acts, such as the negotiation of political
contracts, was taken more or less for granted. Although
men like Locke might postulate a social contract as the
basis of community, they used it primarily as a device to
determine the proper limits of government and made little
effort to investigate the process whereby men actually
acquire the capacity for effective group action. Ever since
that time, however, social conditions in the West have
become increasingly dynamic. The substitution of secular
dualism for the church-state dualism of the Middle Ages
has called for the assumption of active political responsibilities by men previously unacquainted with traditions
of government. Rapid technological changes have repeatedly undermined the traditional bases of human relations.

Under these circumstances, the maintenance of effective community action has emerged as a major political problem. Can large numbers of men be brought, on a conscious rather than on a purely traditional basis, to coöperate for the attainment of common objectives? Can the resulting community be organized in such a way as to exert effective influence on the conduct of government? From the eighteenth century onward these have appeared ever more clearly as the crucial questions of politics.

The peculiar importance of Rousseau in the history of political thought arises from the fact that he was the first to focus attention squarely on these issues. For all his reputation as a daring innovator, Rousseau was well acquainted with the writings of earlier political theorists, and much that he did in the field of politics was little more than a restatement of traditional points of view. The concept of the social contract, which forms the title of his most famous political work, had long been part of the standard repertory. Although the concept of the general will was rather more original, it also owes much to Montesquieu and other earlier writers who had already emphasized the importance of the general spirit of the community as a factor in politics. To a greater extent than his predecessors, however, Rousseau believed that political life depends on the willing and active participation of the community as a whole. He was also fully aware of the difficulties standing in the way of effective community action. His theory of the general will was an attempt to solve these difficulties. Even within its own terms, this attempt was not wholly successful. Since Rousseau's genius was artistic and intuitive rather than logical and systematic, the creation of a comprehensive and consistent theory was beyond his powers. But granted that his exploration of the general will raised more problems than it solved, it had the supreme merit of directing attention to basic political issues. Consummate literary gifts united with passionate personal conviction to produce an impressive statement of the place of the community in modern political life. From that time onward, the problem of the general will has never ceased to be a major preoccupation of Western politics.

The nature of Rousseau's political thought can only be understood with reference to the circumstances of his personal life. Although most political theorists reflect in some measure their own private experiences, their work is usually significant to the extent that those experiences are themselves typical of the aspirations and needs of the time in which they are writing. In the middle of the eighteenth century, however, when Rousseau was at the height of his career, there was little or nothing in the contemporary scene to suggest the need for a thoroughgoing analysis of the problem of community. The political awakening of the masses, which was to make this the crucial problem of nineteenth-century politics, did not begin to get under way until the time of the French Revolution, and even then was rather slow in developing. For the time being, social conditions were comparatively stable. Because of their overwhelming interest in the maintenance of order, most people were willing to accept absolutism as the proper form of government, and saw no need to spend their time examining its foundations. Rousseau's preoccupation with the problem of community action cannot be explained, therefore, as a reflection of contemporary needs. By the peculiarities of his own character and experience, Rousseau was set apart from the men of his time. Those peculiarities are an indispensable clue to the interpretation of his political thought.

One of the circumstances which separated Rousseau from most of his associates was the fact that he was Swiss. Although most of his adult life was spent in France he was a citizen of Geneva, one of the few remaining republics in a world of absolute monarchies, and never ceased to be proud of his republican heritage. As an obscure but enfranchised member of a sovereign community he had been brought up in the tradition of a society where active participation in politics was the right of all free men. It is true that the power of an ambitious aristocracy had reduced that privilege to virtual insignificance. Continuing movements of popular protest showed, however, that the democratic spirit of the past was not yet wholly dead. As the son of an independent member of the lower middle class, Rousseau fell heir to the democratic tradition. This did much to color his conception of politics. At a time when most intellectuals were willing to regard themselves as the loyal and obedient subjects of absolute monarchs, Rousseau was never able to accept the idea that men should be anything less than active and responsible members of a sovereign political community. This in itself would have been enough to keep him hopelessly apart from the prevailing currents of eighteenth-century thought.

But the decisive element of Rousseau's personal history lay in the fact that he was a complete social misfit. One of the symptoms of the social disintegration of modern times has been the emergence of the figure known as the Bohemian, an artist or intellectual who fails to conform to the conventional pattern of social behavior and withdraws into a private environment of his own choosing. Rousseau was one of the earliest representatives of this modern type. As the son of a Swiss artisan, he would normally have followed the career of a rising young apprentice in one of the skilled trades for which his native city was notable. Unfitted for this by the haphazard and undisciplined upbringing of his early years, he abandoned the attempt and became a vagabond. After many years of irresponsible wanderings his native talents came to the fore, and won him a respected place among the intellectual lights of Paris. But even though Paris brought him success, it never gave him contentment. The art of getting along with other people, the rudiments of which are normally learned in childhood, was too complicated to be mastered in middle life by a man like Rousseau, whose pathologically nervous constitution gave way in the end to actual insanity. Although many influential people were genuinely fond of him, and tried to further his interests, the normal frictions of social life were more than he could endure. His awkwardness and touchiness in personal relations alienated many of his friends, and made it impossible for him to follow the conventional pattern of a successful literary career. The only way for him to find peace was to withdraw from ordinary social intercourse into a life of rural seclusion. Unlike the majority of his fellow intellectuals, he was unable to make an acceptable adjustment to the requirements of contemporary society. The gulf which separated him from other leading figures of the Enlightenment was strikingly expressed by his friend Diderot, when he said that Rousseau was a lost soul. This personal tragedy did more than anything else to determine the character of his writings.

As a man whose own contacts with social life had been uniformly troublesome, Rousseau naturally came to conceive of the problem of politics in terms of the relationship between the individual and society. His attitude on the matter, like that of most Bohemians, was curiously bivalent. Impressed by the absolute need for freedom to express his personality, he sometimes felt that the proper course of action was to reject society entirely. This mood was characteristic of his nonpolitical writings, and forms the justification for his reputation as a founder of modern romanticism. The educational theories set forth in his *Emile,* for example, were explicitly directed toward the object of developing an individual personality to the point where it would be capable of self-expression in isolation from the corruptions of contemporary society. Like most people who have been deprived of a basic human satisfaction, Rousseau was strongly aware, on the other hand, of the value of what he was missing. His unhappy personal experience had convinced him that the establishment of a satisfactory relationship between the individual and the community was impossible under the conditions existing in contemporary Europe. The possibility still remained, however, that a different constitution of society might provide an answer to the problem of securing effective community action without at the same time frustrating the will of individuals. Unquenchable yearning for a society in which he himself might have participated was the motive of his excursions into the field of politics.

The work which first brought Rousseau to the attention of the general public was an essay upholding the thesis that primitive societies are superior to societies with a higher degree of civilization. This preference for the primitive, which remained a favorite theme of his subsequent writings, was largely due to the belief that the problem of reconciling individual and group action had been solved in the life of earlier communities. Modern anthropologists know that the rigid training to which people are subjected in many primitive communities tends to produce a high degree of social integration. By favoring the development of socially acceptable personality traits, this training makes it possible for most individuals to accept their traditional roles with a minimum of personal conflict. During the course of the eighteenth century, Europeans were beginning to have some knowledge of the primitive cultures then existing in other parts of the world. But even though this knowledge had some influence on Rousseau, his conception of the primitive, like that of most of his contemporaries, was mainly based on the study of classical and biblical history. The city states of classical antiquity, like the primitive tribes known to modern anthropology, were small and well-integrated societies. Educated from earliest youth in a framework of common traditional values, the citizens of these communities were able to work together for the attainment of common objectives without feeling that their desires were being sacrificed in the process. As a statement of the conditions actually existing in ancient times, this picture is oversimplified, and does scant justice to the elements of coercion and conflict implicit in the life of the city state. Traditional accounts of ancient history offered considerable support, however, for the proposition that the ancient Greeks and Romans had at one time achieved an unusually harmonious pattern of social adjustment, and that subsequent class conflicts were due to the decline of earlier and sounder customs. Rousseau wel-

comed these accounts because he felt that they showed the
way to an ideal solution of the problem of politics. By an-
alyzing and generalizing the principles underlying these
so-called primitive societies, he hoped that it might be possible to illustrate and perhaps even to overcome the inadequacies of contemporary Europe.

Rousseau's idealization of primitive life was summarized
in his concept of the general will. The idea of considering
politics exclusively in terms of will was a daring innovation. Prior to Rousseau even the severest critics of political
absolutism had generally assumed that governments were
justified if they could be shown, in the light of some acceptable standard, to be acting for the best interests of society. The important thing was not to discover what people
wanted, but to find out what was good for them. For Rousseau, however, it was not enough to show that acts of government were objectively correct. The problem for him
was to find a society in which the group could act without
frustrating the will of any individual. This can happen
only if acts commanded by the government are at the
same time willed by every single member of society. Reasonable or not, a command which does not correspond
with a general or all-embracing will is bound to entail
some measure of personal frustration. Since frustration is
the ultimate evil, it follows that no act of government is
legitimate unless it conforms to the general will. In primitive societies, as Rousseau envisaged them, everything is
done on the basis of a shared community of purpose. By
erecting the whole structure of his political theory around
the concept of the general will, he expressed his conviction
that this is the only acceptable basis for social life.

Any such statement of the problem of politics would

seem to result in a hopeless dilemma. The logical implications of the concept of the general will lie in the direction
of anarchism. If no government can act unless the will on
which its action is based is shared by the entire community, it would apparently follow that there could never be
any legitimate occasion for the coercion of individuals in
the interests of society. There have, indeed, been philosophical or religious anarchists who believed that social
life can be maintained without coercive means, but Rousseau was not one of them. Convinced that men can only be
free when governed in accordance with the general will,
he was at the same time willing to admit that no government can be effective without the use of force. As he himself wrote in a well-known phrase, there are times when
men must be "forced to be free." But how can a government use force against a member of society, and at the
same time claim that its action is based on a general will in
which that self-same member continues to participate?
This paradox lies at the center of Rousseau's political
thought.

In order to resolve it, Rousseau was forced to undertake
a more extended analysis of the nature of human volition.
How can a man come in conflict with a general will in
which he himself participates? Obviously this can happen
only if he is capable at one and the same time of desiring
two mutually incompatible ends. This state of mind is not
uncommon. The desire to have cake and eat it too is a well-
known aspect of human behavior. Many people would
like, for example, to be defended by a large navy without
at the same time having to pay taxes. When a man in this
position is visited by the tax collector, his state of mind is
complex. As a private person planning his own personal

budget he would like to evade taxation. As a citizen interested in the performance of a public function he realizes that taxes must be paid. If his efforts at tax evasion land him in jail, his will cannot be said to have been entirely frustrated. His will as a private person has been thwarted in order that his will as a citizen may prevail. Since coercion under these circumstances is used for the accomplishment of purposes freely desired by the victim himself, it is not entirely meaningless to say that the man has been forced to be free.

Rousseau's distinction between the "general will" and the "particular will," which plays such an important part in the development of his political thought, is an elaboration of these ideas. According to his statement of the problem, a man is free as long as he lives under a government which conforms to the general will. A government which seeks to accomplish results desired by the entire community serves to increase rather than to decrease the range of individual satisfactions. But the accomplishment of these results frequently comes in conflict with other interests of the individual. Though they may desire the same end result, people often differ as to the means whereby it ought to be accomplished. Even when they are agreed on means as well as on ends, they may try to avoid their proper share of the costs of social action. Under these circumstances there is a conflict between the general and the particular will which can be resolved only by forcing the particular will to give way to the general. This may involve a certain frustration of individual desires. But as long as it is done for purposes desired by the individual himself, the sense of frustration is never quite complete. A patriotic American may try for personal reasons to keep out of the army as long as he can, and still have the satisfaction, once he is caught in the draft, of knowing that he is contributing to the defense of a community he would like to see preserved. Certainly he is less severely frustrated than a Polish nationalist who, as a member of a racial minority, has been similarly forced to serve in the army of a nation he would like to see destroyed. Although some sacrifice of individual freedom is implicit in any form of social action, that sacrifice is reduced to a minimum when it is demanded only for the accomplishment of purposes desired by the entire community. This was the measure of freedom demanded by Rousseau when he said that the only legitimate form of coercion is coercion dictated by the general will.

This theory deserves the closest attention, for it lies at the basis of most subsequent developments in the theory and practice of liberalism. Modern constitutional democracy believes with Rousseau that all men have the right to express themselves in the field of politics. But if people develop points of view radically at variance with those of the rest of the community, society will fail to maintain the cohesiveness necessary for effective action. Under the conditions of free government it is impossible to cope with the resistance of any considerable minority which fails to share in the general interests of the community. Before the creation of the Irish Free State, for example, Irish nationalists were able to use their democratic rights to hamper the operation of the British parliamentary system. Thus modern liberal theorists, like Rousseau, are faced with the problem of maintaining a government which will be capable of acting without at the same time arousing an important number of citizens to a feeling of irreconcilable frustration. When the general will is strong, people are able to accept a good deal of coercion without becoming seriously embittered. But this is true only if the government confines itself within the limits of action set by the existing level of community agreement. The experiment of national prohibition in America had, in the end, to be abandoned because a substantial number of people, feeling that the regulation of diet was not one of the functions required of the national government, disobeyed the law so freely as to create a hopeless problem of law enforcement. Unless it is willing to abandon the methods of constitutional democracy and apply the coercive measures of a totalitarian state, no government can act unless the purposes of that action are in some measure shared by all members of the community. When he said that political freedom depends on the general will, Rousseau was stating the basic principle of modern liberalism.

Once the importance of the general will is granted, the question arises as to how it can be brought into existence. On this point there is an element of confusion in Rousseau's thought which reflects in a curiously prophetic way the central conflict of twentieth-century politics. The problem centers on the interpretation of his famous phrase, "The general will is always right." This can be taken on the one hand to mean that will is not general unless it is also right. Belief in the rational process as the only enduring source of agreement among men has been a persistent factor in the history of Western civilization. The idea of natural law is an expression of this belief. Modern liberalism, with its emphasis on freedom of opinion and discussion, rests on a similar conviction that any enforced unity, no matter how complete, is objectively inferior to the unity which emerges from the rational negotiation of opposing points of view. On the other hand it is possible to say that rational standards are irrelevant to the formation of will, and that will becomes right simply by reason of the fact that it is widely shared. This is the point of view adopted by modern totalitarians, who regard all differences of opinion as a fatal impairment of social unity and feel that all necessary measures of propaganda and coercion should be used to prevent such differences from emerging. In Rousseau's own writings the ambiguity of the phrase, "The general will is always right," was never clearly resolved. His concept of the general will has therefore served as the starting point for endless controversies.

Although Rousseau himself never faced the issue squarely, the moralistic quality of his thought tended on the whole to lead him in the direction of objective rationalism. Profoundly influenced by Plato and other rationalistic philosophers, he believed that the nature of man is inherently good, and that the proper function of politics is to find means for the expression of that natural goodness. His preference for the primitive was largely a moral judgment. Like many other moralists, he felt that the arts and luxuries of civilization tend to corrupt the moral nature of man. In the reckless pursuit of wealth and power, men lose those traits of sympathy and mutual understanding which constitute the natural basis of social life. Rousseau believed that the social harmony of primitive communities was due to the fact that simple conditions gave unlimited scope to the inherent goodness of human nature. The general will emerging in such communities was not a substitute for but an expression of the innate moral capacity of men. When Rousseau said, therefore, that the general will is always right, he was implying not that generality is the sole criterion of rightness, but that rightness is the true basis of generality. To say, as some interpreters have done, that he regarded mere will as the highest value of human existence, is to do scant justice to the moral preoccupations which underlie the structure of his political thought.

The rationalistic element in Rousseau's concept of the general will appears most clearly in his attitude toward the problem of law. If he had felt that the mere fact of common agreement was in itself a sufficient basis for political life, he could hardly have failed to recognize the legitimacy of any act desired by society as a whole. He always insisted, however, that the general will was not the same thing as the will of all, and that it could only express itself in the form of general legislation. Although a specific act of government, such as the popular election of a magistrate, might represent the unanimous agreement of every member of the community, he regarded it as a manifestation of the particular rather than of the general will. This point of view is an extreme but characteristic reflection of the normal Western tendency to legal rationalism. The idea that the process of legislation, which forces men to think in general rather than in specific terms, is intrinsically more rational than the process of administration, was well-known even in the time of Aristotle. Though a man might be influenced in his own choice of secretaries by a personal and instinctive preference for blondes, it would be hard for him to find rational justification, even in his own mind, for a general rule excluding all brunettes from secretarial employment. The typically Western belief that the best government is a government of laws rather than of men is based upon this simple psychological experience.

This belief was thoroughly shared by Rousseau. Convinced that the general will is always right, he at the same time held to the traditional view that all specific decisions, even when they are the decisions of a unanimous community, are apt to be wrong. True rationality is possible only when men transcend their particular interests and prejudices and devote themselves to a consideration of general problems. Legislation is the only form of community action which offers full expression to the rational element in human nature. It is therefore the only form of action which can properly be ascribed to the general will.

Although Rousseau has often been described as a prophet of absolute democracy, his concept of the general will leads to an uncompromisingly dualistic view of politics. The proponents of absolute democracy, confident in the unlimited political capacity of the people, believe that responsibility for the conduct of government should lie directly in their hands. For Rousseau, on the other hand, the maintenance of a rigorous distinction between society and government was a matter of the highest importance. The function of the community as a whole, as expressed by the general will, is purely normative. Its task is to formulate the moral consensus in acts of legislation, and to see that that legislation is enforced by the government. Whenever it is dissatisfied by the way in which an existing government is executing its mandate, it has the right to dismiss that government and replace it by another. Under no conceivable circumstances is it possible, however, for the general will itself to perform the functions of government. An act of administration, even in those rare cases where it is performed by the entire citizen body rather than by specially selected magistrates, can never be anything more

than an act of particular will. In Rousseau's political
thought the general will, as the supreme representative of
the moral interests of the community, occupies a position
similar to that which the church, as the supreme representative of the spiritual interests of mankind, had occupied
in the political thought of the Middle Ages. Like the medieval church it has the right to instruct and if necessary to
change the administrative organs of government. Just as
the spiritual quality of the church was always endangered
whenever it tried to take over the functions of the state, the
general will ceases to be general as soon as it tries to take
over the functions of government. Rousseau believed that
a proper conception of politics depends on the maintenance of an absolute dualism of society and government.
His distinction between the general and the particular will
could hardly have led to any other conclusion.

The value of Rousseau's analysis has been confirmed by
the experience of modern liberalism. From the eighteenth
century onward, responsibility for the administration of
society has become increasingly the province of state bureaucracies staffed by trained civil servants. With the advance of modern technology, the idea of direct government by society as a whole has become even more fantastic
than it would have been in the time of Rousseau. The con-
current development of public opinion has made it possible, however, to place limits on the exercise of bureaucratic power. As representatives of the moral consensus
of the community, many parliaments have succeeded in
establishing authority over the agencies of government,
holding them to the execution of commonly acceptable
legislative standards. Like the church-state dualism of the
Middle Ages, the resulting dualism of society and govern-

ment has given rise to extremely difficult problems. On the one hand there has been a tendency for the representatives of society to invade the field of government by dictating not only the general objectives but also the specific methods of administrative action. Pressure politics and the spoils system are characteristic examples of the way in which constitutional democracies have sometimes interfered with the conduct of government. On the other hand there has been a tendency for civil servants, by exploiting the weakness and inexperience of popular representatives, to pursue their own lines of policy in defiance of popular control. Thus the problem of maintaining an effective balance between popular and bureaucratic forces has been no less difficult than the corresponding medieval problem of maintaining an effective balance between church and state. But in spite of all difficulties, the lines laid down in Rousseau's distinction between the general and the particular will have pointed the way to a viable form of political dualism. The result has been to give a new lease of life to Western civilization.

The significance of Rousseau's theory is not confined, however, to the light it throws on constitutional democracy. To a greater extent than any other writer of his day he was aware of the obstacles to effective group action. This led him to adopt many positions which are curiously prophetic of modern totalitarianism. The theory and practice of constitutional democracy rest on the assumption that people are able by a process of rational negotiation to reach a degree of common agreement sufficient for the maintenance of social life. In the course of the nineteenth century this assumption was justified by the experience of many Western countries. In other times and places the attempt to produce such agreement has proved more difficult, and has encouraged different views with regard to the rational nature of man. Although Plato believed in the supreme importance of reason in the conduct of human affairs, his discouragement with the current state of Athenian politics brought him to the conclusion that the number of people capable of true knowledge was extremely limited, and that society could be unified only if an intellectual aristocracy, by the use of myths and other irrational devices, was able to impose its ideas on the rest of the community. Similar discouragements in recent times have stimulated the growth of totalitarian doctrines which go even further in their acceptance of force and fraud as instruments of social integration. Rousseau himself, though unacquainted with modern totalitarianism, was thoroughly conversant with the writings of Plato, and the social situation in which he found himself was no less discouraging than that faced by his illustrious predecessor. None of the peoples of eighteenth-century Europe was as yet prepared to assume the burdens of free government. From Rousseau's standpoint the current scene was a spectacle of hopeless corruption. In spite of his faith in the natural goodness of man, he was accordingly forced to take a rather pessimistic view of the political capacity of men. This made him not only one of the earliest exponents but also one of the earliest critics of modern liberalism.

Rousseau's ultimate disbelief in the power of reason is shown in his exaggeratedly monistic conception of the general will. If an effective public opinion is to emerge from the processes of rational discussion it is necessary that society itself be organized on a pluralistic basis. Various groups within the community must be allowed to develop and clarify their own views, and then given the opportunity to negotiate with other groups for the discovery of a mutually acceptable compromise. Under the conditions of modern constitutional democracy, political parties and representative parliaments have provided an essential part of the machinery needed for this purpose. The destruction of that machinery has been one of the key objectives of the totalitarian attack on liberalism. This lends peculiar interest to the fact that Rousseau was if anything even more firmly opposed than modern dictators to the pluralistic organization of society. Like all totalitarian theorists, he was unable to share the liberal belief that a general will can emerge from the mutual intercourse of organized particular wills. For him every particular will was a threat to the purity of the general will, a threat to be eradicated as rapidly as possible. His fear of political parties was especially violent. As one of the traditional devices of aristocratic government, representative bodies might be tolerated. Rousseau regarded them, however, purely and simply as organs of government, and denied them any significance whatsoever as instruments for the expression of the general will. Like all other governmental agencies, parliaments were magistrates with a private will of their own, a private will essentially dangerous and antagonistic to the general will of the community. The general will itself can never be delegated, but must always be exercised by the unorganized mass of the population. These beliefs, which lie at the center of Rousseau's political thought, represent a totalitarian ideal of social integration. Nothing could be further from the theory and practice of constitutional government.

Having rejected all other means for the organization of public opinion, Rousseau was forced, like the modern totalitarians, to fall back on the phenomenon of leadership. Leadership is necessary, of course, to any form of political life. Under the conditions of constitutional democracy, it appears in the guise of an outstanding capacity for negotiation, clarifying and modifying the spontaneous impulses which emerge from the experience of various parts of the community. To Rousseau, however, the leader appeared not merely as a collaborator with but as the actual creator of society. This conception, like so many other elements of his political thought, was based on the study of ancient history. The traditional accounts of early days are filled with the exploits of men like Moses or Lycurgus or Numa, who were supposed to have founded the greatness of their respective peoples by uniting them under wise and enduring systems of legislation. Although modern historical scholarship has thrown more than a little doubt on the validity of this tradition, it was still accepted at face value in the time of Rousseau. He seized upon it as the only possible answer to difficulty in which he, like the totalitarians of our own day, had been placed by reason of his doubts as to the political capacity of ordinary men. Even though people were not able to achieve social integration by their own efforts, they might still be brought together through common devotion to the personality of a single outstanding leader. In ancient times there had been great legislators who, by inducing previously disunited men to follow the same laws, had made it possible for subsequent generations to live under the rule of an effective general will. An equally wise legislator might be able to perform the same service for the men of Rousseau's time. This was the only answer he could see to the problem of making the general will an operative factor in the life of modern Europe.

With the concept of the legislator, a powerful strain of irrationalism incorporated itself in Rousseau's political thought. He was not, to be sure, prepared to go as far as the modern fascists in believing that the necessity of social integration justifies the leader in using every available means for the attainment of his ends. Rousseau's personal hatred of coercion was so overwhelming that he could not imagine any circumstances in which it would be proper to use force against any individual who did not already share the purposes toward which that force was being directed. He therefore insisted that the legislator should act by persuasion only, without the slightest admixture of coercive power. But the fact that the legislator's relations with other men were persuasive did not prevent them from being irrational. Although his legislative measures, like those of the Platonic philosopher king, were in themselves based on a rational perception of what was best for society, Rousseau's legislator could not hope to win the consent of ordinary men by a process of rational demonstration. His hold over society was based in part on the magnetic attraction of his own personality, and in part on conscious fraud. In order to secure initial acceptance for his proposals, the legislator should play on the superstitious prejudices of the masses, telling them that his message came from heaven and that any infraction of the new legislative system would be punished by the gods. Respect for the law should be perpetuated, moreover, by a host of impressive ceremonies and customs which, however meaningless in themselves, would give the people an unquestioning devotion to the way of life laid down for them. For all his belief in the natural goodness of man, Rousseau did not think that ordinary people could be trusted to recognize the truth when it was shown to them, or to continue following it thereafter on a purely rational basis. This curiously bivalent conception of human nature does more than anything else to explain the ultimate confusion and inadequacy of his political thought.

Because of his surrender to irrationalism, Rousseau was unable, for the same reasons which later operated in the case of fascism, to find an acceptable answer to the problems of modern politics. Modern conditions call for the creation of political units which are increasingly large and complex. In Rousseau's time the tiny city state of Geneva had already been reduced to an anachronism by the rise of states like France. Since that time these states in turn have been rendered obsolete by the emergence of continental powers. The task of modern politics has been to keep pace with this development by providing the basis for ever-widening forms of social integration. The tendency of irrationalism, on the other hand, is restrictive. Although fascist dictatorships, by demagogic appeals to national or race prejudice, have been able to bring particular communities to a high degree of totalitarian unity, the exclusive nature of their ideology has made it impossible for them to extend the limits of those communities by any means less exhausting or more reliable than absolute coercion. Similar limitations were characteristic of Rousseau's political thought. Although the cosmopolitan spirit of the eighteenth century was helping to draw the various peoples of Europe to closer social unity, he regarded this as a symptom of corruption. The ideal political unit for him was a small self-contained community, about the size of Geneva, united by an exclusive devotion to its own particular traditions. He believed that the general will could never be operative until all the other states of Europe had been reduced to comparable dimensions.

Recognizing the need for larger units of political integration Rousseau did, to be sure, suggest that many small states ought to be reassembled in the form of federal associations. This idea was incompatible, however, with his totalitarian conception of society. The intrinsic difficulty of solving the problem in his own terms probably explains the fact that, although he made an attempt to write a book on the theory of federalism, the work was never completed. Federalism demands that local communities transcend their particular interests in a comprehensive community of purpose. Since Rousseau believed that the general will can operate only when men give absolute and undivided loyalty to the traditions of their own particular community, the possibility of any wider form of sociability was logically excluded. The result was to give his idea of the state, like the parallel doctrines of modern fascism, a hopelessly anachronistic appearance.

As far as Rousseau himself was concerned, the result of his excursions in the field of political theory was to produce a mood of unmitigated pessimism. Though he believed that a legislator was needed to make the general will effective, he had to admit that legislators, in his sense of the term, were the rarest of phenomena. A personality strong and wise enough to create a state by a process of pure persuasion was nothing less than a miracle. Even on those rare occasions when such a miracle took place, moreover, Rousseau believed that it would usually be ineffective. Most peoples, especially in modern times, are too deeply sunk in corruption, too firmly set in their own perverse habits, to be willing to change their way of life in response even to the wisest and most persuasive of appeals. With the possible exception of Calvin of Geneva, the only successful legislators known to Rousseau were figures of the remotest period of antiquity, living among people whose social conditions were still simple and whose habits were as yet relatively unformed. In the Europe of his own day, Rousseau felt that Corsica alone was sufficiently primitive to offer any real prospect for the creation of an effective general will.

It is true that he recognized one small ray of hope for a wider reformation of contemporary politics. Even in highly corrupt societies there may be revolutionary crises which, like some illnesses in the life of the human organism, produce a sort of amnesia, shaking men out of their habitual ways and preparing them for the acceptance of new views. If a genuine legislator should happen to appear at such a time, he might be able to produce results.

Rousseau felt, however, that revolutions of this sort were hardly less rare than legislators. Since the possibility of reformation rested on the highly improbable coincidence of two separate miracles, the chances were that Europe would never escape from the fetters of corruption. Rousseau's view of history was consequently dominated by a profound sense of pessimism. The general tendency of mankind is not to progress but rather to decline from earlier levels of perfection. If men cleave to their ancient usages they may continue to enjoy some of the virtues of an earlier and purer stage of human society. If they break away from the past the chances are that they will become increasingly corrupt. Pessimistic conservatism, in the last analysis, was Rousseau's own answer to the problem of politics.

But in spite of the conclusions he himself drew from it, his concept of the general will actually served as an inspiration to the liberal position in politics. Like many other writers who are weak in the capacity for systematic exposition, Rousseau was in the habit of clothing his momentary enthusiasms in bold and striking phrases, leaving doubts and qualifications to emerge in the course of subsequent discussion. This made it easy for his readers to remember the phrases and to forget the qualifications. When the French Revolution made it necessary to reconsider the foundations of political order, the proposition that men are born free, yet are everywhere in chains, became the rallying cry of popular discontent. Reminded that sovereignty rests in the general will, people everywhere were encouraged to rise against established governments, without giving a second thought to the fact that Rousseau himself had regarded Corsica as the only place still potentially capable of freedom. Belief in the natural goodness of man encouraged new classes of society to break the bonds of tradition and to assume the responsibilities of political action, untroubled by Rousseau's own pessimistic doubts as to the political capacity of ordinary men. When Marx, in a later revolutionary crisis, told the workers of the world that they had nothing to lose but their chains, he was echoing the familiar words of the *Social Contract*. Even to this day the writings of Rousseau, the conservative pessimist, serve as an inspiration to democratic optimism. This is his primary significance in the history of political thought.

The nature of Rousseau's contribution to the development of modern liberalism is nowhere more clearly visible than in the social philosophy of Kant. At the beginning of his career Kant was an aristocratic rationalist, convinced that the highest gifts of reason are bestowed upon a few men only, and that ordinary people are incapable of making significant contributions to the more important phases of human existence. Acquaintance with the writings of Rousseau changed his point of view and gave him new respect for the dignity and capacity of average men. This feeling dominated his later writings in the field of moral and political philosophy. His talent for systematic exposition was devoted to the task of amplifying and refining the fugitive flashes of Rousseau's imaginative insight. In his hands the concept of the general will became the weapon for a searching analysis of the essence of liberal politics.

The main feature of Kant's reinterpretation lay in his reëvaluation of the place of reason in society. In line with the general tradition of Western rationalism, he believed that reason is largely concerned with the making of general rules. The categorical imperative, which asserts that a man should act in such a way that his behavior could be conceived as a universal rule of action, is allied to Rousseau's principle that the general will can only be expressed in the form of general legislation. But instead of confining this principle, as Rousseau did, to acts of the community as a whole, Kant regarded it as a universal standard of moral action, applicable to individuals and lesser groups as well as to the state. This made it possible for him to overcome the artificially rigid distinction between the general and the particular will which did so much to vitiate the political thought of his predecessor. In all human activities, including the activity of sovereign states, men have a tendency to extend the limits of sociability by allowing the assertion of their own rights to be modified in the light of a growing appreciation of the comparable rights of others. Although Kant no less than Rousseau was aware of the fact that expressions of the moral consciousness are modified in practice by endless imperfections and corruptions, he differed from his predecessor in believing that the urge to social integration is strengthened rather than weakened by the experience of conflict. Through contact with the alien and hostile will of other individuals, men gradually awaken to the necessity of discovering some mutually acceptable basis for common action. Through similar contacts, groups also learn to get along with other groups for the accomplishment of mutual objectives. For Kant, therefore, the conflict of particular wills was not the enemy but the instrument of social integration. Law is not a miraculous gift handed down in perfection by a god-like legislator, but the gradually evolving product of the accumulated experience of ordinary men. All forms of individual and group action are capable of contributing to that experience. Because of his belief in the gradual evolution of the general will, Kant took a pluralistic view of society. This made it possible for him to escape the difficulties and disappointments which accompanied the totalitarian monism of Rousseau.

Above all, it enabled Kant to express the theory of the general will in a form compatible with the expanding requirements of modern civilization. As long as the problem of social integration was conceived in terms of the maintenance of an exclusive community tradition, there could be no hope of reconciling popular government with the growth of cosmopolitan consciousness. In the Middle Ages the church owed its moral authority to the fact that it represented in a real and special sense the unity of Western civilization. The power of modern liberalism has likewise been derived in large measure from its position as a cosmopolitan movement, mobilizing the conscience of Western peoples in a concerted attempt to master the forces of bureaucratic absolutism. If Rousseau's totalitarian view of society had been the only valid interpretation of the problem of the general will, no such development would have been conceivable. Reinterpretation along the lines laid down by Kant has enabled modern liberalism to overcome these difficulties. By conceiving of social integration as the function of indefinitely evolving social experience, free play can be given to the socially creative faculties of men. In his essay on *Perpetual Peace*, Kant offered the hope that human reason, slowly awakened to the need for common action, would one day lead to the creation of a general will sufficiently strong and comprehensive to bring all peoples within the framework of a federal world state. Although this hope has yet to be realized, it represents the ultimate aspiration and forms the ultimate strength of the liberal conception of politics.

But for all its inadequacy as an analysis of the methods of constitutional democracy, Rousseau's theory of the general will is valuable as a statement of the underlying objective of modern liberalism. Although parliaments and other organizational devices may be necessary instruments for the expression of public opinion, they are meaningful only insofar as they bring the moral consensus of the community to bear on the conduct of government. Preoccupation with the mechanics of political action is likely to make men lose sight of this all-important fact. In the Middle Ages the moral authority of the church, which alone gave it the capacity to limit the power of the state, was constantly endangered by institutional inertia. Periodic waves of revolutionary enthusiasm, as in the time of St. Francis, were needed to purify the hierarchy of abuses and to revitalize the spiritual unity of Christendom. Under modern conditions similar problems emerge in connection with the organization of secular society. Constitutional machinery set up for the purpose of mobilizing public opinion tends to become an end in itself for the people who have a vested interest in its operations. As Rousseau put it, any particular group of men, including parliamentarians and party bosses, tends to develop a particular will of its own, distinct from the general will of the community. If society is to maintain the moral authority needed to enable it to act as a check on government, institutional inertia must from time to time be overcome by movements of drastic reform. The history of liberalism consists, therefore, in a series of revolutionary crises. In response to a newly awakened political consciousness, previously inert groups of the population have repeatedly succeeded in revitalizing and enlarging the area of effective community by breaking through the bonds of established constitutional legitimacy. Although Rousseau's dislike of representative machinery, and his insistence that the general will cannot be delegated, cannot be taken as a sufficient guide to the problem of modern politics, they serve at least as a useful corrective to the opposite error of regarding mere machinery as the essence of constitutional democracy. The basic problem is to keep the institutions of government in line with the expanding moral consensus of the community. The concept of the absolute and inalienable sovereignty of the general will still stands as a valid statement of the objective of liberal politics.

5

The Awakening
of the Middle Classes

The first stage in the development of modern liberalism came with the rise of the middle classes. Ever since the later Middle Ages, well-organized groups of merchants and craftsmen had dominated the life of European cities. For a time they had been able, through institutions like the Hanseatic League, to play an independent role in politics, contending with kings and feudal lords on terms of substantial equality. Although the triumph of absolute monarchy deprived most cities of their onetime freedom of action, the urban middle classes remained an important factor in the life of society. As the allies of territorial princes in their struggle with the feudal nobility, individual members of this group took a leading part in the creation of modern state bureaucracy, and won a corresponding share of public prestige and profit. The rise of material prosperity which followed the period of religious warfare offered still further opportunities for advancement. By the end of the seventeenth century, therefore, the middle classes of Western Europe were firmly entrenched as an influential and self-respecting group, conscious of their own importance, and determined to maintain their interests in the face of hostile pressures. When the policies of absolute monarchs proved in the course of the eighteenth century to be incompatible with their purposes, their atti-

tude grew critical and ultimately revolutionary in character. Inspired by a new faith in the value and potentialities
of secular society, they subjected the state to organized
social pressures comparable to those once exerted by the
medieval church. Their energy and devotion were responsible for the first successful attempt to restore the dualistic
tradition of Western civilization on a purely secular basis.
Although the ideas and institutions which guided them in
this enterprise, being based on the experience of a rather
narrow social group, were insufficient to create an all-embracing general will, they formed the starting-point for
later democratic developments. Thus the awakening of
the middle classes stands as the first great milestone in the
history of modern liberalism.

Although the revolutionary culmination of the eighteenth century appeared at the time as a sudden and unpredictable outburst, it was the product of forces which
had long been maturing in the body of Western civilization. Ever since the end of the period of religious warfare,
Europe had been moving rapidly in the direction of a
thorough technological revolution. Modern science, established on firm foundations through the efforts of men like
Newton, was beginning to show its promise as a weapon for
the understanding and control of man's natural environment. New methods of commercial and colonial exploitation, which had already reduced many parts of the world
to the condition of European tributaries, were providing
new opportunities for the accumulation of wealth. The
productive capacity of Western industry was being enhanced by a series of technological inventions which
marked the first stages of what later came to be known as
the industrial revolution. For people capable of partici-

pating in these developments, the time offered unlimited
prospects of advancement and profit. Sooner or later, however, every attempt to make use of novel opportunities
came in conflict with the existing social order. Religious
and political censorship, inherited from the days when the
church was the authoritative center of intellectual life,
was a constant threat to the growth and dissemination of
scientific learning. Commercial enterprise was hampered
by a complex maze of local and international trading
restrictions, relics of the days when economic intercourse
had for the most part been confined to narrow local areas.
The rights of guilds and other monopolistic organizations,
acquired at a time when the transmission of traditional
skills had been the basis of production, stood as a constant
barrier to the adoption of progressive industrial techniques. Institutions which had been adequate to the needs
of a relatively static society could hardly meet the requirements of a more dynamic age. The result was friction
which in the end could be resolved by nothing less than a
revolutionary crisis.

Consciousness of the emerging conflict was restricted,
however, to a comparatively narrow group. Participation
in the more advanced forms of intellectual and economic
activity was possible only to people who had a fair degree
of intelligence and education, and who at the same time
were willing to break away from the routine of established
tradition. This meant that the possibility of profiting by
revolutionary change was largely confined to members of
the urban middle classes. In most of the countries of eighteenth-century Europe the mass of the population consisted
of an illiterate peasantry devoted to the time-honored
traditions of an ancient way of life. At the other end of the

social scale the landowning nobility and gentry, while
enjoying the advantages of a more ample education, were
similarly absorbed in the performance of traditional ruling-class functions, and showed little interest in exploring
novel opportunities. Outside of England and a few other
exceptional communities, law and custom generally for-
bade them to participate in any form of commercial or
industrial enterprise. Scientific and literary activities were
less completely tabu, and individual noblemen employed
their advantages of wealth and education to play a distinguished role in the intellectual life of the period. This
was especially true of France, where the overwhelming
boredom of court life, to which great landowners had been
drawn by a deliberate royal policy of keeping them away
from their estates, led many weary courtiers to find solace
in intellectual pursuits. On the whole, however, the more
ambitious members of the middle classes were the people
best prepared to exploit both the intellectual and the
economic possibilities of the new era. Long acquaintance
with the problems of commercial and industrial life, and
the possession of relatively abundant resources of liquid
capital, gave them a marked advantage in the more experimental forms of economic enterprise. Good education
combined with an inquiring habit of mind made it possible for them to take an active part in the exploration of
new fields of learning. Thus the eighteenth century was an
age of peculiar opportunity for the middle classes. Insofar
as the existing order prevented the full exploitation of that
opportunity, they above all were the people to feel the
need for drastic reformation.

As a small minority more or less excluded from the responsibilities of government, the middle classes were in

no immediate position to express their grievances through direct political action. By the end of the seventeenth century, however, they were beginning to acquire a fair amount of independent power. In the earlier phases of modern capitalism, merchants and manufacturers had been dependent on state assistance for the inauguration of large-scale business ventures. Public or semipublic trading corporations, like the British and Dutch East India companies, and publicly owned and operated manufacturies, like the porcelain factory at Sèvres in France, were typical agencies of economic progress in the early modern period. In the intellectual realm, the need for royal or aristocratic patronage condemned middle-class writers and artists to a similarly dependent position. As long as these conditions continued, the middle classes could hardly aspire to genuine freedom of action. By the end of the seventeenth century, however, the situation was beginning to change. Through institutions like the Bank of England, ample resources of capital and credit became available for the support of private as well as of public enterprise. By controlling these resources, already greater than the limited revenues of states, outstanding merchants and financiers, operating from such international centers as London or Amsterdam, were able to draw the threads of economic leadership into their own hands. Intellectual leadership tended at the same time to shift from the chilling atmosphere of etiquette-ridden courts to the freer and more vivacious air of private salons, which rose to their highest peak of international influence in eighteenth-century Paris. Many successful members of the middle classes used their newly acquired wealth and leisure to patronize and participate in this exciting world of art and letters, associating on terms of equality with like-minded recruits from the landowning nobility. With the growth of a sizable reading-public for books and periodicals, gifted authors like Voltaire and Dr. Johnson were even able to support themselves by their writing, without depending on the favor of wealthy patrons. In intellectual as well as in economic matters, the middle classes of the eighteenth century had already gone a long way toward acquiring independent forms of social organization. This made them an increasingly powerful factor in the life of the time.

To produce significant results in the face of an entrenched absolutism something more than this was needed, however. If the Roman Empire had previously been forced to share its power with the Christian church, it was due to the fact that the Christians, with all their institutional weaknesses, were united by a passionate devotion to a common faith. Convinced that their gospel of other-worldly salvation was the only possible answer to the needs of humanity, this small minority was able to impose its own terms on the masters of the world. The salons and banking communities of the eighteenth century, though operating on a purely secular plane, were in much the same position as the congregations of early Christianity. As the agencies of a scattered and unrespected minority, they could never hope to make their views prevail until they had succeeded in inspiring the middle classes as a whole with an effective fighting faith. To provide the bases for such a faith was the objective of eighteenth-century thought.

This need was filled by the intellectual movement known as the Enlightenment. It derived not from the work of any single man, but from the coöperative endeavors of several generations of political and social thinkers. Although writing in many different times and places, all were concerned with the problem of releasing the creative forces of the period from the restraints of an outworn social system. Since this problem had many different aspects, there was room for a considerable range of interests and opinions among the several individuals who contributed to the movement. Adam Smith, the Scottish economist, was mainly concerned with the issue of free trade. Voltaire struck telling blows against the stupidities of literary and intellectual censorship, while Beccaria confined himself to the question of criminal-law reform. Regional variations, corresponding in many cases with peculiarities of the local situation, were also characteristic of the schools of thought which prevailed in particular countries. Since the economy of France was overwhelmingly rural, the leading group of early French economists, known as the physiocrats, were primarily interested in the rationalization of agriculture, while the English utilitarians, in a land of wide-ranging commercial interests, tended to concentrate on the rationalization of international trade. But with all their variations, the proponents of the Enlightenment are less notable for their differences than for their similarities. The needs and aspirations of the middle classes in all countries were more or less the same. Common experience gave rise to common doctrines which in their totality constitute the philosophy of the Enlightenment.

The faith which united the members of this school of thought was a belief in the possibility of terrestrial happiness. Although orthodox Christianity had never been wholly indifferent to the problem of relieving the lot of

men on earth, it had taught that suffering is an inescapable consequence of the fall of man, and that the final
hope of happiness lies in the promise of a heavenly after-
life. The philosophy of the Enlightenment was a direct
challenge to this conception. It is true that the philosophers did not necessarily deny the possibility of a blissful
life after death, and some of them continued to practice
the Christian religion. Because of their confidence in
modern science and technology, however, their attitude
toward the problem of terrestrial existence was remarkably optimistic. Although modern medicine was still in its
infancy it was beginning to show something of its capacity
to overcome the ancient curse of disease and suffering.
New techniques of commerce and manufacture had already done so much to raise the living-standards of the
West that the ultimate elimination of poverty seemed a
reasonable expectation. The result of such experiences was
a new conception of the nature and destiny of man. According to the faith of the Enlightenment, the earth was
designed by a benevolent God not as a place of penitential
suffering, but as a scene of human happiness. Although an
event like the Lisbon earthquake might lead the caustic
wit of Voltaire to satirize the extreme optimism of those
who asserted that this was the best of all possible worlds,
all were agreed that the terrestrial life of man was capable
of becoming far more pleasant and prosperous in the future than it had ever been in the past. To minimize pain
and suffering, and to maximize happiness, was the proper
goal of human existence. This was the humanitarian faith
which inspired the eighteenth-century Enlightenment.

But if happiness was the divinely appointed end of
secular life, why was it not yet being attained in practice?

Christianity had explained the evils of the world as a consequence of sin, and had taught that the conquest of sin through grace was the only way of overcoming those evils. The philosophers of the Enlightenment offered a parallel solution to this perplexing problem. According to them, the failure of past generations to realize their potential happiness was due not so much to sin as to ignorance, and reason rather than grace was the appointed instrument of their salvation. Through the gift of reason, God had made it possible for men to understand the laws of the universe, and to accommodate their behavior to the benevolent requirements of the divine plan. In the earlier stages of history men had experienced great happiness by living in accordance with the simple laws of nature. Most eighteenth-century thinkers, like Rousseau, were attracted by the picture of a highly idealized primitive society peopled by "noble savages," for they saw it as the promise of what life could be in a world stripped free of corruption. In the course of time men had had the misfortune, through the operation of causes never fully explained, of falling away from the guidance of reason. Powerful individuals found that they could increase their own apparent happiness at the expense of the general welfare by keeping other people in ignorance. Kings and priests waxed fat by coercing their followers into the payment of tribute. Bigotry and superstition became a vested interest, defended with all the united resources of church and state. Centuries of suffering were the consequence of this unnatural situation. Reason still remained, however, as a force capable of restoring humanity to the conditions of that happier life which was its natural birthright. To overcome ignorance through the liberation of reason was the eighteenth-century solution to the problem of human existence.

The philosophers of the Enlightenment were not content, however, to set up the goal of a humanitarian heaven on earth, and to assert the efficacy of human reason as a means of reaching that goal. If the middle classes were to generate the kind of energy required for a thoroughgoing attack on absolutism, it was necessary to inspire them with the conviction that the triumph of their cause was not only possible and desirable, but also inevitable. In this respect the men of the eighteenth century betrayed a habit of mind which had long been enshrined in the traditions of Western civilization. The reformers of other cultures have generally been willing to work without being assured in advance that their efforts will meet with complete or lasting success. In ancient China, for example, successive generations of Confucian sages have been content to labor for the restoration of lost ancestral virtues, undeterred by their clear-sighted and realistic conviction that all human achievements, including their own, are imperfect and subject to decay. For men brought up in the Judaeo-Christian tradition, however, resignation to the fatalities of historical existence is a matter of extreme repugnance. The idea that history is not a meaningless series of recurring cycles, but a drama with a unique and happy ending, is implicit in the story of creation, redemption, and resurrection. Through the influence of Christianity, the Western world had grown used to the idea that all secular miseries would end with the second coming of Christ and the establishment of an eternally perfect kingdom. When the men of the Enlightenment directed their attention from religious to secular activities, their apoca-

lyptic hopes were bodily transferred from the spiritual to
the secular realm. Although an occasional unhappy eccentric, like Rousseau, might deviate from the normal
optimism of the period, people generally continued to take
it for granted that perfection was the predestined end of
history. To formulate this religious belief in secular terms
was one of the characteristic problems of the Enlightenment.

The idea of progress was the eighteenth-century answer to the problem. Before that time most people had
assumed that the facts of decay and death were just as
much a part of secular life as the facts of birth and growth.
The bases, however, for a more optimistic conception had
been gradually accumulating in the course of Western
history. Ever since the Dark Ages, European society had
been trying to relearn the arts of classical civilization. By
the eighteenth century this development had gone so far
that men began, for the first time in more than a thousand
years, to be conscious of the fact that they were more
accomplished than the ancients. In natural science, in
medicine, in the military arts, and in various other fields,
modern discoveries made the writings of classic authorities increasingly obsolete. In literature and art, where
questions of relative excellence are less open to empirical
demonstration, the prestige of antiquity was more enduring. Toward the end of the seventeenth century, however,
people finally found the courage to challenge the supremacy of the ancients even in this field. The extraordinary
interest aroused by the so-called war of the ancients and
the moderns is due to the fact that this celebrated literary
controversy represented the final stage in the liberation of
the Western mind from an age-old sense of inferiority.

Secular history no longer appeared as a painful effort to recapture the lost glories of Greece and Rome, but as a triumphant progress toward ever-rising levels of perfection. The idea was so novel and exciting that it took powerful hold on the imagination of the West. One of the most triumphant statements of this doctrine, Condorcet's *Outline of the Progress of the Human Spirit,* was written at a time when the author was himself a fugitive from the guillotine of the French Revolution. Although the results of the movement he had helped to create were, from an immediate personal standpoint, somewhat discouraging, nothing could shake his confidence in the inevitability of human progress. His attitude was typical of the spirit of the Enlightenment.

The doctrine of progress was valuable not only as a means of raising the morale of the middle classes, but also as a means of undermining the self-confidence of their opponents. Of all the obstacles met by reformers, none is more troublesome than the human tendency to cling to long-established habits. The fact that a given custom or institution has been in existence for a long time raises a certain presupposition in its favor, leaving the burden of proof on those who wish to see it altered. The normal relationship between old and new is reversed, however, for anyone who believes in the progressive character of history. If the tendency of human affairs lies in the direction of constant improvement, it follows that new ideas and institutions ought on the whole to be better than those which stem from an earlier stage of historical development. This does not mean, of course, that every harebrained scheme is necessarily worthy of adoption. Even the men of the Enlightenment, with their passion for modernity, never went so far as to deny that the present as well as the past is a proper subject for rational criticism. What the idea of progress did was to shift the burden of proof. Whereas the tendency formerly had been to assume that old things were good until new ones had been shown to be better, the presumption now was that old things were bad unless it could be proved that new proposals were worse. This justified unusual freedom in the criticism of established habits. In England this attitude found typical expression in the writings of the utilitarians, who asserted that all ideas and institutions, no matter how ancient and respectable, should be judged in terms of their demonstrable ability to satisfy current needs. The position of other revolutionary thinkers, even when expressed in different words, was substantially the same.

In view of the fact that modern science and technology, for all their promise, were still in a fairly primitive stage of development, such confidence in the possibility of immediate reformation would seem to have been a trifle premature. It should be remembered, however, that the eighteenth-century view of progress was based not on the nineteenth-century conception of historical evolution, but on the timeless mathematical premises of seventeenth-century science. Of all the current achievements of modern learning, Newtonian physics was the discovery which most thoroughly captivated the imagination of the Enlightenment. By applying certain mathematical hypotheses to the observed movements of heavenly bodies, Newton had succeeded in explaining a large range of terrestrial and celestial phenomena in terms of a few extremely simple laws of motion. This outstanding accomplishment gave rise to an exaggerated view of the rational simplicity

of the universe. The average supporter of the Enlightenment assumed that the whole of creation was a perfectly
economical mechanism constructed in accordance with a
limited number of rationally comprehensible laws. For
men of intelligence and good will, the discovery and
application of those laws should be a fairly easy matter.
Once this had been done, the problems of human existence would be solved for all time. Unlike the scientists of
later generations, who conceived of progress in terms of
the slow and patient accumulation of empirical data, the
more influential thinkers of the eighteenth century believed in the possibility of achieving final perfection
through the sudden introduction of rationally intuited
hypotheses. This gave their revolutionary optimism an
uncommonly persuasive basis.

The intellectual atmosphere of the eighteenth century
produced a distinctive type of personality. The extraordinary popularity enjoyed by Benjamin Franklin, both at
home and abroad, owed much to the fact that he impressed his contemporaries as the ideal embodiment of
what men ought to be. As an enterprising writer, printer,
and publisher, he had raised himself from poverty to
affluence by his own unaided efforts. Endowed with an
insatiable curiosity and an untiring zest for living, he had
participated actively in the intellectual life of the time,
and was known as the author of several important discoveries and inventions. Born and raised in a country
where the older traditions of European society were comparatively weak, he was able to view religious and political questions with a fresh and critical eye. It is true that
his mind in many respects was characterized by a degree
of superficial practicality which prevented him from ap-

preciating some of the more complex aspects of human experience. In this, too, he was a true representative of the age in which he lived. In a period of impending revolution, the great need is for men whose capacity for energetic and self-confident action is uninhibited by the endless perplexities and qualifications which attend the more subtle manifestations of philosophic thought. The capacity of the Enlightenment to inspire people with this particuar type of enthusiasm is a true measure of its success as a revolutionary doctrine.

In one important respect, however, the thought of the eighteenth century was less clear-cut and simple than it seemed. This was due to the persistence, in a newly secular form, of one of the characteristic dilemmas of Western religion. Christianity, particularly in its Western version, is the resultant of a rather unstable balance between self-regarding and other-regarding motives. With its emphasis on the supreme importance of individual salvation, it has tended, on the one hand, to heighten the moral consciousness of the individual at the expense of the community. Christ's injunction to His disciples that they must abandon their families and follow Him is an illustration of the ruthless moral egoism implicit in the Christian message. The respect accorded to monks and hermits, and the attempt to encourage the introspective tendencies of ordinary men through institutions like the confessional, are manifestations of a deep-seated conviction that the true source of religious vitality lies in the development of the individual conscience. Along with this individualistic tendency, however, the Christian religion contained a powerful social element. One of its loftiest aspirations was the desire to unite all men within an all-embracing community of love and charity. To maintain an effective balance between these opposing forces has been the critical problem of practical Christianity. With the rise of the Enlightenment this problem, far from being resolved, was carried over from the religious to the secular plane of action. This accounts for many of the real complexities which underlie the apparent simplicity of eighteenth-century thought.

Perhaps the most obvious characteristic of the period was its exaggerated individualism. At a time when emerging intellectual and economic forces were coming into conflict with the traditions of an older society, it was natural for supporters of the new movement to lay great emphasis on the need for individual freedom. Just as the creative vitality of Christianity had resided in the religious energy of its individual saints, the hope of the Enlightenment rested in the rationalizing energy of its individual scientists and enterprisers. This led to a radical assertion of the right of the individual to pursue his own rational interests without regard for the restraints traditionally imposed by society. The sensationalist school of psychology, then at the height of its influence, rested on the assumption that men are born without moral or social ideas of any sort, and that all subsequent developments of the human personality are the product of purely self-regarding attempts to minimize the painful and to maximize the pleasurable sensations of the individual human organism. According to this theory, society is a mechanical aggregate of sentient individuals all of whose actions are motivated by the pursuit of rational self-interest. With the advance of secularization, therefore, the Christian doctrine of the supreme value of the individual soul was transformed into an equally uncompromising doctrine of the value of the individual sentient body. The result was a marked heightening of the individualistic tendency which had always been one of the characteristic features of Western civilization.

In accordance, however, with the dualistic habit of Western thought, this emphasis on self-regarding motives was counterbalanced by an equally drastic reassertion of the other-regarding aspects of human life. Although modern scholars, in their reaction against the abuses of nineteenth-century individualism, have sometimes tended to lose sight of the fact, this was one of the all-pervasive phases of the Enlightenment. The leaders of the movement were inspired by the belief that their principles would increase the happiness not only of peculiarly gifted individuals, but also of society as a whole. Just as the Christians had previously dreamed of a day when all mankind would be united by a universal law of love and charity, the men of the eighteenth century were captivated by the vision of an age when all humanity would enjoy the common blessings of freedom from want and pain. That this was no pious platitude, but a passionate conviction, was demonstrated by innumerable acts of humanitarian devotion. When admiring contemporaries paid tribute to Franklin as an ideal representative of the age they were mindful of the fact that he was a well-known philanthropist, whose time and money had been given to the creation of an amazing number of welfare organizations. This attitude of social responsibility was widely shared. Appalled by the spectacle of human suffering, many men and women cheerfully descended into the hell of hospitals and prisons to devote their lives to the mitigation of such

horrors. Disturbed by the prevalence of ignorance, others
gave themselves with equal selflessness to the cause of
popular education. Although the more extreme forms
of humanitarian heroism, like the more extreme forms of
saintly devotion, were beyond the capacity of ordinary
men, they were widely admired as an expression of the
contemporary moral sense. Without due recognition of
the other-regarding motives which gave rise to these
developments, the nature of the eighteenth-century Enlightenment can never be understood.

The humanitarian element was so strong, indeed, that
it sometimes threatened to destroy the meaning of individualism itself. This threat to the balance of Western
dualism is nowhere more clearly visible than in the writings of Jeremy Bentham. Inspired by the analogy of Newtonian mechanics, the English utilitarian believed that
the pleasures and pains of men, like the mass and velocity
of physical objects, are capable of quantitative measure-
ment in terms of a single, universally applicable standard.
This led to a conception of human welfare which had the
effect of subordinating individuals to the operation of an
imaginary science of social statistics. According to the
Principles of Morals and Legislation, the supreme end of
life is to secure "the greatest good of the greatest number," setting off the pains of one individual against the
pleasures of another in such a way as to produce the largest possible net quantity of human happiness. The natural
tendency of men is to maximize their own particular
pleasures by all available means, even when those means
involve a net loss to the happiness of the community as a
whole. Under these circumstances, the community has a
right to introduce a new element into the calculations of

individual self-interest. By estimating the precise amount of pleasure to be derived from the various forms of anti-social action, and by imposing legal penalties exactly painful enough to outweigh that pleasure, the enlightened legislator has it in his power to make the hedonistic calculus of selfish men coincide with the higher interests of society. But if penal law is the only force capable of preserving the general welfare against individual selfishness, it would seem to follow that the state rather than the individual is the ultimate source of moral authority. A similar view of human nature led Hobbes, in an earlier crisis of English history, to develop a theory of uncompromising state absolutism. The logical implications of utilitarianism, as expounded in the juristic writings of Bentham, are essentially Hobbesian.

Fortunately the individualistic element of eighteenth-century thought was rather stronger than these utilitarian formulas would suggest. Although the men of the Enlightenment were fond of describing human nature in terms of virtually unqualified egoism, their view of the individual was at the same time marked by a degree of rationalistic idealism which made it unnecessary for them to appeal to the state as the sole defender of human values. Most of them believed that benevolence and sympathy were normal expressions of the rational nature of man. Any really enlightened person, according to this view, will take pleasure in doing good to others, and will find it painful to cause pain. In a rational attempt to maximize his own happiness, therefore, the individual will generally behave in a socially acceptable fashion. Although this strand of rationalist idealism was particularly strong in thinkers who, like Godwin or Kant, had been in contact with pietist and other Christian circles, it played a part in the thought of most eighteenth-century rationalists. Bentham himself, while tending to minimize the pleasures of benevolence, was never committed to the position that fear of legal penalties is the only motive for decent behavior. Altogether, the leaders of the Enlightenment were disposed, in much the same fashion as their Christian predecessors, to take a rather balanced view of the self-regarding and other-regarding factors in human nature. This made it possible for their political thought to develop along the traditional lines of Western dualism.

In order to reconcile these opposing elements, however, it was necessary to discover a form of social organization in which individualistic and humanitarian values could find simultaneous expression. Medieval Christianity had solved the corresponding religious problem through the institution of the church. The purpose of that institution was to provide a framework within which the religious genius of spiritually gifted individuals could be made to contribute to the salvation of all mankind. After an elaborate process of selection and training, men with a special religious vocation were entrusted with functions of pastoral leadership. Others were encouraged, in a monastic life of prayer and contemplation, to acquire spiritual merits which, according to the prevailing view, would redound not only to their own credit, but also to the credit of the society which supported them. Under the protection of the Holy Ghost, the religious efficacy of these institutions was divinely guaranteed. The search for a correspondingly efficacious form of secular organization was one of the most important features of the eighteenth-century Enlightenment.

The answer to this need was found in the concept of the free market, a secular institution guaranteed not by the Holy Ghost but by the equally divine and immutable principle of the natural harmony of interests. The market itself was an ancient institution which had long played a central part in the life of the middle classes. Most of the cities of Europe grew up in localities where traders and craftsmen had found it convenient to congregate for the purpose of offering their wares to the surrounding rural population. From the beginning the power of the urban middle classes had depended not, like that of the feudal lords, on their ability to force subjects to pay tribute, but on their capacity to meet the requirements of customers on a basis of voluntary negotiation. When the eighteenth century brought the middle classes to a new peak of social aspiration, it was natural for them to look upon the market as the likeliest instrument for the satisfaction of their ambitions. Now the peculiarity of market relations, insofar as they are not tainted by extraneous coercive factors, is that they occur only when both parties to the agreement feel that they have something to gain thereby. In other words, they represent a field of action within which the individual enterpriser is able to succeed only on the condition that his efforts are beneficial to others as well as to himself. The philosophers of the Enlightenment seized upon this fact as a clue to the solution of their problem. Under the conditions of absolutely free negotiation it would be possible for rational men, without ceasing to pursue their own individual purposes, to develop a system of social relations which would tend to maximize the welfare of society as a whole. Newtonian science had familiarized people with the conception of a vast aggregation of heavenly bodies which, by responding to the attractive and repulsive powers of mass and motion, were able to move in perfect harmony according to the mathematically simple plan of the Divine Maker. This made it easy to suppose that a vast aggregation of individual men, known as humanity, by responding to the attractive and repulsive powers of rational self-interest, was likewise intended by a benevolent Creator to live in perfect harmony according to the simple rules of the free market. Like the Christian church in the field of religion, the market was the institution which seemed to have been divinely ordained for the reconciliation of self-regarding and other-regarding elements in the secular life of man. The purpose of the church militant had been to insure the benevolent operation of the Holy Ghost within the terrestrial city of God. The function of the free market was to insure the operation of the equally benevolent principle of the natural harmony of interests within the realm of secular history.

As an instrument for the satisfaction of middle-class needs, this conception was nowhere more useful than in the field of economics. Progressive enterprisers of the eighteenth century, as masters of the most efficient commercial and productive techniques of the period, were intrinsically in a favorable competitive position. Whenever they tried to offer their goods and services, however, they were frustrated by the fact that craft guilds, public and semi-public corporations, local tariff units, and other established institutions possessed a wide range of monopolistic powers which made it impossible to enter many potentially profitable fields of competition. The principle of the free market allowed middle-class enterprisers to attack these restrictions not merely as defenders of their own class interest, but as supporters of the welfare of humanity at large. According to the more influential schools of eighteenth-century economics, the supreme economic goal of man, considered in his capacity as a consumer, is to buy the best possible goods and services at the lowest possible price. Legal restrictions, insofar as they have any effect at all, can only serve to limit freedom of choice, compelling purchasers to pay higher prices for inferior merchandise. Thus the establishment of a free market coincides with the economic interest of consumers. In his capacity as a producer, on the other hand, the supreme economic goal of man is to produce the largest possible quantity of pleasurable goods and services with the least possible expenditure of painful effort. Unrestricted competition, by insuring the ultimate disappearance of high-cost producers, bestows the highest rewards of economic life on those who are relatively efficient in the use of labor and material. A free market serves, therefore, to create a natural harmony of interests between producers and consumers. Through the operation of unrestricted competition, the desire of consumers to minimize the cost of their purchases, and the desire of producers to maximize the efficiency of their labor, are simultaneously and automatically achieved. This was the eighteenth-century solution to the problem of economic welfare. By applying the concept of the natural harmony of interests, economic theorists were able to satisfy the individualistic aspirations of the middle classes without doing violence to the humanitarian tendencies of contemporary thought.

A corresponding line of argument was also used to support those members and associates of the middle class whose primary interests lay in the direction of intellectual rather than of economic action. Like the merchants and manufacturers with whom they were associated, the scientists and publicists of the Enlightenment were confident of their ability to stand the test of competition with the proponents of rival doctrines. Unfortunately the absolute monarchs of the period, as heirs to the heresy-hunting traditions of the medieval church, still claimed the right to prevent the propagation of ideas inimical to the established order. Although these claims were not on the whole particularly well-enforced, prison and exile had been the lot of many eighteenth-century authors, and all had suffered more or less from the dangers and inconveniences of official censorship. Revulsion against these experiences encouraged the development of an intellectual version of the economic doctrine of free trade. During the religious controversies of the seventeenth century, exceptional men like John Milton and Roger Williams had already come forward with the proposition that the religious interests of mankind would prosper best by allowing every variety of religious opinion to circulate freely, submitting rival doctrines to the conscientious judgment of men. This concept of religious toleration was adopted by the Enlightenment, and used as the basis for a more comprehensive theory of intellectual freedom. According to this theory, the goal of intellectual life is to maximize the discovery and diffusion of rationally verifiable truth. If all forms of opinion are allowed to compete freely, the rational judgment of individuals will ultimately suffice to distinguish truth from error. The imposition of legal restraints, by excluding potentially useful ideas from the scope of rational discussion, forces the public to accept an inferior in-

tellectual product, and deprives the producers of an inval-
uable chance to improve the quality of their work. In the
intellectual as well as in the economic realm, the men of
the Enlightenment believed that the maintenance of free-
market conditions was indispensable not only from the
standpoint of their own particular interests, but also from
the standpoint of the general welfare. Belief in the existence of an ultimate rational harmony enabled them in
both cases to reconcile the opposing claims of self-regarding and other-regarding action.

Confidence in the divinely appointed efficacy of the
free market served, in much the same way as medieval
confidence in the efficacy of the church, to encourage a
radically dualistic conception of society. According to the
eighteenth-century view, all the really significant values
of human life, both economic and intellectual, are the
products of individual initiative. Under the benevolent
operation of the natural harmony of interests these values
become available to humanity through the automatic
operations of the free market. Governmental action, insofar as it attempts to interfere with these operations, can
have no other effect than to decrease the sum of human
happiness. This estimate of the relationship between
society and government is equivalent, on the secular
plane, to the medieval estimate of the relationship between church and state. Secular society, like the church, is
an autonomous organization capable of acting through
institutions of its own. The ends of humanity can only be
defined and achieved through the agency of these institutions. Modern governments, like the medieval state,
have no legitimate concern with, and no capacity for the
creation of positive values, and must be content to accept

those values as a gift from the sister organization. This aspect of the Enlightenment is nowhere more clearly expressed than in the writings of Thomas Paine. Flatly asserting that all human welfare is the product of society, and all human misery the product of governments, he believed that the powers of government, in the interests of humanity, should be constantly checked and controlled by the superior moral authority of society. Even in the heyday of the medieval papacy, the dualistic aspiration of Western civilization had never been more drastically revealed.

But with all their emphasis on the moral supremacy of society, the leaders of eighteenth-century thought were not disposed to deny the necessity of government. Although an occasional enthusiast like Godwin, inspired by overwhelming faith in the possibilities of rational negotiation, might be willing to adopt a strictly anarchist position, the great majority agreed that a certain amount of coercive power was indispensable. Medieval churchmen had preached the duty of obedience to secular authority on the ground that the power of the state was necessary to protect the sacred work of the church against the dangers of lawless violence. The philosophers of the Enlightenment ascribed a similar value to the state as a guardian of the free market. The concept of a free market involves the idea of a place where men can negotiate on a voluntary basis, undeterred by fear of coercion. During the Middle Ages, market towns generally grew up in the shadow of castles, since military strongholds then offered the only available areas of security against the depredations of robber bands. When subsequent advances in political and military technique made it possible to organize defense on a national and even on an international scale, national and international markets arose in their turn. Without the protection afforded by an appropriate type of political organization, no system of markets could long continue to endure. This fact was appreciated by political theorists of the eighteenth century. Confident though businessmen and intellectuals might be regarding their ability to hold their own in peaceful competition with others, they had no reason to suppose that their talents would serve them equally well in a free-for-all contest with gangsters. The protection of markets against force and fraud, including the enforcement of contractual obligations, had long been recognized as a function of organized government. As long as governments were willing to confine themselves to the performance of this function, the men of the Enlightenment were no less disposed than medieval churchmen to preach the duty of obedience.

At this late date it is hardly necessary to emphasize the fact that this narrow conception of the functions of government is an oversimplification of the problem of politics. The eighteenth-century view of society was based on the idea that all the creative energies of man were capable of being absorbed in a rationalized and individualistic pursuit of wealth and learning. Within the external framework of a politically guaranteed free market, enlightened self-interest was expected to induce self-seeking individuals to participate in a mutually advantageous course of voluntary negotiation, and thereby to create the conditions of an effective general will. This confidence in the spontaneous social efficacy of individual reason was unrealistic, and soon broke down under the impact of practical experience. In the period of the Enlightenment itself, occasional warnings had been voiced against the inadequacy of the prevailing conception. The difficulty of achieving social harmony by rational demonstration was recognized not only by the artistic intuition of Rousseau, but also by the critical intelligence of Hume. By the end of the eighteenth century this early skepticism had already found classic expression in the restrained and realistic rationalism of Kant. But as far as the average run of the Enlightenment was concerned, these were voices crying in the wilderness. Once the state had been reduced to its proper function as guardian of the free market, most people believed that all the problems of social existence would be spontaneously resolved. To rescue men from the consequences of this illusion has been one of the important functions of modern political thought.

The historic function of the Enlightenment, however, was not to create a ready-made solution to the problem of liberalism, but to furnish the initial impetus for further liberal experiments. The limitations of eighteenth-century philosophy made it all the more suitable for the performance of its appointed role. To most people the idea that man is an animated calculating machine, rationally weighing the advantages of every possible line of action, would seem unrealistic to the point of grotesqueness. Man is too much a creature of impulse and habit ever to act exclusively in this fashion. To progressive members of the middle class, on the other hand, this conception of human nature was by no means unappealing. The writers who developed these theories were themselves professional intellectuals, a group of men particularly apt to exaggerate the importance of rational inquiry as a function of human life. The audience to which they addressed their

work was composed of intelligent merchants and manufacturers, whose daily business was governed by shrewd
calculations of profit and loss. To such people there was
nothing intrinsically improbable about the notion that
man is a rational machine operating in terms of the hedonistic calculus. The limitations of their own personal
experience corresponded exactly with the limitations of
the prevailing view of human nature. This made it possible, at a time when the middle classes were the only
people in a position to challenge the power of the absolute
state, for the philosophy of the Enlightenment to serve as
the basis for an effective revolution.

With all its inadequacies, moreover, the conception of
the free market had the virtue of pointing the way to more
satisfactory lines of future development. Originally created in response to the needs of a rather narrow class, the
elements of this conception were so broadly formulated
that they were also capable of stimulating the desire for
wider forms of community action. The idea that all men
have equal rights, although originally conceived in rather
negative terms of legal equality, was a powerful incentive
to the growth of democratic aspirations in other fields of
experience. The idea that institutions must be subject at
all times to criticism in the light of their continuing utility,
an idea originally developed to meet the revolutionary
aspirations of the middle classes, was a powerful weapon
in the hands of those who later sought to satisfy the needs
of other social groups. Above all, the idea that human
welfare is to be sought not by methods of force and
repression but by a process of voluntary and mutually
profitable negotiation, an idea implicit in the eighteenth-
century preference for social as contrasted with govern-

mental action, was admirably suited to the encouragement of future attempts to integrate rival class interests within the structure of an all-embracing general will. All these were lasting contributions to the development of modern liberal thought.

6

The Emergence
of Liberal Constitutionalism

The ultimate consequence of the middle-class awakening was to create a secular basis for the revival of Western constitutionalism. This result did not appear, however, until the end of a long and painful period of political experimentation. At its inception, the philosophy of the Enlightenment was distinctly apolitical in character. Like their Christian forebears, the leaders of early eighteenth-century thought were concerned with the welfare of a society independent of and superior to political institutions. This made them regard the organization of the state itself as a matter of relative indifference. As long as a state, however constituted, was willing to guarantee society in the performance of its supremely important functions, they were ready to give it their unquestioning allegiance. Repeated disillusionment alone could teach the enlightened middle classes that suitable political institutions are necessary to keep the state within its appointed limits. Modern constitutionalism is the product of that hard-won experience.

If the middle classes had been powerful enough to follow their own inclinations, the history of Western politics would never have moved in the direction of constitutional democracy. During the later Middle Ages, when merchant and craft guilds had controlled the politics of independent

cities, absolute aristocracy had been the normal instrument of government. Political power in most of these cities
fell into the hands of a limited circle of patrician families,
who exercised it to the exclusion of other elements in the
community. When the eighteenth century brought the
middle classes a new opportunity for self-assertion, their
political attitude remained similarly aristocratic. It is true
that the philosophers of the Enlightenment believed in
the equal enjoyment of legal rights by all men. In response
to the claims of the hereditary nobility that some men are
naturally superior by birth, they also laid emphasis on the
proposition that superiority is primarily a matter of education, and that all men are equally capable of improvement by proper educational methods. This faith in education, which led to the establishment of libraries, schools,
mutual improvement societies, and other institutions of
popular education, did much to foster the ultimate spread
of democratic feeling. For the time being, however, it was
almost as aristocratic in its political implications as the
earlier belief in superiority by birth. Whatever the possibilities of future development might be, the immediate
fact was that only a limited number of people enjoyed the
advantages of an ample education. The ability even to
read and write was still the privilege of a minority. Under
these circumstances it was easy to conclude that the exercise of political power, though directed toward the
welfare of all mankind, should remain in the hands of the
educated few. If the men of the Enlightenment had been
free in their choice of political means, the chances are
that aristocratic absolutism would have become the predominant form of government.

Fortunately the conditions of eighteenth-century Eu-

rope were such that there was no serious possibility of inaugurating purely aristocratic experiments. Although the
middle classes were strong enough to make themselves
felt, they were by no means capable of assuming sole responsibility for the direction of society. The maintenance
of social order depended on the existence of an elaborate
civil and military bureaucracy, and on the functioning of
a predominantly agrarian economy. With the latter the
urban middle classes had little or no contact, and their
hold on the former, above all on the army, was much less
than that of the traditional ruling classes. As a relatively
small minority enjoying no great social prestige, they
could hardly hope, as in the more favorable environment
of the medieval city state, to lay formal claim to a monopoly of political functions. In their own chosen field of market competition, their skill and energy were unrivaled.
Outside of that field they could not act without the co-
operation of other social groups. This made it impossible
for them to dream of founding an exclusively middle-class
absolutism.

The relative weakness of the middle classes did not immediately lead them, however, in the direction of constitutional government. Their position was such, indeed, that
their interest for the time being was rather to increase than
to decrease state authority. As far as they were concerned,
the all-important problem was to liberate intellectual and
economic markets, as rapidly and as thoroughly as possible, from the restraining influence of traditional institutions. So radical an attack on vested rights called for an
uncommonly drastic and uninhibited assertion of the
power of the sovereign state. Ever since the end of the
Middle Ages, the theory of sovereignty had been the main

ideological weapon of those who sought to rationalize the life of society in the face of ecclesiastical, feudal, and other traditional forces of resistance, while constitutionalism had been the defense of those who wanted to preserve the traditional order. Hatred of the traditional order was the mainspring of the Enlightenment. During the greater part of the eighteenth century, therefore, the most extreme supporters of state absolutism were to be found in the ranks of enlightened philosophers.

In view of the fact that the middle classes themselves were not strong enough to control the exercise of political authority, their eagerness to exalt the power of the state might seem at first to be rather surprising. Their confidence in the power of reason was so great, however, that they had no doubt of their ultimate ability to direct the use of sovereign authority along lines of their own choosing. Their attitude was much the same, indeed, as that previously adopted by the Jesuits, whom the eighteenth-century philosophers rightly regarded as their own most dangerous rivals. After a few tentative experiments in the direction of constitutionalism, the Jesuits had decided that their interest was to support absolute monarchy. Confident in their capacity, as agents of the Holy Ghost, to appeal to the religious conscience of sovereigns, they exalted the power of princes in the expectation that they would be able to use that power as an instrument for the advancement of the true faith. The men of the Enlightenment, supported by a comparable confidence in the power of human reason, reached similar conclusions. Sincerely believing that no rational man could fail in the long run to recognize the validity of their arguments, they felt that any sovereign authority, however constituted, would ultimately use its power for the furtherance of enlightened interests. This made it possible for them to encourage the growth of absolutism without fearing that the powers thus created would operate to their disadvantage.

Up to the time of the American and French revolutions, enlightened despotism was the form of government most widely favored by the leaders of eighteenth-century thought. In England, where power rested in the hands of a parliamentary oligarchy, it was possible for a man like Bentham, at the beginning of his career, to hope that the oligarchy itself would prove strong and enlightened enough to accomplish the task of radical reformation. In most countries, however, monarchs were the effective centers of state authority, and it was to them that the reformers generally turned for help. Their preference for monarchy may also have owed something to the fact that, for all their confidence in the possibilities of rational persuasion, the work of converting a single strategically placed individual to the cause of the Enlightenment looked easier than any corresponding attempt to convert a larger number of less well-educated men. The English philosopher-statesman Bolingbroke, toward the beginning of the century, had expressed a preference for enlightened despotism in his *Idea of a Patriot King*, which maintained that the factional strife and corruption of the British oligarchy called for a vigorous reassertion of royal power by a wise and benevolent monarch. This attitude was characteristic of the philosophers of the Enlightenment. Although Voltaire and his contemporaries admired the religious toleration and intellectual freedom of England, they felt no urge to follow Montesquieu in regarding the British constitution as a model of progressive government. Like Rousseau, they were interested not in the establishment of a system of checks and balances, but in the creation of a homogeneous society responsive to the dictates of a single sovereign will. They differed from Rousseau, however, in believing that the will of an individual monarch rather than the corporate will of a larger community was the force most likely to serve reformatory needs. Enlightened despotism was their solution to the problem of contemporary politics.

For a time the wisdom of this conclusion was apparently justified by the event. This was due to the fact that the interests of eighteenth-century monarchs coincided, up to a certain point, with the interests of the middle class. Realizing that the military strength and peacetime revenues of their kingdoms largely depended on the prosperity of industry and commerce, intelligent and successful rulers tried to support the more progressive elements of the business community in their struggle against the vested rights of communes, guilds, and other traditional organizations, and used their sovereign prerogatives rather freely to curtail or destroy those rights. In an age, moreover, when intellectual life was largely dominated by the forces of the Enlightenment, ambitious monarchs like Frederick the Great of Prussia and Catherine the Great of Russia, found that they could enhance their prestige considerably by appearing as the friends and patrons of philosophers. With princes brought up in a long-established tradition of social responsibility, the humanitarian spirit of the age was often capable of generating a good deal of genuine reformatory enthusiasm. All this led to the simultaneous appearance, in most of the major dynasties of Europe, of sovereigns who seemed well qualified to answer to the name of enlightened despot. In addition to Frederick and Catherine, rulers in Austria, Spain, and other unlikely countries became known as vigorously progressive reformers, ruthlessly rationalizing the economic and administrative structure of their kingdoms. It is true that some of their reforms were less than satisfactory from the middle-class point of view. In the face of stubborn conservative opposition, moreover, apparent victories often proved to be more or less ephemeral, the work of many an enlightened despot being undone by his less enlightened successors. On the whole it can be said, however, that the trend of events at this time was distinctly favorable to middle-class interests. In the light of what had already been accomplished, there seemed to be no reason to believe that the ideals of the Enlightenment could not be realized through the agency of enlightened despotism.

The American Revolution was the event which first suggested the need for a different approach to the problem of politics. Throughout the eighteenth century the British colonies in North America had been growing increasingly dissatisfied with the hindrances to commercial and industrial development imposed upon them by the mercantilist policies of the mother country. In their attempts to secure greater freedom of action, the disaffected groups tended to ignore the authority of parliament, appealing directly to the king for the relief of their grievances. This was not, however, an expression of the contemporary faith in enlightened despotism. The political ideas of the American colonists were a product of their English constitutional heritage, and had little relation to the absolutist conceptions of the Enlightenment. Although they rejected the claims of the British parliament to rule over them, their own claims rested on the traditional right of Englishmen to enjoy the protection of a parliament of their own choosing. Unfortunately, the parliamentary oligarchy of Britain showed little inclination to abandon its power in favor of a local American parliament, and appeals to the king brought reformatory proposals no nearer to fruition. George III was too far away, and too deeply engrossed in his attempts to dominate the political life of England to have either the capacity or the inclination to meet the needs of his colonial subjects. The resulting tension finally led to a revolutionary crisis. This crisis opened the way to a radical reorientation of eighteenth-century politics.

The immediate effect of the American Revolution was to stimulate the growth of absolute democracy. It is true that the older constitutional tradition, with its marked aversion to the concentration of power in the hands of any single authority, never disappeared from the American scene. The circumstances of the struggle with England were such, however, as to require a sudden increase of popular participation in politics. Although many of the objectives of the revolution, particularly the abolition of mercantilist restrictions, were calculated to serve the commercial interests of merchants and plantation owners, the propertied classes were by no means unanimous in accepting the advisability of revolutionary action. Weakened by Tory disaffection, middle-class revolutionists were in no position to overcome their opponents without the support of other elements of the community. This necessitated an appeal to the principle of popular sovereignty. Proclaiming the right of the people to take political affairs in their own hands, skillful democratic agitators like Samuel Adams were able to stir up a vigorous revolutionary movement among the lower orders. At a time when king and parliament, and many even of the prosperous middle classes, had proved deaf to the most persuasive reformatory arguments, simple artisans and farmers had responded freely. This suggested that the common people were the real repositories of reason and virtue, and that the cause of rational reform involved placing the largest possible measure of authority in their hands. In the writings of men like Jefferson, this democratic point of view found ardent and persuasive spokesmen. For leaders of the revolutionary persuasion, absolute democracy rather than absolute monarchy appeared as the most effective agency of enlightened government. This belief has remained down to the present time as one of the persistent strains of American political thought.

The course of events soon served, however, to rid many middle-class revolutionaries of the belief that rational persuasion would insure popular acceptance of enlightened principles. In most of the American states, which enjoyed virtually unlimited powers of self-determination under the original articles of confederation, authority fell in the hands of more or less popularly elected legislatures. But the conduct of these legislatures, both during and after the revolution, left much to be desired from the middle-class standpoint. The Enlightenment taught that the welfare of society depends on the elimination of all trade barriers. And yet, though the revolution itself had been in large measure a protest against British mercantilism, state legislatures promptly set up tariffs and other hindrances to interstate and foreign trade. The Enlightenment taught that the maintenance of a stable circulating medium, and the enforcement of contractual obligations, were indispensable to the functioning of a rational market economy. In response to the desires of a large debtor class, however, most of the states proceeded to enact measures for the reduction or cancellation of debts, partly through the reorganization of judicial personnel and procedure, and partly through the encouragement of currency inflation. Although the power of the majority was not yet complete, it was effective enough to express many needs and aspirations unknown to the enlightened view of government and society. Short and tentative as the experiment had been, the incompatibility between absolute democracy and middle-class interests was already quite apparent.

The result was to alienate most leaders of middle-class opinion from the idea of political absolutism, and to revive their traditional faith in constitutional government. Although many prosperous people were convinced, with Hamilton, that the people were "a great beast," the beast was too strong to be overcome by an exclusive assertion of middle-class authority. The only hope was to limit the powers of democracy in such a way that popular majorities could not act without some regard for the interests of a middle-class minority. Under the circumstances then prevailing, this hope, though slender, was by no means desperate. As heirs to the tradition of English politics, most Americans had always thought of liberty in terms of the legal limitation of government. Separation from the mother country had served to enhance rather than to detract from the strength of that tradition. As colonists restive under the exactions of a foreign parliament, and as pioneers eager to create a new world without official interference, Americans had never had a chance to forget the dangers of political authority. The doctrines of Locke and Montesquieu, antiquated as they might seem in terms of

British and continental experience, still formed the basis
of American political thought. At the time of the revolution, the traditions of constitutional government had probably retained more vitality in America than in any other
part of the Western world. This gave the middle classes of
that country a unique opportunity to counteract the dangers of absolute democracy by inaugurating constitutional experiments.

The capacity of American statesmen to make use of this
opportunity was demonstrated in the constitutional convention of 1787. Although the proposals which emerged
from the Philadelphia deliberations were the product of
many compromises, the general purpose of the gathering
is clearly visible in the provisions of the final document. In
order to repress the harmful activities of existing state governments, it was necessary to provide a central authority
strong enough to guarantee the conditions of free enterprise throughout the country. This meant the transfer
from state to federal agencies of the ultimate power to deal
with questions of military defense, to regulate commerce,
and to establish those weights and measures, especially the
monetary standard, necessary for the operation of a stable
market economy. The right of states to impair contractual
obligations was also restricted by specific constitutional
prohibition. But even though the need for strong federal
authority was clear, the danger that such an authority
might fall into unsuitable hands was also recognized.
Without daring to exclude people already in possession of
the franchise from voting in federal matters, the framers
sought to weaken the impact of democratic forces by making senatorial and presidential elections indirect rather
than direct in character. If all else failed, a strict separa-

tion of executive, legislative, and judicial powers, combined with the presidential veto and other applications of the principle of checks and balances, was relied upon to prevent the federal government from following certain state governments along the road to absolute majority rule. Thus the principles of earlier constitutionalists, skillfully adapted to the requirements of the local scene, served to protect the middle classes against the more pressing dangers of absolute majority rule.

Once the constitutional document had been drawn up, the next problem was to secure its adoption by constitutional conventions meeting in each of the several states. Since the proceedings in Philadelphia occurred behind closed doors, the general public had had no way of knowing the theoretical and practical arguments in favor of the new proposals. The task of winning public acceptance accordingly fell to a number of political writers, by far the most important of whom were the authors of *The Federalist*. Designed for the special purpose of encouraging ratification in the doubtful and indispensable state of New York, this work soon gained recognition as the classic statement of early American constitutionalism. It is true that the theories there propounded were not particularly original. In setting forth the need for strong central authority to combat the dangers of national disintegration, the authors were able to draw upon the thought and experience of earlier federal systems, particularly significant examples of which appeared in the pages of ancient and medieval history. In justifying the advantages of checks and balances and the separation of powers, the American writers were doing little more than to appeal to a tradition which went back through Montesquieu and Locke to the ancient historian Polybius. But the fact that these ideas were already familiar served rather to increase than to decrease their persuasiveness. The main task of political pamphleteers is to mobilize familiar notions in support of desired objectives. In the complex process of political and ideological manoeuvering which preceded the adoption of the American constitution, the authors of *The Federalist* were able, by the forceful marshalling of familiar arguments, to play a substantial role.

The result of these efforts was to establish one of the most enduring constitutional structures of modern times. It is true that the American constitution was not in all respects as successful in resisting majority pressures as the framers themselves had hoped. The growth of political parties, for example, soon had the unexpected effect of nullifying the aristocratic institution of indirect presidential elections. This development was counterbalanced, on the other hand, by the no less unexpected development of the supreme court, under the leadership of Chief Justice Marshall, into a powerful organ for the control of popularly elected presidents and congresses. In devising a constitutional system for the future it is impossible to expect absolute accuracy of prediction. But the men of the Philadelphia convention were an unusually capable and level-headed lot, soundly grounded in the theory and practice of politics, and most of their guesses were shrewd guesses. Few people have ever been more successful in devising a system which would manage both to satisfy contemporary needs and to provide a basis for future growth. When subsequent social developments, as in the time of President Jackson, led to the emergence of new political forces, the constitution proved flexible enough to allow these forces to express themselves without producing a revolutionary crisis. The fact that America is still living under this, the oldest of all written constitutions, is the highest possible tribute to the wisdom of its creators. Their work is one of the outstanding political achievements of eighteenth-century politics.

The outcome of the American Revolution was a matter of more than local significance. Intrinsically the event was not, to be sure, an affair of great moment. The American colonies were as yet no more than a small and unconsidered outpost on the frontier of Western civilization. The problems faced by the American revolutionists were a good deal simpler, moreover, than the corresponding problems of Europe. Except for the external restraints imposed upon it by the mercantilist policies of England, the new world was still too young and too fluid in its social relationships to suffer as much as the older continent from outworn institutions. This made it possible for the American Revolution, once the initial difficulty of separation from England had been met, to develop along comparatively peaceful lines. But even though the analogy between American and European conditions was far from complete, the news from across the sea could hardly fail to have widespread repercussions. After a century of tranquillity, during which the power of established governments had nowhere been significantly challenged, a revolutionary population had arisen and won reforms denied by legitimate authorities. This example was a standing invitation to revolutionary action in other parts of the world.

France was the first country to feel the impact of these developments. In some measure this was due to the fact that the French, as allies of the colonists in the later phases of the revolutionary war, had come in direct contact with American experience. Unusual dissatisfaction with the possibilities of reform within the existing political order was the real consideration, however, which made the American example particularly appealing to the French middle classes. Although enlightened despotism elsewhere had proved to be a reasonably useful ally of the Enlightenment, special conditions had made it practically useless in France. Ever since the time of Louis XIV, the policy of the French monarchy had been to curb the rebellious tendencies of the upper nobility by incorporating them in the royal administration. As a result of this policy, the holders of hereditary privilege had become so firmly entrenched in the royal court and in the public services that they were able, to a greater extent than in most countries, to stifle the expression of reformatory impulses on the part of the monarchy. Even when the pressure of accumulated abuses brought the nation to the verge of bankruptcy, the inertia of a privilege-dominated administration was strong enough to frustrate the efforts even of so well-meaning a minister as Turgot. Experiences like this made it clear that enlightened despotism could never become an effective instrument of middle-class action in France. This encouraged Frenchmen to look with ever-increasing favor on the American alternative of reform by revolution.

In France even more than in America, however, it was necessary to carry out the revolution on a broadly democratic rather than on a purely middle-class basis. The French middle classes did not have the advantage of living in a fluid commercial and pioneering community with a well-established tradition of political freedom. They were part of an ancient and comparatively stable society consisting mainly of peasant agriculturists, and dominated by the relics of an entrenched feudal nobility. Their only hope of success lay in their ability, as spokesmen for the people as a whole, to mobilize the forces of popular, and above all of agrarian discontent which had been slowly accumulating against the exactions of the *ancien régime*. From the beginning, therefore, middle-class proponents of revolution had to think in democratic terms.

This found expression in the history of the third estate. In 1789 the estates general, the French counterpart of the English parliament, was summoned by the king, for the first time in more than a century, to deal with the problem of national bankruptcy. Since the third estate in France, as in most continental parliaments, represented the interests of urban communities, the hopes of middle-class reformers centered in that particular branch of the assembly. Under the traditional system of procedure, however, the third estate would have been powerless to accomplish anything against the opposition of the other two estates. This difficulty was overcome by ascribing superior rights to the third estate, not as representatives of the middle class alone, but as representatives of the entire nation. This claim proved to be so convincing that the third estate was allowed on this occasion to elect twice as many delegates as either of the others. When the estates assembled, the third estate then proceeded to demand that the old system of having each estate meet and vote separately, like the two houses of an American congress, be abandoned in favor of joint meetings in a single national assembly. Since the aspirations of the Enlightenment were shared not only by the whole of the third estate, but also by a substantial minority of nobles and clerics, the effect of these changes was to place the assembly in the hands of a clear reformist majority. Thus the enlightened middle classes succeeded, through the adoption of a democratic ideology, in acquiring a powerful revolutionary weapon for the accomplishment of their purposes.

The resulting opportunity was exploited to the full. On August 4, in a single session of wild enthusiasm, the whole traditional complex of class privileges was abolished, making all Frenchmen equal in the sight of the law. Shortly thereafter the special privileges of various localities were handled in an equally drastic fashion with the abolition of all historic units of regional government, and the establishment of a uniform system of departmental administration. Old and inconvenient weights and measures, many of them local in scope, were replaced by a simple and uniform metric system. Through the efforts of the national assembly and its successors, the spirit of enlightened rationalism was able, in these and in many other fields, to effect a thoroughgoing reform of social and political life. Within a remarkably short space of time a vast array of traditional abuses and inconveniences disappeared for good. The most optimistic hopes of eighteenth-century rationalism seemed to be in process of fulfillment.

This experience called for a reorientation of the political thought of the Enlightenment. At a time when absolute monarchy had remained unresponsive to middle-class persuasion, an assembly which spoke in the name of the people had proved to be singularly ardent in the cause of reform. This led most progressive thinkers to conclude that popular majorities rather than kings were the authorities most amenable to rational argument, and that absolute democracy was preferable to enlightened despotism as a solution to the problem of government. In the writings of men like Paine and Bentham, a democratic interpretation of history became the order of the day. According to this theory, the evils of society derive from the fact that kings and other members of the ruling classes have a natural interest in maintaining their own privileges at the expense of the community as a whole. Against this interest, humanitarian arguments can never hope to make a deep or lasting impression. The mass of society, on the other hand, has everything to gain and nothing to lose by following the dictates of right reason. The possibility that majorities themselves might be interested in gaining a privileged position through the political exploitation of minorities, a possibility fully recognized in Rousseau's theory of the general will, was generally disregarded. Although their onetime trust in enlightened despotism had collapsed, the philosophers of the Enlightenment had as yet lost little of their confidence in the persuasive powers of reason. Convinced that a properly instructed people could not fail to support the middle-class conception of human welfare, they now felt that the solution of all political problems lay in the establishment of absolute majority rule. Like the preceding theory of enlightened despotism, this was a typical expression of eighteenth-century rationalism.

In France as in America, however, the course of events soon cast a chill on the hopes of the Enlightenment. As time went on it became evident that the middle classes could not long control the revolutionary forces which they themselves had evoked. Emphasis on majority rights was safe enough in the early days, when the lower and middle classes were still at one in their desire to escape the burdens imposed by the privileges of the nobility and of the clergy. Once the bulk of these privileges had been swept away, however, the situation of the middle classes became increasingly difficult. Many people, having gained their main objectives, turned conservative and lost interest in the prosecution of further reforms. This was especially true of the peasantry, which was delighted to escape the exactions of feudal landlords but preferred in other respects to abide by traditional ways. Other groups became excessively radical, and demanded changes which were no longer in harmony with the ideas of the middle-class Enlightenment. Extremists like Buonarroti and Babeuf began appealing to the unpropertied urban masses by asserting that equality of property was no less important than equality of legal status as a basis for human liberty. Although voices of this sort were few, they were significant as an indication that the revolution was moving beyond the point where it could be dominated by strictly middle-class conceptions. As time went on, the right of enlightened reformers to speak in the name of the sovereign people became increasingly dubious.

In America, as we have seen, the effect of similar difficulties was to turn the current of middle-class thought in the direction of constitutional government. In France this same conclusion, though ultimately reached, was delayed for a time by the circumstance that the political tradition of that country offered little encouragement to the adoption of constitutional methods. Frenchmen for generations had been accustomed to the rule of absolute kings. When the revolutionary experience with majority rule proved disappointing, their immediate tendency was to look for an alternative form of personal absolutism. The turning point came in 1795, when the unpopular revolutionary

authorities extricated themselves from an awkward position by ordering a rising young general named Bonaparte
to turn his guns on a mob of angry Parisians. From that
time onward it was obvious that no reformist government,
in the face of domestic insurrection and foreign invasion,
could hope to survive without the support of the armed
forces. In 1800 the situation reached its logical conclusion
in the coronation of Bonaparte as emperor. A single individual had once again been entrusted with absolute authority to determine the destinies of France.

The Napoleonic experiment in enlightened despotism
proved hardly more successful than its predecessor in
meeting the requirements of the Enlightenment. It is true
that the process of rationalizing social and governmental
procedure, a process so notably begun in the revolutionary
period, continued with marked success under the leadership of the emperor. Administrative organization reached
a hitherto undreamed of stage of perfection. A single admirably developed code of law, the Napoleonic code, took
the place of an outworn and chaotic legal system. The Napoleonic conquest of Europe had the effect, moreover, of
encouraging the adoption of French reforms throughout
the greater part of the continent, thus bringing the
achievements of the Enlightenment within the reach of all.
The only trouble was that Napoleon's preoccupation with
military exploits involved costs which could not be justified from the utilitarian standpoint of the prosperous middle classes. The peasants of France, whose sons were dying
by the thousands to satisfy the needs of an insatiable military machine, were willing to support Napoleon as long as
they could share in the glory of his victories. Even after his
defeat the magic of the Napoleonic legend continued for

generations to exercise a remarkable hold on the imagination of the French masses. But the idea of military glory had no place in the hedonistic calculus of eighteenth-century rationalism. Once the obstacles to free enterprise had disappeared, the middle classes asked nothing more of government than that it should leave them to the enjoyment of their economic and intellectual opportunities. The Napoleonic system of military expansion called for an ever-increasing degree of taxation, trade regulation, and censorship. Although Napoleon was more energetic than the Bourbon kings, his energy found expression in ways which could not be reconciled with rationalistic humanism. Once again the method of enlightened despotism had shown its inadequacy for the accomplishment of middle-class purposes.

The result was to force French liberals, in much the same fashion as the Americans of a preceding generation, to take refuge in the principles of constitutional government. It is true that the ideal of democratic absolutism was not abandoned by all supporters of the Enlightenment. In England, which had not experienced the evils of revolutionary and Napoleonic despotism, it was possible for a man like Bentham to place his hopes in absolute majority rule. For most of the middle classes, however, all forms of absolutism were discredited. When the power of Napoleon was broken by England and her allies, the more prosperous members of this group were generally willing to accept a Bourbon restoration. Since the new regime was unable to command any considerable measure of popular enthusiasm, this in itself was calculated to reduce the power of the French state. But the middle classes by this time were so deeply suspicious of despotism in general that they

were unwilling to rely on Bourbon weakness as the sole defense of their interests. Only a constitutional monarchy
was now acceptable. Although the constitutional tradition
of France itself, as of most continental countries, had been
pretty well destroyed by centuries of absolutism, a model
of limited kingship was available in England. This model
was promptly adopted by middle-class thinkers as an answer to their needs. When Louis XVIII came to the throne
he had to issue a charter guaranteeing all citizens in the
possession of certain important rights, and sharing his
power with a two-chamber parliament after the English
fashion. When his reactionary successor, Charles X, tried
to disregard these limitations and return to the practice of
absolute kingship, the outcome was the revolution of 1830
and the selection of a new monarch who was willing to
rule under constitutional conditions of an even more
stringent sort. Constitutionalism by this time had become
so much a standard part of middle-class doctrine that men
were willing to fight rather than to see it destroyed. After
many painful adventures, the philosophy of the Enlightenment had reached its final solution to the problem of politics.

To an even greater extent than in the case of America,
the adoption of constitutional government in France
meant the abandonment of exclusive pretensions on the
part of the middle classes. When confidence in the power
of reason had been at its height, it had been possible to
dream of a world in which the views of the Enlightenment
would be universally triumphant. Constitutionalism, on
the other hand, involved the acceptance, on terms of equal
partnership, of other groups with other points of view. The
lower classes could, to be sure, be rather more easily disre-

garded in peasant Europe than in pioneer America. This made it expedient, in the earlier stages of French constitutionalism, to restrict the franchise to a comparatively narrow group of electors with high property qualifications. The resulting middle-class advantage was more than counterbalanced, however, by the fact that France, unlike America, was the home of a landed aristocracy still too rich and powerful to be challenged with impunity. The restoration could take place only on the basis of an uneasy compromise between middle-class and upper-class interests. To provide the political framework for such a compromise was the first great task of French constitutionalism.

The classic theoretical expression of this particular phase of French history appears in the writings of Benjamin Constant, whose *Course on Constitutional Politics* is the best systematic exposition of the argument for constitutional monarchy. In its underlying principles this work was quite traditional. Like the Americans of *The Federalist*, Constant based his conception of political liberty on a theory of the separation of powers already thoroughly popularized by English revolutionists of the seventeenth century. His importance lay in the skill with which he was able to adapt that theory to the circumstances of contemporary politics.

According to his doctrine any properly constructed government should have not three but five separate and mutually balancing parts. By the early nineteenth century the development of the British cabinet system had made it obvious, as it had not been in the time of Locke, that responsibility for the administration of a modern state rests in the hands of cabinet ministers rather than those of the

king himself. Constant accordingly made room for kingship by recognizing, in addition to the familiar executive
power, a so-called royal or neutral power, vested with the
task of overseeing the maintenance of constitutional government as a whole. The position of a modern English
king, who is expected to assume active responsibility only
in times of political or constitutional crisis, but remains as
a lasting symbol of constitutional morality, is a fair example of what Constant conceived the neutral power to be.
The realities of contemporary political life were also reflected in his treatment of the legislative branch of government. Recognizing the necessity of safeguarding the interests of rival social classes, he defended the proposition that
the work of legislation ought to be entrusted to two equal
chambers, the one representing hereditary position, the
other property. In view of the fact that no legislation
could pass without the consent of both chambers, this
meant that the aristocracy and the wealthy middle classes
were both protected against the adoption of legislative
policies on any other basis than mutual consent. This,
together with the familiar judicial power, gave Constant
a grand total of five separate organs of government. Although the general principle was not new, the unusual
elaborateness of this particular application is evidence of
the fear with which French liberals were now disposed to
regard the possibility of absolute government.

Under a political system which gave so much power to
the aristocracy, the middle classes did not feel, however,
that the possession of a virtual legislative veto would suffice to guarantee their position. Nothing less than the
absolute exclusion of government from certain forms of
activity would satisfy their minimum demand for eco-

nomic and intellectual freedom. Although many civil liberties were incorporated in the charter of the restored monarchy, the fact that this charter had been issued as an act of royal authority, and might conceivably be withdrawn in the same way, tended to make the legal situation somewhat precarious. Constant met this situation by a fresh appeal to the principle of natural law. A large part of his work went to show that there are certain types of action which no government, constitutional or otherwise, can legitimately undertake. According to this theory, the purpose of government itself is to guarantee men in the possession of such basic rights as freedom of speech, freedom of contract, and the right of private property. Any government which attempts to interfere with these rights is acting beyond its legitimate competence, and need not be obeyed. Although it may be convenient and desirable, as in the bill-of-rights amendments to the American constitution, or in the French declaration of the rights of man, to embody these principles in the form of a specific legal enactment, right reason is sufficient to support the validity of such limitations even when they are not expressly guaranteed in a constitutional document. The attitude of the American supreme court in voiding legislation under the due-process clause has frequently been close to Constant's point of view. By the early nineteenth century the political consciousness of middle-class liberals was so strongly developed that they were unwilling to abide by the result of any political process which failed to reflect their basic aspirations. Constant is the classic exponent of this particular stage in the evolution of modern liberalism.

This trend was characteristic not only of France and

America, where it first made its appearance, but also of the Western world in general. On the continent of Europe the hope of the middle classes everywhere centered in the establishment of constitutional systems, usually monarchies after the French pattern. After many discouraging setbacks this hope was generally realized. In England, where the power of the monarch had already been limited to the verge of extinction, the problem was to gain control of a parliament long dominated, on the basis of narrowly limited voting rights and the rotten-borough system, by the great landowners of the nation. This objective was won in 1832, when the threat of revolution induced the aristocratic parliament to pass a drastic reform act abolishing the rotten-borough system and admitting persons with middle-class property qualifications to the exercise of the parliamentary franchise. When the resistance of the aristocracy seemed too great to be overcome in any other way, the middle classes often followed in the footsteps of the French and American revolutions by appealing to the power of the masses. Fear of the rapidly growing democratic movement, which enjoyed the support of leading utilitarians, had much to do with the passage of the British reform act. What the middle classes really wanted, however, was not the triumph of majority rule but the establishment of limited constitutions in which they themselves, if not actually dominant, would at least have the power to veto undesirable acts. This was the basis of their devotion to the principles of constitutional government.

Adequate as these arrangements may have been from the standpoint of the Enlightenment, they provided no final answer to the problem of modern politics. The ultimate object of eighteenth- and early nineteenth-century thought, like that of the medieval churchmen, was to place institutional limits upon the exercise of state power. The effectiveness of the medieval solution depended on the fact that the church was an all-embracing organization capable of mobilizing the total moral force of the Christian community against the abuses of kingship. If parliaments were to become similarly effective in controlling the activities of modern bureaucracies, it was necessary that they should acquire a comparable position as spokesmen for the entire secular community. Even in its final constitutional form, the political thought of the Enlightenment provided no sufficient basis for the attainment of that end. Although the middle classes might be content with an arrangement which limited government to the task of guaranteeing free markets, experience had shown that this negative conception had no strong appeal for other potentially important groups. People less well equipped to prosper under the conditions of individual competition could hardly be expected to sacrifice themselves in defense of such a system. The rapidity with which the bourgeois monarchy of France was overthrown in 1848, and the ease with which Napoleon III was able to gain popular support for the establishment of a second empire, was in itself an indication of the fact that the whole structure of middle-class liberalism rested on dangerously narrow foundations. Fundamentally the ideas of the Enlightenment, though proclaimed in the name of all humanity, were an expression not of the general will but of a specific class interest. As long as the practice of constitutional government was bound up with these ideas, there could never be any hope of making parliaments an effective check on bureaucratic power.

With all their limitations, however, these early experiments had the value of creating an institutional basis for the evolution of modern democracy. Although Rousseau had been in advance of most men of his time in recognizing the need for an all-embracing general will, he had been unable to think of a practicable way to bring it into existence. The constitutional theorists who succeeded him, for all their unawareness of the problem itself, unconsciously pointed the way to a solution. Rousseau had seen that a general will cannot operate if minorities, like the slaves in ancient Athens, are coerced by majorities. In their desire, under the conditions of monarchical restoration, to protect themselves against the possible preponderance of aristocratic power, the middle classes had to take the lead in defining those areas of governmental action, such as the protection of private property, which they and the aristocracy both considered desirable, and in imposing specific constitutional prohibitions against any attempt to act outside the area of common agreement. Conscious of the fact that the general will must conform to the common interests of the entire community, Rousseau had insisted on the active and equal participation of all men in the direction of political life. The necessity of coöperating with landowning aristocrats forced the middle classes to encourage the formation of bicameral parliamentary bodies in which both groups were represented, and in which everything had to be done through a process of mutually satisfactory negotiation. Through party leadership, parliamentary committees, and other empirically discovered devices, people gradually learned the art of welding discordant interests into effective parliamentary majorities, and of using those majorities, through budgetary and other procedures, as a check on the power of bureaucracies. Since their parliamentary position depended on electoral victories, party leaders also found it necessary to use their conciliatory arts on the electorate, uniting diverse elements in support of mutually acceptable personalities and programs. Although the attempt at first was not to create a general will embracing the whole of society, the necessity of finding a basis for common agreement between aristocratic and middle-class elements of the community provided an occasion for the development of ideas and institutions which later could be used in a wider social context. When the pressure of subsequently awakened social groups made it necessary to extend the franchise beyond its original limits, accumulated experience in the arts of negotiation and compromise was available to facilitate the work of bringing these groups within the framework of parliamentary government. Thus the institutions of early nineteenth-century constitutionalism, though designed for the comparatively limited purpose of reconciling the interests of a divided ruling class, actually became the basis for the creation of a comprehensive general will. The social and political developments which led to this result are the history of modern liberalism.

7

The Conservative Reaction

The awakening of the agricultural classes was the second great stage in the evolution of modern liberalism. We have already seen that the vigor of aristocratic resistance to middle-class pretensions had much to do with the emergence of liberal constitutionalism. That resistance was the product of a political movement known as the conservative reaction. Like the philosophers of the Enlightenment, the theorists of conservatism had no original desire to institute constitutional government. Their purpose was to defend the traditional structure of rural society against the impact of the middle-class revolution. Convinced that the needs and interests of that society were identical with the welfare of humanity, they sought, in much the same way as the exponents of enlightened despotism, to impose their views on the rest of the population through the use of absolute power. Their ultimate acceptance of parliamentary government was due not to any love of constitutionalism but to the failure of their original pretensions. But if their contribution to modern liberalism was involuntary, it was none the less substantial. By inspiring the rural classes to resist the forces of the Enlightenment, they aroused an important section of the population to political self-consciousness. Following on the heels of the middle-class awakening, the conservative reaction made it necessary to face the problem of creating a secular society based not on the particular will of a single social group, but on the general will of a complex community. This was its contribution to the development of modern liberal politics.

The history of modern conservatism begins in the years immediately following the outbreak of the French Revolution. Up to that time the landowning aristocracy, absorbed in the privileges and duties of a hereditary ruling class, had felt so sure of their position that they had allowed the philosophers of the Enlightenment to dominate the world of letters by default. As long as no one interfered with their accustomed way of life, most of them were too busy and self-assured to think of entering the field of political controversy. When the revolution was upon them, however, many able members of this group began to apply their talents to theoretical questions. It is characteristic that Maistre and Bonald, the two leading exponents of early French conservatism, were both men in their early forties who had never written anything for publication until the revolution abruptly tore them from their place as minor members of the hereditary public service. A revolutionary crisis was likewise needed to induce Edmund Burke, at the age of sixty-one, to take time off from his labors as a member of the British parliamentary oligarchy and compose his first comprehensive work on political philosophy. As soon as they began to devote their attention to the matter, these men had little difficulty in challenging the philosophy of the Enlightenment. Their efforts soon laid the foundations for a vigorous reassertion of the conservative position in politics.

Although the leaders of the conservative reaction came from the aristocracy, they were able to speak for a social group more numerous and important than the hereditary ruling class. As the product of an urban environment, the philosophers of the Enlightenment had never had any real appreciation of the needs and aspirations of the rural population. The aristocracy, on the other hand, was primarily a rural landowning group, sharing many interests and experiences with other members of the agricultural community. It is true that some aristocrats, through the practice of absentee ownership, had lost contact with the peasantry. In regions where the evils of absenteeism were particularly prevalent, hostility to the privileges of noble landlords provided the basis for an alliance between the peasants and the revolutionary middle classes. But most aristocrats were still active agriculturists with an unimpaired tradition of leadership in their local communities. Even in France, where royal policy had forced great noblemen to live away from their estates, there were certain districts, like the Vendée, where the local gentry were able to lead the peasantry in stubborn rebellion against the revolutionary republic. In other countries far larger sections of the aristocracy were in a position to exercise local influence. Since the peasantry at this time formed a majority of the total population of Europe, substantial power lay within the grasp of anyone who could organize them as an active political force. This was the challenge and the opportunity of the conservative reaction.

From the standpoint of other members of the community, the great defect of the middle-class revolution was its tendency to upset the habitual bases of social life. Habit rather than choice is the normal basis of human action. Learning to do new things in a new way is such hard work that no one has energy enough to do very much of it at any given time. To the extent that it involves the abandonment of settled habits, therefore, innovation is painful. This particular element of cost was neglected in the hedonistic calculus of the Enlightenment. Impressed, for example, by the rational simplicity of the decimal system, revolutionary legislators had no qualms about disrupting the routine of daily life by forcing people to cope simultaneously with a new set of metric weights and measures, with a decimal currency, and with an unfamiliar republican calendar. Preoccupied with the advantages of technological progress, enlightened economists were willing to allow the discoverer of new methods of production to deprive less efficient producers of their traditional livelihood, immediately and without compensation, through the operation of free competitive markets. For intelligent and adaptable members of the middle class, the costs of change were not excessive in comparison with the profits. For those who had to bear the brunt of innovation, the situation was disastrous. Absolute adaptability to the requirements of a constantly changing society is an impossible standard of behavior for ordinary men. Failure to recognize this fact was the essential weakness of the eighteenth-century Enlightenment.

Of all the members of contemporary society, the agricultural classes were the ones who stood to suffer most from the ruthless progressivism of early liberal thought. In its emphasis on rational calculation and social mobility, the Enlightenment was a reflection of urban rather than of rural experience. Life in an environment of cosmopolitan intercourse and changing fashion teaches men to adjust their minds to novel currents of thought, and to adapt their labor to the demands of fluctuating markets.

In a world where social contacts are loose and casual, people are relatively free to determine their movements in accord with the dictates of individual self-interest. As far as the urban population was concerned, therefore, the idea of a society based on calculating individualism was not entirely false. As applied to the conditions of rural society, however, the presuppositions of early liberalism were grotesquely unrealistic. Generations of quiet village life had done nothing to prepare eighteenth-century peasants for the task of understanding and dealing with unfamiliar problems. Devoted to the cultivation of traditional crops by traditional methods, they were incapable of adjusting their labor to a fluctuating economy. Intimately wrapped up in the social life of a specific community, and owing their livelihood to the productivity of a specific piece of land, they were less free than other people to move about in search of favorable employment. All this made it impossible for them to profit by the opportunities, and exposed them to all the disadvantages, of a dynamic social order. Under conditions of free competition, new manufacturing processes might appear at any moment to destroy their village handicrafts. Imports from outside regions might suddenly arrive to undersell their agricultural products. To compensate for such losses within the framework of a traditional peasant economy was impossible. Thus the philosophy of the Enlightenment, for all its value as an expression of urban interests, was hopelessly at variance with the needs and experience of the agricultural classes.

The task of the conservative reaction was to defend the traditional values of rural life against the forces of urban progressivism. This could be done only by denying the

validity of the early liberal concept of progress, and by
asserting the value of social stability as a factor in human
welfare. The writer who went farthest in this direction was
the Vicomte de Bonald, whose *Theory of Power* is notable
as one of the more radical statements of the conservative
position. In its abstract and pseudomathematical method
of argumentation, this curious work was closer to the spirit
of the Enlightenment than to the historical empiricism of
most contemporary conservatives. But the premises to
which this method was applied were different from those
adopted by the eighteenth-century philosophers, and led
to different results.

Accepting the hedonistic assumption that happiness is
the proper goal of secular existence, Bonald attempted to
show that happiness itself is a function of social stability.
He then proceeded, with all the rationalistic self-confidence of a Newtonian social scientist, to prescribe the
conditions necessary for the creation of a static society.
Although the resulting picture bore a suspicious resem-
blance to the *ancien régime* of France, it was an *ancien
régime* purged of all the dynamic features of its historic
prototype. A rigid and all-embracing caste system, designed to insure the hereditary transmission of every possible function, was to form the basis for all social and
political relations. Because of their inherently dynamic
character, commerce and industry were to be discouraged
in favor of peasant agriculture. Calculated social policies
were to maintain the level of population at an unvarying
optimum. Balance of power principles were to provide
a permanent guarantee against changes in the world of
international affairs. By applying the methods of a fully
rationalized political and social science, Bonald believed

that it would be possible to maintain society forever in an absolutely static condition. This was his answer to the problem of maximizing the happiness of men.

Although Bonald's work is interesting as an indication of the conservative emphasis on stability, it was too extreme to be influential. People generally tend, even in the face of rapidly changing circumstances, to cling to the ideas and preconceptions of the age in which they were born. In order to gain a hearing for new conceptions, therefore, it is necessary to present those conceptions in a form which does the least possible violence to established modes of thought. The success of the Enlightenment was due to the fact that most of its theories were a reinterpretation of familiar Christian doctrines. Subsequent theorists could not hope to succeed unless they made a similar attempt to reinterpret the doctrines of the Enlightenment.

By the time of the French Revolution, the idea of progress had been dominating the minds of men for several generations. Few educated people were entirely impervious to its influence. Continuing achievements in the field of science and learning made it unlikely, moreover, that it would lose its appeal for many generations to come. Although some might reject the extreme revolutionary optimism of the Enlightenment, and deplore the disruptive consequences of excessive change, the promise of new triumphs in the conquest of man's natural environment was too attractive to be lightly abandoned. The only hope for conservatives under these circumstances was to adopt the idea of progress as their own, and then to reinterpret it in a conservative direction. Because of his failure to do this, Bonald was unable to found an effective school of modern conservative thought.

For anyone acquainted with country life, the easiest way to conceive of progress is in terms of organic growth. In the artificial environment of a great city, where apples grow on grocery shelves and most things can be bought or made according to human specifications, it is natural to believe that nothing is beyond the capacity of skillful and inventive men. The idea of progress in its original form was an expression of this urban point of view. In the natural environment of the countryside, however, the potentialities of human action are more limited. A shoe-maker can start making shoes whenever he finds a customer, and if he is in a hurry there is nothing to prevent him from working overtime. An agriculturist must wait for the proper moment before he begins planting, and nothing he can do thereafter will make the crop ripen ahead of its appointed season. Inventors, once they have completed the designs for a new machine, can have it built immediately. Breeders must work for generations to carry out their ideas for the improvement of a particular strain of cattle. Far from being entirely free to create his own conditions, the farmer must be content to help things grow in accordance with their own inherent laws of development. Gathering the produce of vineyards and orchards planted by his fathers, and planting new trees which will never bear in his own lifetime, he learns to think of human welfare in terms of the coöperative effort of successive generations. Progress for him is a matter not of sudden innovation but of gradual accumulation. Rural experience leads, therefore, to a concept of organic growth which is poles apart from the mechanistic rationalism of the eight-eenth-century philosophers.

The function of conservative theory was to use this organic conception as the basis for a fundamental rein-terpretation of the early liberal idea of progress. The theo-rists who most clearly recognized this fact were Joseph de Maistre and Edmund Burke. Unlike Bonald, both of these men had a certain measure of sympathy for the progres-sive spirit of the age in which they lived. Before the out-break of the French Revolution, Burke's career as a leg-islator had been that of a cautious but persistent reformer. By his speeches on the conciliation of the North American colonies, he had identified himself with the cause of the American Revolution. He had also played a leading part in the trial of Warren Hastings, the first of a long series of attempts to overcome the abuses of British administration in India. Although Maistre's previous career had been less notable, an atmosphere of mild reformism is likewise characteristic of his works. Appalled, however, by the revolutionary extremism of the Enlightenment, both men became early and vigorous opponents of the French Rev-olution. In the same year, and under practically identical titles, each published a book expressing his concern about the current trend of developments in France. The point of view of these two books was not in all respects identical. Maistre was a deeply religious thinker with an orthodox Catholic conception of the nature and destiny of man, while Burke, without being impervious to religious in-fluences, was content to rest his case on a more purely secular basis. But in their common attempts to counter-act the spirit of the Enlightenment both men relied on an eloquent and persuasive statement of the organic conception of progress. This made them the most widely influential spokesmen of the early conservative reaction.

The starting point of their argument was a radical rejection of abstract, pseudomathematical reason. The philosophers of the Enlightenment had assumed, on the analogy of Newtonian physics, that the application of a few rationally intuited laws would suffice to solve the problems of human existence. A peasant subject to the unpredictable vagaries of wind and flood, and forced to cope with the individual idiosyncrasies of living organisms, is in a better position than the average city man to recognize the oversimplification implicit in this point of view. Thus Maistre and Burke were appealing to an important range of human experience when they challenged the rationalistic assumptions of eighteenth-century thought. According to them, man and nature alike are so complex that no mortal mind can hope to understand the full consequences of any given action. Christian theology had always taught that man is a weak and imperfect creature, incapable by his own efforts of comprehending the divine order of the universe. The conservative reaction, whether explicitly as in the case of Maistre, or implicitly as in the case of Burke, was a reversion to the Christian conception of human nature. Both theorists felt it wise, however, to rest their case on empirical as well as on dogmatic grounds. Denying the practical possibility of basing reformatory action on abstract general principles, they ventured to predict that the revolutionary movement would have consequences entirely unforeseen by its own self-confident supporters. These predictions were by no means uniformly fortunate. On the ground that there was "too much deliberation, too much humanity" in the idea of planning a national capital, Maistre offered to bet a thousand to one that the currently projected city of Washington would never become the seat of government in the United States of America. But if the conservatives went too far in denying the possibility of rational calculation, their position was a useful corrective to the opposing exaggerations of revolutionary optimism. The philosophy of the Enlightenment grossly overestimated the power of abstract reason. To deflate its pretensions was the initial task of modern conservative thought.

This attack on eighteenth-century rationalism did not go so far, however, as to deny the possibility or importance of progressive achievement. Although Burke and Maistre were sure that the mind of man could never reduce the universe to a comprehensible system, they were strong believers in the value of empirical action. The fact that they, unlike the general run of enlightened philosophers, had had a good deal of direct political experience may well have had something to do with their empirical and anti-theoretical point of view. According to their analysis of human nature, practical responses to practical problems are the basis of human achievement. An individual in the course of his daily life encounters a number of specific difficulties. Guided by intimate experience of his own immediate environment, he proceeds by a process of trial and error to look for a solution. If the solution stands the test of time, he adopts it as a general rule of conduct. Imitated by his neighbors and handed down to his descendents, the rule crystallizes in the form of tradition. Tradition, by providing men with a ready-made solution to certain problems, leaves them free to apply their energies to the solution of new difficulties. Since man is a weak and imperfectly rational creature, with no real knowledge of the causes and consequences of any action, each separate step is slow and tentative. Transmitted in unbroken succession from person to person and from generation to generation, modest discoveries nevertheless mount up to an impressive total. By experiencing the social inconveniences of unregulated passion, men gradually evolve usages of etiquette and morality. By adding invention to invention, they develop the arts of civilization. Maistre and Burke were largely in agreement with the eighteenth-century proposition that progress is the normal tendency of history. Where they differed from the Enlightenment was in insisting that empirical experience rather than abstract reason is the instrument of progressive accomplishment.

This emphasis on tradition made it possible to use the idea of progress itself as the basis for an attack on the spirit of the Enlightenment. As long as people continued to think of society in mechanistic terms there was no logical limit to the possible extremes of revolutionary action. If a watchmaker has the inventiveness to design and the skill to execute a superior timepiece, there is no reason why he should not immediately scrap his old models. The reformatory optimism of the early liberals was due to the fact that they regarded society, like a watch, as an inert mechanism susceptible to instantaneous revision by the rational will of men. But if civilization is a product of gradually accumulating tradition, organic rather than mechanistic analogies immediately suggest themselves as a clue to the proper understanding of history. The progress of humanity is a process extending over many generations. Like a plant or animal it can be fostered and encouraged, but never

forced beyond the limits of its own nature. Since the skill
and intelligence of living men are insufficient to replace
the achievement of past generations, progress depends on
the continuity of tradition. A social reformer, like a conscientious farmer, will always try to improve the organism
under his care. Maistre and Burke were willing to admit
that there were imperfections and abuses in the existing
state of society, and recognized the need of patient efforts
to eliminate those abuses. Where the French Revolution
went wrong, in their opinion, was in trying to force the
tempo of social change to a point incompatible with traditional continuity. An experienced cattle breeder knows
that it would be disastrous to treat his animals in such a
way as to jeopardize the life of the herd. Impatient interference with the traditional structure of society is equally
dangerous to the welfare of humanity. All living things
enjoy at best a precarious existence. A few minutes will
suffice to fell a tree which represents a century of growth.
Deluded by an unrealistic faith in the possibility of rational reconstruction, the philosophers of the revolution
were preparing to lay the axe to the traditional roots of
civilization. By destroying rather than developing the
achievements of the past, they threatened not merely to
retard the rate of human progress but to cause a regression
from which it would take long centuries to recover. This
was the conservative answer to the revolutionary optimism
of the Enlightenment.

Although the concept of organic growth, like the earlier
concept of mechanistic rationalism, had its roots in the
experience of a particular class, its appeal extended beyond the limits of that class. The excesses of the French
Revolution gave rise to a mood of doubt and revulsion on

the part not only of the agricultural population but also of most other members of the community. Ugly manifestations of mob violence and terrorism made thoughtful spirits everywhere begin to fear the consequences of relaxing the restraints of traditional morality. As the dream of an immediate heaven on earth gave way to the harsh realities of Napoleonic warfare, the limitations of rationalistic calculation became increasingly apparent. New doubts as to the intellectual and moral capacities of men made it necessary to formulate a new conception of human nature. As an answer to that need, the conservative doctrine of progress was able to effect a rapid and lasting revolution in the presuppositions of Western thought.

The romantic movement, which began to dominate the world of letters at this time, was a characteristic reflection, among other things, of the conservative revolution. Classical literature had proceeded on the Newtonian principle that art is an exemplification of universal laws. According to classical critics, the function of the artist was to select and formulate the raw material of experience in such a way as to produce works exemplifying the abstract and rationally verifiable rules of artistic perfection. The romantics, on the other hand, insisted on the right of every living organism to express itself in accordance with the laws of its own particular nature. Where their predecessors had tried to discover universal truths, and to analyze typical forms of behavior, they stressed the unique and personal aspects of human character. Unlike the classical tragedians, who used history as a convenient means of illustrating ageless problems such as the conflict of love and duty, they cherished the past for its own sake, attempting to recapture the individual flavor of exotic times and peoples. The novels of Sir Walter Scott, with their loving re-creation of the days when knighthood was in flower, were a typical romantic product. As a reaction against the rationalistic uniformity of the classical world, the romantics yearned for the color and multiplicity of a universe teeming with the endless variety of organic life. In some cases this attitude led to immediately conservative conclusions. Thus Chateaubriand justified the Bourbon restoration by recalling the romantic association of royalty with the historic glories of France. But even when the romantics were not politically conservative, their emphasis on personal and historic individuality helped to reinforce the conservative attack on eighteenth-century rationalism. Thus the triumph of romanticism served as an indirect but powerful confirmation of the conservative position.

The rise of historicism, which took place at the same time, had much the same effect. In their attitude toward history the philosophers of the Enlightenment had been closely akin to the classical tragedians. Confident in the possession of universally valid laws, they had regarded the past not as something to be understood and appreciated for its own sake, but as a convenient storehouse of examples and warnings for the benefit of those who might stray from the path of right reason. Periods like the European Middle Ages, which had persisted in religious bigotry and other forms of unenlightened conduct, were either neglected or condemned. Toward the beginning of the nineteenth century, however, a different attitude toward history, and above all toward the Middle Ages, began to make its appearance. Newly impressed with the importance of traditional continuity, students in various fields found that they could increase their understanding of many problems by a sympathetic investigation of historical origins. The German jurist Savigny, distressed by the revolutionary rationalism of the Napoleonic code, devoted his life to a study of the historical development of modern civil law. Following his lead innumerable scholars, in an attempt to justify the peculiarities and explain the needs of particular institutions, began tracing the historical antecedents of nations, classes, ideas, and other social forces, thus laying the foundations of modern historical science. Through the use of comparable historical methods, students also succeeded in raising disciplines like linguistics and geology to the status of exact sciences. The movement reached its culmination in 1859, when the publication of Darwin's *Origin of Species* showed that even the forms of animal life, previously regarded as fixed creations, were a product of historical evolution. By the middle of the nineteenth century, historical empiricism had definitely replaced mechanistic rationalism as the prevailing mode of Western thought. From that day to this, the evolutionary view of progress has never ceased to play a leading part in the intellectual life of the West.

Intrinsically, the conservative theory of progress was not a political doctrine. Like the philosophy of the Enlightenment, it was an attempt to define the inalienable rights of society in a form which would be equally applicable against the encroachments of any type of government. It is true that the conservatives, with their traditionalist view of society, differed from the early liberals in their opinion as to the proper scope of state action. Regarding the individual as the true source of progress, the Enlightenment had believed that the free market, which gives the widest possible range to individual initiative, was the only institution necessary for the organization of society, and urged that the state confine its activities to the defense of that institution. The conservatives, on the other hand, believed that tradition-bearing groups rather than isolated individuals are the primary agents of progress. For them the organization of a truly progressive society depended not merely on the existence of a single institution, the free market, but on the maintenance of a wide variety of traditional associations. To defend and foster all these associations was the function of properly conservative states. But even though this might involve a relatively large range of positive state action, traditionalism agreed with the philosophy of the Enlightenment in regarding society rather than the state as the primary source of human welfare. Like the exponents of medieval dualism, the conservatives were supporters of an autonomous social order whose interests took precedence over the interests of any political authority. As long as those interests received due consideration, specific questions of political organization were logically a matter of indifference.

But if the logic of conservative theory lay in the direction of social dualism, political contingencies led its supporters to place an extremely one-sided emphasis on the power and importance of the state. We have already seen that the philosophers of the Enlightenment, in their desire to use political power for the purpose of establishing a free market, were initially inclined to support absolute monarchy. Since the long-run power of the rural population, in a world of expanding commerce and industry, was substantially less than that of the middle classes, the conservatives were even more painfully aware of the need for state support. Deprived of the protection of the monarchy, the French aristocracy had been unable to maintain itself against the forces of the revolution. Only the restoration of the Bourbons, supported by the united armies of Europe, made it possible for them to return from penniless exile to a position of importance. Under these circumstances it was natural for them to exaggerate the role of political authority in the maintenance of social order. One of the most curious and unsatisfactory features of Burke's writings is his tendency to assume that none of the arts and graces of civilization could possibly survive the death of Marie Antoinette. Other conservatives were more extreme in supporting the view that an all-powerful monarchy is indispensable to the maintenance of traditional values. To an even greater extent, therefore, than in the case of early liberalism, the initial tendency of conservatism was to upset the balance of Western dualism in the direction of state absolutism.

At the present time, the idea of an alliance between aristocracy and monarchy is not especially surprising. Actually the attempt to form such an alliance was a radical departure from the tradition of European politics. Ever since the end of the Middle Ages, the authority of kings had been a force operating in the direction of radical innovation. In the interest of an ever-increasing rationalization of political and social life, ambitious monarchs had never hesitated, within the limits of their power, to upset the traditional bases of society. The development of modern state bureaucracies was a centuries-long assault on the traditional independence of manors, guilds, parliaments, and other ancient institutions. Since the middle classes, as the leading exponents of technological efficiency, had generally supported and contributed to the royal war against tradition, the eighteenth-century idea of enlightened monarchy was compatible with middle-class habits of thought. The aristocracy, on the other hand, was the hereditary enemy of monarchy. As the chief beneficiaries of a waning social order, they had always opposed the attempts of upstart royal servants to reduce the traditional privileges of landowners and parliaments. Accustomed to running their own localities in their own way, they resented the centralizing power of the modern state, frequently resisting it with acts of open rebellion. One of these rebellions, known as the Fronde, had taken place in France itself as recently as the seventeenth century. Although the authority of the monarch had prevailed, the Frondist spirit was not dead. Suspicion of and hostility to the power of kings was one of the inveterate elements of the aristocratic tradition. When conservative theorists spoke in favor of absolute monarchy they were flying in the face of all the past experience of the class whose interests they were trying to defend.

Under the conditions then prevailing, however, the idea of a tradition-defending monarchy was by no means fantastic. Although the institution of kingship had tended in the past to be revolutionary rather than conservative in character, the French Revolution had deprived most European kings of the opportunity to play their accustomed role. Their traditional allies, the revolutionary middle classes, had become permanently disillusioned with the potentialities of enlightened despotism, and were now unwilling to support anything more than a narrowly circumscribed form of constitutional monarchy. Although some rulers might be content to reign on these terms, it went against the grain of men long used to absolute authority. This left them with no alternative but to join the conservative camp. Many monarchs and aristocrats had recently been fellow sufferers in exile. The fact that kings, like noblemen, owed their position to hereditary right also served as a common bond in a period when hereditary claims were subject to rational criticism. All this made it relatively easy for monarchs, now that the possibility of revolutionary initiative had slipped from their hands, to forget the revolutionary exploits of their ancestors, and to regard themselves as the divinely appointed defenders of an unchanging traditional order. Granted the impossibility of gaining middle-class support, no absolute ruler could hope to maintain his throne without satisfying the demands of the aristocracy. This made it possible for aristocratic theorists to accept absolute monarchy without jeopardizing their position.

In their acceptance of royal absolutism, the aristocracy never succeeded, however, in shaking off their deep-seated distrust of kings. This gave a curiously ambiguous character to their theory of monarchy. In order to counteract the danger of popular revolution, conservative theorists like Maistre and Bonald found it necessary, on the one hand, to proclaim the duty of absolute and unconditional obedience. Apart from Maistre's half-hearted suggestion that an appeal to the pope might provide an acceptable way of deposing particularly outrageous rulers, they were unwilling to admit the legitimacy of any attempt to curtail the sovereign authority of kings. In order to counteract the dangers of royal unreliability it was necessary, on the other hand, to discourage sovereigns from acting on their own responsibility. Conservative theorists accordingly took great pains to point out that monarchs have little or nothing to do with the actual conduct of government. Since no one man can run a country unaided, all states, whatever their legal form, are aristocracies in fact. The function of kingship is to lend authority to the aristocratic administration. By impressing common people with the duty of obedience, and by inspiring aristocrats to devote their united efforts to the state, the traditional prestige of monarchy provides a unique basis for political stability. "The word KING," said Maistre, "is a talisman, a magic power which gives to all talents and forces a central direction." A similar emphasis on the psychological importance and practical impotence of kingship is also characteristic of Bonald's political writings. The history of the *ancien régime* in France had shown that legally omnipotent monarchs are incapable of overcoming the will of a well-entrenched aristocratic administration. To revive and perpetuate this curiously qualified form of absolutism was the object of conservative politics.

The theories of Maistre and Bonald were reasonably acceptable to the aristocracy. As the basis for an appeal to other elements of the community they were less satisfactory. Although the name "king" had not yet lost all its traditional magic, the attempt to use it as a cover for absolutism ran counter to the prevailing trend. The French Revolution had acquainted Europe with the idea of freedom. For the middle classes, the removal of external restraints on individual action was the hallmark of social progress. The abolition of aristocratic privileges had given the peasantry also a certain sense of the value of liberty. Like the desire for progress, the desire for freedom by this time was so powerful that political theorists could hardly afford to neglect it. In order to be effective, conservative theorists had to face the necessity of incorporating the idea of freedom within the structure of their political thought. Because of their failure to accomplish this, men like Maistre and Bonald were incapable of providing the basis for a widely influential statement of the conservative position.

The man who finally undertook this task was the German philosopher Hegel. Unlike the majority of the earlier conservative theorists, Hegel was not a member of the aristocracy. In his earlier years, moreover, he was strongly attracted by the philosophy of the Enlightenment. Traces of this early liberal influence remained throughout his work. His emphasis on legal rights was at variance, for example, with the patriarchal ideas of most German conservatives, and made him *persona non grata* to the more hidebound representatives of the Prussian Junker class. In his ultimate capacity as a university professor, on the other hand, he had a share in the official responsibility of training candidates for the Prussian civil service, and rapidly assimilated the conservative point of view. This varied experience found expression in his later political writings. Although the purpose of these writings was to provide a philosophical justification for the conservative Prussian monarchy, Hegel's firsthand acquaintance with the philosophy of the Enlightenment made him genuinely aware of the power of its leading ideas. To incorporate those ideas as far as possible within the framework of conservative thought was the guiding principle of his later work. This enabled him to present the theory of modern conservatism in an uncommonly sophisticated light.

The need for a conservative reinterpretation of eighteenth-century liberalism was particularly urgent in post-Napoleonic Prussia. It is true that Germany, as the region which had suffered most from the religious wars of the seventeenth century, had generally tended to go further than other countries in welcoming royal absolutism as a defense against disorder. Because of this tradition, the German princes had been able, in the period of conservative reaction, to assume a leading place in the attack on constitutional monarchy. Even in Germany, however, the course of royal absolutism was not easy. Educated Germans had always been susceptible to the intellectual influence of France. As the favorite battleground of revolutionary and Napoleonic armies, many regions had also come in direct contact with the ideas of the French Revolution. In Prussia, where the recent patriotic revival had led, under the direction of men like Baron Stein, to the adoption of many enlightened reforms, the influence of middle-class liberalism was particularly strong. During the first decades of the nineteenth century, when Hegel was doing his work, liberal ideas were continuing to win many converts among the middle and upper classes. University students and faculties were especially prone to liberal infection. As a professional academician, Hegel was fully aware of the fact that the concept of freedom possessed great powers of attraction for the educated youth of Germany. To capture this idea for the benefit of conservatism was the underlying purpose of his later political writings.

In response to the challenge of the Enlightenment, Hegel boldly attempted to demonstrate that loyalty to an absolute state is in itself the highest form of freedom. His most important political work, *The Philosophy of Law and Right,* is an argument in support of that proposition. As insistently as any product of early liberalism, the book starts from the premise that freedom is the most important thing in the world. History, indeed, is nothing more than a succession of steps leading toward the progressive realization of that idea. But freedom is not, as the men of the French Revolution believed, a mere question of liberating men from negative legal restrictions. The right not to be prevented from entering a butcher shop adds nothing to the liberty of those who have no money to lay on the counter. No man is truly free unless he has power to accomplish his purposes. Positive freedom depends on positive power. Since no one man can ever be as powerful as a group, it follows that the positive freedom of the individual is great in proportion to the power of the group with which he is associated. Under modern conditions, the most powerful form of association is the absolute state, as represented by such institutions as the Prussian monarchy. To enhance the power and authority of political absolutism is, therefore, the only course for anyone who is genuinely interested in the progress of human freedom.

Like the philosophy of the Enlightenment, the concept of positive freedom was an attempt to rationalize the needs of a particular social class. The proposition that positive state action is indispensable to the accomplishment of individual purposes ought logically to have led Hegel to adopt a constitutionalist position. If the power of a group, as Rousseau had already pointed out, is to serve rather than to thwart the purposes of its members, that power must be used in accordance with the general will of the group. In adopting the idea of freedom as a primary consideration, Hegel logically committed himself, to the necessity of finding ways and means for the establishment of popular control in politics. The conservative classes knew, however, that they could direct the powers of an absolute monarchy more easily than they could direct the powers of any other type of government. As far as they themselves were concerned, freedom and absolutism were not incompatible. This social fact was the tacit premise of Hegel's political thought. The middle classes, knowing that their economic power was sufficient to enable them to work their will under competitive conditions, had been willing to argue that the institution of the free market was the necessary and sufficient basis of freedom for all men. The conservatives, realizing that their main strength lay in the control of royal administration, made similar claims for the institution of absolute monarchy. In both cases, the needs of a particular class took on the guise of a universal theory of politics.

One further step was needed, however, before conservatism could become an effective answer to the philosophy of the Enlightenment. The Western mind, long nourished on the apocalyptic hopes of Christianity, has a deep-seated repugnance to any theory which neglects to crown the history of mankind with a promise of ultimate triumph. Failure to recognize and provide for this sentiment was one of the major weaknesses of early conservative thought. At a time when the middle classes were strong in the faith of progress, conservative writers had been able to offer their followers no comparable inspiration. Although men like Maistre and Burke might demonstrate that progress within a traditional framework was possible, they did not claim that it was inevitable. The fear that visionary reformers might succeed in undoing the work of civilization haunts every page of their writings. But hope rather than fear is the normal legacy of Christian civilization. Unless the conservatives could learn to face the future in a more hopeful spirit, there was no prospect that they would be able to match the vigor of their revolutionary opponents.

In this respect also, Hegel was the man who succeeded in remedying the defects of the earlier conservative position. This was the ultimate significance of the *Philosophy of History* which was written in the period when Hegel was still a liberal, but acquired new meaning in the light of his later political thought. The idea that the course of human events follows a definite and predictable pattern has always had a considerable power of attraction for the Western mind. In the first centuries of the Christian era, Western Christianity had already produced one monumental work along these lines in Augustine's *City of God*. During the later Middle Ages, this tendency bore fruit in the writings of men like Joachim of Floris, who justified the hopes of contemporary reformers and mystics by explaining that terrestrial history was about to enter the last of three divinely predestined and progressively improving stages, the age of the Father, the age of the Son, and the age of the Holy Ghost. Hegel justified the conservative position by a similar appeal to the inalterable laws of history. By demonstrating that the most advanced form of the modern state, identified in his later writings with the Prussian monarchy, was the last of three predestined stages in the evolution of mankind, he showed the triumph of conservatism to be not only desirable but also inevitable. This made it possible for him, unlike the majority of earlier conservatives, to face the challenge of the Enlightenment in a mood of inspiring self-assurance.

The Hegelian interpretation of history rests on a philosophic principle known as the dialectic, a term derived from the Greek word for conversation or debate. The basic principle of the idealist school of philosophy, to which Hegel belonged, is that the visible world is a reflection or embodiment of eternal and unchanging ideas. According to the theory of the dialectic, the process by which those ideas become manifest in reality is not accidental or capricious, but follows fixed laws of development analogous to the process of intellectual debate. When a man starts an argument, he begins by stating a proposition, or thesis. Since no one is likely to be entirely correct in his initial formulation of a problem, the chances are that this thesis will be partly right and partly wrong. This encourages an opponent to make a contradictory statement, or antithesis, which likewise contains no more than a partial element of truth. This sets the stage for a debate which tests the strength and weakness of both positions. As a result of this experience, both protagonists abandon the more untenable features of their original statements. This makes it possible for them to agree in the end on a revised statement, or synthesis which includes the valid and excludes the invalid features of the two initial propositions. But even though the synthesis is more nearly true than its predecessors, it is also likely to contain an element of error. It therefore becomes the thesis of a new debate, inviting the opposition of a new antithesis, and contributing to the formulation of a still more adequate synthesis. Thus the dialectical process, endlessly repeated, serves as the instrument for progressively closer approximations to the realization of ideal truth.

Hegel's confidence in the inevitable triumph of conservatism rested on the proposition that modern absolutism represents the final stage in the dialectical realization of the idea of freedom in history. It is true that the dialectical process, with its endless succession of progressively higher syntheses, is logically incompatible with any sort of historical finality. The apocalyptic leanings of Western civilization are so strong, however, that the illogicality of ascribing an end to an endless process did not disturb Hegel in the least. According to his analysis of history, the realization of the idea of freedom required three successive stages of historical experience. In the beginning human beings lived in vast slave states, like the ancient Egyptian and Assyrian empires, where no one but the despot himself had any reason to regard state power as a means for the accomplishment of his purposes. The first partial realization of the idea of freedom took place in the city states of ancient Greece. Although a substantial slave population remained in the same position as before, the organization of the political community made it possible for free citizens to express themselves through political action, and thus to associate the idea of freedom with the idea of political loyalty and obligation. The imperfection of continuing slavery made it necessary, however, that the Greek world, considered as a thesis, should encounter the opposition of an antithesis, in the form of the Roman Empire. Through the influence of Christianity and other forces, which broke down the old distinction between slaves and citizens, the idea of moral responsibility extended to all men, but only at the cost of loosening the ties of loyalty to the state. The result was the Germanic empire, a synthesis which finally realized the idea of freedom by uniting and reconciling the best features of its predecessors. In the modern world the

Roman idea of moral responsibility has reached fulfillment in the abolition of slavery, and in the recognition of the civic capacity of all men. Through the development of the modern idea of sovereignty, moreover, the entire population has achieved a sense of loyalty and devotion to the state comparable to that evoked, from citizens only, in the ancient Greek polis. Thus the modern state represents the final realization of the idea of freedom in history, and will continue for all time as the perfect basis for the political life of mankind.

Considered in terms of its own objectives, Hegel's political philosophy was a failure. Like the philosophy of the Enlightenment, it was an attempt to prove that an institution favorable to the interests of one particular class was nothing less than the final goal of history. For people who did not happen to belong to the favored class, the demonstration was unconvincing. The middle classes, strong in the field of economic competition, felt no temptation to abandon their belief in the free market as the proper instrument of freedom. Other groups, finding that they were unable to control the operations either of free markets or of absolute monarchies, began to look for other means of accomplishing their purposes. Although subsequent theorists, above all the Marxists, found it useful to borrow many elements from the Hegelian system, their conclusions were at variance with the conservative position. As a means of inspiring aristocratic resistance to middle-class pretensions, Hegel's political theory had some value. As a final solution to the problem of Western politics, it was unable to win general acceptance.

Precisely because of its failure, however, the conservative reaction was able to play an important part in the evolution of modern liberalism. If either the aristocrats or the middle classes had succeeded in gaining exclusive control over the state, modern parliaments would never have been able to take over the functions of the medieval church as defenders of Western dualism. The value of conservative theory lay in the fact that, by inspiring rural resistance to the urban forces of the Enlightenment, it provided modern society with one of the elements necessary for the establishment of an internal balance of power. Although efforts to revive absolute monarchy were temporarily successful, repeated middle-class revolutions made it clear that this was no longer a practical solution to the problem of politics. The vigor of aristocratic and other forms of resistance made it equally clear, on the other hand, that middle-class absolutism was also impossible. The resulting stalemate compelled both groups to accept the position of competitors within a single constitutional framework, using parliamentary power as a means of safeguarding their respective interests. Instead of relying on their capacity to influence kings, aristocrats found it desirable to mobilize rural sentiment in support of their policies. Instead of relying on their capacity to dominate free markets, the middle classes had also to descend into the arena of competitive politics. In their search for votes, radicals and conservatives began vying with one another in extending the franchise to allied classes of the community. Although the theorists of conservatism, like the men of the Enlightenment, had no interest in constitutional democracy, constitutionalism was the actual consequence of their success in arousing the agrarian classes to political self-consciousness. This was their contribution to the development of modern politics.

8

The Awakening of the Urban Proletariat

The awakening of the urban proletariat was the third great stage in the evolution of modern liberalism. During the eighteenth and early nineteenth centuries, when cities were small and largely commercial in character, opposition to the philosophy of the Enlightenment found its main support in the rural population. All this changed with the advent of the industrial revolution. As manufacturing cities grew in size and importance, a large class of factory workers came into existence. These workers, unable to find satisfaction within the framework of the existing order, soon followed the example of their predecessors by developing a revolutionary theory of their own. Convinced, after the apocalyptic fashion of the West, that their particular experience had given them a general answer to the problems of human existence, they also attempted to impose their views on the rest of the population. Although their efforts ended in the usual failure, the result was to arouse a hitherto dormant part of the community to vigorous political life. Along with the middle-class Enlightenment and the conservative reaction, proletarian socialism is one of the forces which have done most to widen the social basis of modern politics. It therefore stands as a significant chapter in the history of modern liberal thought.

The proletariat itself was the product of a curious social

invention of the nineteenth century, an institution known as the labor market. Unlike the workers of former ages, whose rights and duties had been fixed with some degree of stability by local or craft tradition, the nineteenth-century laborer enjoyed no security of employment. According to the economic principles of the Enlightenment, he was simply an individual engaged like any other trader in selling his services to the highest bidder. His right to work, and the conditions under which he exercised that right, were matters of agreement between himself and his prospective employer. If the employer could find others willing to do the work for less money, or if trade conditions made it unprofitable to continue operations, he could terminate the arrangement at any time. If the worker could find no one willing to employ him at his old trade he had either to emigrate to a region where that particular skill was in demand, or else take up another kind of work. Continuous adaptation to the requirements of a fluctuating labor market, subject to all the mysterious hazards of trade cycles and technological change, was the condition of his economic existence. Absolute insecurity of employment was the basic principle of nineteenth-century industrialism. The modern proletariat is the product of this unique experiment in industrial relations.

From the standpoint of technological progress the existence of a large and flexible labor supply was extremely useful. Ever since the beginning of the industrial revolution science and technology have been opening up endless opportunities for economic change. The adoption of newly invented industrial processes and the exploitation of newly discovered resources has required a high degree of occupational and geographical mobility. If people had remained wedded, as in the past, to particular skills and particular localities, it would have been impossible for the industrial revolution to make rapid headway. The spectacular development of nineteenth-century America, for example, could never have taken place in a society where workers were unaccustomed to the idea of emigration. The existence of a fluid labor market enabled modern enterprisers to direct the movements of whole populations in accordance with the requirements of technological change. The proletarianization of the working class was a basic factor in the triumph of industrial civilization.

Like all great social experiments, however, the invention of the labor market was expensive. It involved, in the first instance, a swift and drastic decline in the material standard of living of the working classes. Centuries of experience under the guild and handicraft system had led to the establishment of fairly tolerable conditions of employment. Workers in the various occupations knew the traditional rates of payment for their work, and planned their lives accordingly. This element of security vanished with the coming of the factory system. Since the system itself was new, there were no traditions to govern the wages or working conditions of factory employment. Owners considered themselves justified, in accordance with the principles of market competition, in requiring the largest possible quantity of labor in return for the smallest possible remuneration. Individual workers were too weak and too little experienced in the ways of commercial negotiation to offer effective resistance. In order to avoid starvation whole families, including children no more than five years old, found it necessary to work under unwholesome conditions for as many as sixteen hours a day in return for bare subsistence. Large segments of the population, in a time of expanding material prosperity, were reduced to a standard of living lower than anything previously known. While others reaped the benefits, they experienced nothing but the burdens of the industrial revolution.

Economic impoverishment was only a part, moreover, of the sacrifice demanded of the proletariat. The social disintegration of the working class was if anything an even more disastrous consequence of the factory system. The operation of the labor market tore workers away from the local and occupational associations which had formed the center of their social interests. In order to find work they had to go to big towns and cities and live among strangers in the slums. Families were broken as people migrated from region to region and from continent to continent in search of employment. Although the individuals thus uprooted were able to make new social contacts in their new environments, these contacts were less strong than before, and might be broken at any time in response to shifts in the demand of the labor market. Members of the upper and middle classes were prosperous enough, in a period of increasing social mobility, to keep their families intact and to form new associations with comparative freedom. Workers on the verge of starvation enjoyed no comparable opportunities. For them the process of proletarianization meant social isolation. In this respect also the lower classes were forced to pay more than their share of the cost of industrial progress.

In the face of so intolerable a situation the first impulse of the workers, as of the nobility and peasantry, was conservative. Their old way of life was so much more satisfactory than the new that only the most drastic pressures could force them to enter the labor market. For a time only the dregs of society, the paupers, drunkards, and habitual ne'er-do-wells, could be recruited for factory service. Rather than abandon their villages and crafts, many skilled workers tried to remain in competition by working their hand looms and spindles for longer hours at lower rates of pay. When it became obvious that factory competition was insuperable, many tried to solve the problem by smashing the machines. To an even greater extent than the landowning aristocracy, skilled workers had everything to lose by the triumph of economic liberalism. No spokesman with the eloquence of a Burke appeared to express the woes of a class so uneducated and inarticulate. From their actions it is clear, however, that they were no less interested than Burke himself in the maintenance of conservative traditions.

There could, however, be no real prospect of solving the problems of modern industrialism on a traditional basis. Although the relatively slow rate of discovery in the field of agricultural technique made it possible for the agricultural population to retain much of its old way of life throughout the nineteenth century, the forces of innovation in industry were too strong to be overcome by conservative opposition. Factory methods of production were so much cheaper than the older handicrafts that only the most ruthless and determined political action could have prevented their adoption. The artisans were too weak, both politically and economically, to accomplish that result. By the end of the eighteenth century the factory system was already well established in England. The first half of the nineteenth century brought it to France, the second half to Germany and America. During the present century the progress of industrialism has been even more rapid. The advantages of mechanical production are so obvious that no conservative or reactionary movement has long been able to delay its introduction in any part of the modern world.

Granted the impossibility of maintaining or reëstablishing the older forms of economic life, the only way to safeguard the interests of the proletariat was to provide them with new bases for social organization. If a person is to enjoy freedom, the conditions under which he lives and works should satisfy his social and economic needs. Modern industrialism made the factory the primary institution in the lives of the proletariat. Freedom for the factory worker was therefore a question of organizing the factory community in such a way that it could serve as a vehicle for the expression of working-class interests.

This end could not be attained, however, without a radical change in the principles of nineteenth-century industrialism. Under the theory and practice of early liberalism, the life of all productive units was subject to the dictates of an alien institution, the free market. Industrial control rested in the hands of men for whom profit was the only recognized criterion of successful management. Regarding the factory simply as an instrument for the production of marketable goods, they had no interest in making it serve the welfare of the working community. If the proletariat was to achieve freedom, this absolute subordination to market considerations had to be broken. Just as conservatives had found it necessary to attack the philosophy of the Enlightenment in order to save the life of traditional associations, supporters of the proletariat had to challenge the power of the market in order that a new form of association, the factory community, might develop as an organization for the satisfaction of working-class needs. To insure that development has been the basic problem of the modern proletariat.

The people who made the first serious attempt to solve this problem were the so-called Utopian socialists. In their social background and intellectual habits, these early nineteenth-century writers were themselves a product of middle-class society. But humanitarianism had always been an important element in the philosophy of the Enlightenment, and the abuses of early industrialism were hard to reconcile with the humanitarian point of view. The Utopian socialists were middle-class humanitarians who saw that the existing factory system was not in fact serving the welfare of the working population. This led them to look for means whereby welfare considerations might be made to replace market considerations as a controlling factor in the life of industrial communities.

One possible way of approaching this problem was to reform the factory system by appealing to the humanitarian conscience of factory owners and managers. This was the line adopted in the early writings of the English reformer, Robert Owen. In his own career as manager and part owner of a successful textile factory at New Lanark, Owen had proceeded on the assumption that he was responsible not only for the maintenance of profitable production, but also for the welfare of his employees. A passionate subscriber to the eighteenth-century belief that proper education will bring out the rational potentialities of all men, he devoted himself to the task of making his factory community an ideal environment for the education of factory workers. By providing wholesome housing and working conditions, by giving children time off for attendance at company schools, and by other paternalistic measures in advance of the practice of the time, he tried to insure the development of his employees as rational human beings. His *New View of Society* was an attempt to awaken other employers to a similar sense of social responsibility. By using the humanitarian conscience of the Enlightenment as a check on the operations of a pure market economy, he believed that it would be possible to convert industrialism into a genuine instrument for the welfare of mankind.

The pressure of market competition was too strong, however, to permit any such solution to the problem of the proletariat. Although some employers, like Owen, might be willing to allow humanitarian considerations to stand in the way of profit, the operations of an unrestricted market economy usually made it possible for less scrupulous enterprisers to drive them out of business. It is true that better living and working conditions often paid dividends in terms not only of human welfare but also of production. At a time when most factories were manned by overworked children and drunken derelicts, the extra efficiency of the sober and self-respecting labor force at New Lanark gave Owen himself a competitive advantage which went far toward paying the cost of his social experiments. But even though Owen was an unusually efficient manager, he could not make enough money to satisfy his partners, and had finally to retire. Less able men had even less chance of competitive survival under like conditions. Some employers were both humanitarian and prosperous enough to be satisfied with less than maximum profit. Some also found that a certain degree of paternalism was a sound business investment. Situations of this sort were too rare, however, to constitute a basis for general reformation.

The difficulty of converting the existing order to humanitarian uses suggested the need for a radically different system of production. If market considerations prevented the factory community from developing properly, the obvious solution was to create working communities which would be isolated from the operations of the general market economy. This was the line followed by most of the Utopian socialists. The writings of Fourier, for example, presented detailed blueprints for the organization of economically self-sufficient communities, known as phalansteries. By producing all the goods and services required for the welfare of their members, these communities would escape the necessity of entering into market relations with the outside world, and would thus be free to govern themselves according to the dictates of rational humanitarianism. The Utopians believed that as soon as they had found the means to establish a few experimental phalansteries, the advantages of this method of production would be so obvious that more and more people would withdraw from the world of economic competition to found phalansteries of their own. The result would be a gradual withering away of the market economy, and the establishment of a world order based on voluntarily coöperative working communities. This was the Utopians' cure for the evils of modern industrialism.

The event failed to justify their expectations. During the early part of the nineteenth century a number of Utopian communities were founded in various parts of the world. Owen himself, after the disappointment of his hopes for employer paternalism, played a leading part in one such experiment. But the Utopian socialists, after the optimistic fashion of enlightened rationalists, had exaggerated the possibilities of social planning, and their artificial communities collapsed in the face of unexpected difficulties and dissensions. The concept of communal self-sufficiency was incompatible, moreover, with the requirements of modern technology, which depends on the performance of increasingly specialized functions within a comprehensive system of economic exchange and control. Like the idea of employer paternalism, the idea of Utopian withdrawal was not entirely fruitless. In the form of worker coöperatives, which began at this time to appear in the wake of the Utopian movement, non-market agencies of production and distribution were able to play a modest part in improving the lot of the working classes. Achievements along this line were too limited, however, to provide a satisfactory answer to the needs of the proletariat.

The creation of effective working-class institutions came about in a very different fashion. While the Utopian socialists were vainly trying to create welfare communities according to rational plans, proletarians themselves were evolving a more organic pattern of social organization. Uprooted from their native environments, urban laborers came in contact with one another in the overcrowded intimacy of factories and slums. Common material interests and a common desire for human companionship led to the ripening of new loyalties. Workers everywhere began spontaneously, and with little or no encouragement from enlightened theorists, to organize trade unions for the defense of their interests. Long prohibited as illegal combinations in restraint of trade, these unions had originally to take the form of secret societies. As they grew stronger and more self-confident they proved harder to suppress, and finally gained legal recognition. In England, the first country to experience the full impact of the industrial revolution, the ban on labor unions was lifted as early as 1824. In countries of slower industrial growth similar developments occurred at a correspondingly later time. Everywhere the working classes learned, by a process of trial and error, to develop institutions for the satisfaction of their common needs. The modern trade-union movement had begun.

Tentative and unassuming as they were, unions provided the urban proletariat with a sounder basis for social action than anything the Utopian socialists had been able to devise. As a product of truly organic growth, developed in the light of accumulated experience rather than according to preconceived ideas, they reflected the interests and abilities of working people. The Utopians believed that the creation of desirable social conditions was a responsibility of the enlightened middle classes, and that simple people should live as passive recipients of humanitarian bounty. Even if it had been possible for well-meaning employers or community founders to gain their ends, the result would not have been entirely satisfactory. When Owen, in the interests of worker efficiency, prevented the sale of liquor at New Lanark, he was acting in accordance with the best paternalistic principles, but there was no reason to believe that his workers were pleased by the reform. Men want social institutions not only for purposes of objective welfare, but also as a means of expressing their own desires. Ambitious and able individuals of all classes need a stage on which they themselves can play an active role and gain the social approbation of their associates. In the small villages of earlier times everyone was known to the whole community, and everyone had a reasonable chance of winning some form of social distinction. In the impersonal life of great cities, and in the disciplined regimentation of autocratically managed factories, this basic satisfaction was denied. Only in the trade union did ordinary workers discover a form of association which they themselves could control, and in the service of which they had an opportunity to gain social recognition. Social as well as economic causes contributed, therefore, to the establishment of trade unionism as a vital factor in the life of the proletariat.

But if working-class associations were to convert the factory system into an agency of working-class welfare, it was necessary for them to gain some measure of control over the determination of industrial policy. This called for nothing less than the unification of the proletariat. Although the employees of a particular factory, by strikes and other means, might be able to force concessions from their employers, their gains remained precarious as long as the free market continued to dictate the conditions of industrial survival. Economically speaking, a manager who granted unusually favorable terms to strikers was in the same position as a humanitarian paternalist. To the extent that his concession increased his costs of production, he was in danger of being driven out of business by his competitors. The only way of avoiding this difficulty was to impose the same conditions simultaneously on all competing producers. This involved action not only on a national but even on an international scale. If simultaneous strikes forced concessions from all competing employers in a single country, competition from lower-cost foreign producers might still nullify the resulting gains. As long as international market conditions remained a major factor in industrial production, proletarian action had likewise to assume the character of an international movement. Nothing less would suffice to give the working class effective control over the life of the factory community.

To unite the proletariat on any such scale would have been impossible without the aid of a vigorous political doctrine. Although practical experience might teach the workers in particular factories or localities to recognize the advantages of concerted action, that experience was too limited to produce wider forms of national and international solidarity. In the period of the French Revolution, common devotion to the philosophy of the Enlightenment had given the middle classes the unity and enthusiasm of a successful revolutionary movement. A comparable doctrine was needed to give the proletariat a corresponding degree of disciplined efficiency.

The formation of an effective working-class ideology was comparatively difficult. The creation and dissemination of complex political doctrines requires the services of intelligent and educated men. In the early days of their rise to power, the middle classes had profited by the circumstance that the conditions of commercial life had already produced a substantial group of middle-class intellectuals. When the time came for a comparable effort on the part of the working classes, no similar resources were available. Men forced from earliest childhood to labor fifteen to eighteen hours a day had little chance for intellectual development. Only a few especially able and lucky individuals could hope to rise from such surroundings to a position where they could compete with expensively educated members of the middle and upper classes. In the early nineteenth century the conditions of social mobility were such, moreover, that the few workers who did manage to rise had comparatively little difficulty in gaining admission to the upper ranks of society. Energetic men of any class, in the expansive days of early industrialism, had a reasonable chance of becoming captains of industry. Under these circumstances there was a natural tendency for the ablest and best educated elements of the working class to lose contact with their origins and merge with the interests of higher social groups. This made it practically impossible, in the early days of proletarian socialism, to find working-class intellectuals capable of formulating doctrines of proletarian resistance.

Factory workers were not the only people, however, who felt the destructive impact of the industrial revolution. Nineteenth-century conditions had also produced a fateful cleavage within the ranks of the middle class itself. The strength of the Enlightenment owed much to the fact that its idea of freedom had made an equal appeal to intellectual and to economic interests. The commercial classes of the eighteenth century, partly as a result of stimulating contacts with unfamiliar lands and peoples, had been notable not only for economic enterprise but also for intellectual curiosity. The career of a man like Franklin, half businessman and half scientist, was typical of the age. With the shift from a predominantly commercial to a predominantly industrial civilization, this harmony disappeared. Some members of the middle class began devoting themselves exclusively to economic pursuits, while others concentrated on intellectual matters. The result was to divide the middle class against itself, and to lay the foundation for fresh revolutionary developments.

During the nineteenth century, the prevailing trend of middle-class society lay in the direction of Philistinism. The rewards of industrial enterprise were so great, and competition so fierce, that economic power fell increasingly into the hands of those willing to devote their entire energies to the pursuit of wealth. This led to a progressive narrowing of intellectual interests. For most members of the middle class, money became the sole criterion of success. When they asked how much a man was "worth," they took it for granted that the answer would be a recital of his financial assets. Early industrial management, with its emphasis on the technical and financial problems of a single specific factory, encouraged a state of mind rather more parochial and rigid than that engendered by wide-ranging mercantile activity. Thus the typical figure of the new age was not a man of balanced interests, like Franklin, but a preoccupied captain of industry who looked down upon intellectuals as absurd and impractical dreamers. This became the dominant attitude of the successful middle classes.

Along with this development, however, the nineteenth century also saw a marked increase in the number and importance of professional intellectuals. The extension of literacy created an ever-wider public for literary productions. Whereas the intellectuals of former times, with the rare exception of men like Voltaire and Dr. Johnson, had depended for their livelihood on the support of wealthy patrons, new openings in journalism, education, and the learned professions made it possible for a substantial number of people to earn an independent livelihood by intellectual pursuits. But even though the financial rewards of a successful intellectual career might be considerable, they could not bear comparison with the sums accruing to successful business enterprise. In a society where wealth was the criterion of worth this condemned the intellectual classes to a position of permanent social inferiority. Although a majority of them were recruited from the ranks of the middle classes, resentment against this discrimination led many of them to react against the prevailing standards of middle-class society. Bohemianism, an act of deliberate withdrawal and defiance on the part of artists and intellectuals, became an accepted answer to Philistinism. Thus the rise of industrialism, far from breaking the spirit of the intellectual classes, inspired them with a new willingness to stand on their own feet as exponents of an independent line of action.

This division in the ranks of the middle classes was an important factor in the evolution of the working-class movement. Although some intellectuals might be willing, in much the same fashion as the Utopian socialists, to retire from middle-class society into a Bohemian world of their own devising, others began to explore the possibility of a direct attack on the bases of middle-class society. This led many to turn a sympathetic eye on the plight of the proletariat. Like the working classes, the intellectuals felt the oppression of a system where all values were subordinate to the dictates of a market economy. They also wanted a society where competitive economic power was not the sole measure of the rights and importance of men. To a far greater extent than most workmen they had the advantages of education and intelligence needed for the creation and dissemination of political ideas. This made it easy for them to assume a position of leadership in the working-class movement, and to become the founders of a proletarian school of revolutionary thought.

Of all those who tried to provide the international proletariat with a unifying ideology the most successful were Marx and Engels. Both were typical representatives of the intellectual middle classes. As the son of a prosperous professional family Marx had been educated for an academic career, while Engels was a successful factory manager who succeeded, like Owen, in combining business activities with an interest in social and economic reform. Although German by birth and education both spent the greater part of their adult lives abroad, and regarded themselves as citizens of the world. Since countries like England and France, at the time when they began writing, had gone a good deal further than Germany along the road to industrialization, their work owed rather more to the experiences of those countries than to that of their native land. The *Communist Manifesto*, the first important fruit of their lifelong collaboration, was issued on the eve of the disturbances of 1848 in an attempt to arouse the workers of the world to revolutionary action. To a greater extent than most contemporary socialists, they saw that the problem of the proletariat was international in scope. Their purpose was to create an ideological structure which would encourage the world proletariat to make a concerted assault upon the forces of world capitalism.

Although the philosophy of the Enlightenment was their real enemy, Marx and Engels realized that the problem of revolution had been complicated by the intervening triumph of the conservative reaction. Under the influence of conservative historicism, the idea of historical evolution had become one of the most widely influential principles of nineteenth-century thought. This idea was acceptable not only to conservative traditionalists, who wanted to cushion established institutions against the shock of radical innovation, but also to middle-class industrialists, whose position was so satisfactory that they felt no need for further political changes. But from the standpoint of anyone interested in the creation of a revolutionary movement, the evolutionary hypothesis was embarrassing. In the contemporary intellectual climate no movement could hope to succeed unless it could claim to be the product of gradually evolving historical forces. The essence of revolution, on the other hand, is to make a break with the past. To justify revolution on evolutionary grounds is a task of no small difficulty. The necessity of overcoming this difficulty did much to determine the specific character of modern socialist thought.

The basic discovery of Marxism was that the theory of the conservative reaction could be adapted to the purposes of proletarian action. In Germany there was a group of liberal Hegelians, of whom Feuerbach was perhaps the most notable, who were interested in developing the progressive rather than the conservative implications of the master's philosophy. Contact with this group had been one of the formative influences of Marx's academic career. Although unwilling to follow Hegel to his final conclusions, he found much to admire in the Hegelian approach to the problem of history. The idea of the dialectic, with its sharp alternations of thesis, antithesis, and synthesis, was especially attractive, for it suggested a means of overcoming the antirevolutionary gradualism implicit in most formulations of the evolutionary hypothesis. The dialectical pattern, though applied in Hegel's later writings to support the conservative position, actually implied that conflict rather than growth was the motive force of history. From this one might easily conclude that historical development is a product not of slow and imperceptible changes, but of sudden revolutionary outbursts interspersed with periods of relative stability. Hegel himself had interpreted the progress of freedom in terms of three successive empires, each in turn destroyed by its successor. To anyone interested in demonstrating the creative value of revolution, the dialectical emphasis on conflict was, to say the least, suggestive. Marxism is an attempt to develop the suggestion into a full-fledged theory of proletarian action.

From the proletarian standpoint, the defect of the Hegelian dialectic lay in the fact that its emphasis was political. Workers who had suffered the evils of market competition could easily subscribe to the conservative concept of positive freedom. They found it less easy to believe that the conservative state, with all its power, was an instrument for the realization of freedom. Because of the ability of their aristocratic representatives to control absolute monarchs, the rural population had had some reason to look upon the existing political organization as a guarantor of their interests. The proletariat had no grounds for similar confidence. Although conservatives, as in the case of the British factory acts, might occasionally take the lead in defending the working classes against the worst abuses of middle-class liberalism, their preoccupation with rural affairs, and their love of tradition stood as a barrier to full sympathy with and understanding of the needs of the proletariat. The trade-union movement was more effective than the conservative state as a vehicle of proletarian action. A nonpolitical reinterpretation was needed, therefore, to make the Hegelian dialectic useful to the cause of the urban proletariat.

The materialistic interpretation of history was the Marxian answer to this need. In the philosophy of Hegel the record of human achievement is a dialectical unfolding of the idea of freedom. To a philosopher steeped in the atmosphere of idealism, explaining events in terms of ideas seemed wholly natural. To Marx it was a clear case of putting the cart before the horse. Intense preoccupation with the economic injustices of his time had convinced him that men are dominated primarily by economic self-interest. Hegel believed that ideal forces shape the material world. Marx believed that ideas themselves are a product of the material environment, developed primarily as tools for the satisfaction of economic needs. At any given stage of social and technological achievement there are certain possible means of providing material livelihood. Human thought and behavior adapt themselves to the requirements of this objective situation. Changes in the conditions of material production reveal new opportunities for economic satisfaction, and lead to corresponding alterations of thought and behavior. This material factor is the primary cause of all developments in the scientific, religious, political, and other spheres of human activity. The state itself is only a secondary expression of economic interests. Progress is not, therefore, a matter of successive political empires, but of successive economic systems.

This was Marx's answer to the conservative contention that absolute monarchy was the end of the dialectical process in history.

The Marxian conception of economic determinism, like the early conservative conception of evolutionary historicism, was widely influential. Although the notion that man is primarily governed by economic motives would have seemed fantastic in most periods of history, it was in line with the prevailing trend of nineteenth-century thought. Middle-class Philistinism, with its emphasis on wealth as the criterion of success, had accustomed many people to the idea that economic enterprise was the most important form of human activity, taking precedence over art, learning, religion, and every other form of achievement. The early liberal theory of the market as the positive creator and of the state as the negative defender of progressive values made it especially easy for the middle classes to accept the view that politics is subordinate to economics. In the experience of the industrial proletariat, economic preoccupations were if anything even more obsessive. Men who work fifteen or more hours a day for the bare necessities of life have little time or energy to devote to religious, social, or other noneconomic interests. To anyone on the verge of starvation, the question of food looms large in the imagination. The proposition that men are governed by economic motives was consistent, therefore, with an important range of nineteenth-century experience. This made it possible for the materialistic interpretation of history to exert a profound influence on the intellectual life of the period.

Having eliminated the state as a primary factor in historical development, Marx was free to develop the revolutionary implications of the Hegelian dialectic. According to the principles of dialectical materialism, each stage in the progress of material production offers certain opportunities for economic achievement. Men who happen to be particularly well equipped for the purpose seize control over the currently available instruments of production, and exploit them to their own advantage at the expense of the rest of society. Because of their common interest in preventing others from gaining a share of control, these men constitute a homogeneous economic class. The political, religious, and other ideas and institutions which characterize any given stage of civilization are the product of an overwhelming desire on the part of the ruling class to perpetuate its economic power. But just as every intellectual statement evokes its own antithesis, Marx believed that every stage of economic life is a thesis containing within itself the seeds of dialectical development. In exploiting the economic possibilities of a given situation, the ruling class fails to satisfy the needs of other members of the community. These people, brought together by the common experience of economic exploitation, gradually emerge as a new class which stands in a relation of antithesis to the first. The result is a revolutionary crisis, which leads to the forcible expropriation of the old ruling class, and the establishment of a new system of production. This new system, a synthesis drawn from the economic experience of both preceding classes, becomes in turn the basis for a new civilization. But this synthesis, by arousing new forces of revolutionary opposition, then assumes the position of thesis in a new cycle of dialectical development. The Marxian interpretation of history rests on the principle that class conflict is the mechanism of historical progress. In this way the dialectical method, used by conservatives to justify the duty of obedience to established states, was transformed into an instrument of revolutionary protest.

The value of dialectical materialism from the working-class standpoint lay in the fact that it offered the promise of inevitable victory as a stimulus to united proletarian action. According to Marx's interpretation of the current scene, capitalist society had reached the stage of historical development which made it ripe for destruction. The dominant class of nineteenth-century industrialism were the factory owners. By controlling the instruments of industrial production, they had been able to shape the ideas and institutions of the period in accordance with their class interests. But capitalism had at the same time brought into existence a large mass of propertyless wage earners. Through their common sufferings in factories and slums, these workers were becoming aware of common economic interests. A proletarian class, in other words, was emerging as an antithesis to capitalist society. The conditions of capitalist production were such, moreover, that the proletarians were constantly growing and the capitalists constantly declining in numbers. Marx rightly recognized that the trend of modern industrial development lay in the direction of larger units of monopolistic control. From this he deduced that increasing numbers of small property owners would be squeezed out of the capitalist class and forced down into the ranks of the proletariat. Thus capitalism would satisfy the needs of an ever smaller proportion of the population. In the end the numerical disproportion would become so great that the capitalist system would no longer be able to maintain itself against organized proletarian pressure. The result would be the destruction of capitalist society, the thesis, by its own antithesis, the proletariat, and the creation of a new synthesis in the form of communist society. In this society the technical resources of capitalist industrialism would be directed to satisfying the needs of the working classes. Since dialectical development is the inescapable law of history, this meant that the proletariat could count with absolute assurance upon the realization of their hopes.

But even though he felt the disappearance of capitalism to be inevitable, Marx did not promise that it would come without revolutionary effort on the part of the working classes. A dying social order has considerable power of resistance. Ruling economic groups are in absolute control of the state, with its apparatus of armies, police forces, law courts, and other repressive agencies. The political and social ideas prevailing at any given period are also an expression of the ruling-class point of view, and retain currency long after their proper time through the efforts of journalists, clergymen, professors, and other paid propagandists. Important material and ideological resistances stand in the way of the triumph of the proletariat. According to the materialistic interpretation of history, no class will abandon its economic interests without a bitter struggle. A class which is able, though limited in numbers, to use its wealth to hire mercenary defenders can put up a strenuous fight for survival. Only a violent revolution can suffice, therefore, to destroy the political and economic power of the middle classes.

This theory was an answer to the difficult problem of finding a form of action which was both evolutionary and revolutionary in character. In accordance with the evolutionary tendencies of nineteenth-century thought, the Marxian dialectic teaches that social change is not, as the eighteenth-century reformers believed, a matter of rational choice, but a product of gradual historical development. No amount of conscious effort would suffice to bring a communist society into existence unless a preceding capitalist society had already run its appointed course. This was Marx's concession to evolutionary conservatism. But once the course of evolution has reached a certain point, revolution is necessary to overcome the resistance of a dying social order. This is not a violation but a manifestation of the law of evolutionary growth. In Marx's own phrase, revolution is the "midwife of history," liberating social forces which have ripened in the womb of time. Marxism thus managed to dispose of the conservative theories which had already undermined the intellectual foundations of the eighteenth-century Enlightenment.

Logically, the principle of dialectical materialism should have led Marx to interpret history as an endless series of revolutionary crises. The apocalyptic tradition of Judaeo-Christian thought was still too powerful, however, to allow him, any more than Hegel, to be content with this conclusion. He therefore tried to prove not only that the coming proletarian revolution would be successful, but also that it would be the final stage in the dialectical development of history. The proletariat differed from all previous classes in that it consisted not of a property-owning minority but of the unpropertied masses of mankind. When the proletariat succeeded in seizing the instruments of production, productive capacity would for the first time serve the needs not of a ruling class but of the entire population. Since economic exploitation is the only basis for class antagonism, this would result in the elimination of all class conflicts and the establishment of a permanent classless society. Regarding sin as the source of all evil, the Christians had looked forward to the day when the second coming of Christ, by overcoming the forces of sin, would grant men the bliss of an eternally perfect kingdom. Regarding economic exploitation as the source of all evil, the Marxists offered men the hope of a proletarian revolution which, by eliminating economic exploitation, would insure the establishment of an eternally perfect society. Thus the theory of dialectical materialism ended in the apocalyptic vision of a time when the dialectical process itself would cease to operate as a factor in history.

The apocalyptic character of Marxism rendered it incapable, in its original form, of offering a final solution to the problems of modern politics. To an even greater extent than the philosophy of the Enlightenment, it avoided the consideration of political questions by adopting a quasi-religious faith in the natural harmony of the universe. Although the men of the eighteenth century believed that market competition would automatically serve the interests of mankind, they at least had recognized that coercive state action would be necessary to prevent selfish individuals from violating the conditions of market competition. Marxism, on the other hand, assumed the existence of a harmony of interests so perfect and so unqualified that the problem of politics simply disappeared. Since the members of a single economic class all stand in the same relationship to the instruments of production, their interests are identical. Although coercive power is needed to impose the will of one class on another, it has no place in a society where all men are members of a single social class. Once the revolutionary power of the proletariat had succeeded, therefore, in liquidating the last remnants of the capitalist class, the state would gradually wither away. Marx's concept of class solidarity was so absolute that he was unable to envisage the need for political guarantees against the exploitation of proletarians by other proletarians. This prevented him from giving real consideration to the problem of proletarian politics.

Considered in terms of its own intellectual pretensions, Marxism was a failure. Marx and Engels themselves believed that dialectical materialism was an important scientific discovery. In all their writings they made much of the point that theirs was a scientific socialism, sharply distinguishable from the nonscientific or Utopian socialism of their predecessors and contemporaries. Actually their proposed law of historical development was no more capable of exact scientific demonstration than were the corresponding ideas of Hegel or of the Enlightenment. Before any scientific hypothesis can be accepted it must be shown to correspond with a significant range of empirical experience. No such verification was offered in support of the Marxian dialectic, which rested at best on nothing more than the single historical example of the French Revolution. Reacting against the restrictions of an outworn feudal order, the middle classes of eighteenth-century France had developed a unified class-consciousness which enabled them to rebel against that order and set up a new system expressive of their own class interests. By assuming that this one episode was typical of historical development in general, the Marxian dialectic gave the proletariat hope that they in turn would come one day to enjoy a similar opportunity. Economic analysis of contemporary capitalist developments did something to bolster up that hope. But when it came to investigating the more remote past for similar examples of the dialectical process, the Marxians were strangely silent. No convincing attempt was made to show that the middle classes had been a necessary product of feudal society, or that feudal society had emerged as the antithesis to a preceding economic order. Application of the dialectical pattern to still earlier stages of history was even more disappointing. Though masquerading as a scientific hypothesis, the Marxian theory was an act of faith which could not stand the test of scientific investigation.

Unfounded as they may have been, however, the scientific pretensions of Marxism had a good deal to do with its ultimate success. In the middle of the nineteenth century, science enjoyed a quasi-religious prestige. The achievements of natural science were so spectacular, and at the same time so mysterious to the layman, that people were ready to believe almost anything that might be promulgated in its name. Scientific socialism, by promising the working classes that their struggle against the injustices of the labor market were bound to end in victory, gave them the self-confidence and assurance indispensable to organized political action.

The scientific pretensions of Marxian thought also had the advantage of encouraging the adherence of middle-class intellectuals to the proletarian movement. It is true that, on any strict interpretation of the theory of economic determinism, it would have been natural to assume that all members of the middle class would have to share the same ideas and suffer the same fate. Because of their respect for science, however, the Marxists were willing, in the case of intellectuals, to admit an element of free will into their generally deterministic system. Through the use of scientific intelligence, individuals from any class might transcend the limitations of their own class experience. Recognizing, as a consequence of historical and economic studies, the necessity and desirability of the proletarian revolution, they could escape the fate of their own class by joining forces with the proletarian movement. Just as Marx and Engels had risen above the limitations of their middle-class origins to become intellectual leaders of the proletariat, other individuals might also find the way to scientific salvation. For discontented members of the intellectual middle classes, this prospect was attractive. Scientific socialism thus provided an excellent means of uniting intellectuals and proletarians in a common revolutionary effort.

To a greater extent than any other theory, Marxism helped to stimulate the awakening of the urban proletariat. Like the philosophy of the Enlightenment and the conservative reaction, Marxism was a class doctrine, reflecting the needs and experience of a particular social group. Discontent with the abuses of a market-dominated factory system had led factory workers to the conclusion that their welfare depended on their ability to control the instruments of industrial production. Just as the middle classes had found that the free market, and the rural classes that the conservative monarchy was the social institution best adapted to their ends, the urban proletariat felt that their own class associations were the only reliable agencies of working-class control. Marxism encouraged these developments by teaching that the welfare of humanity depended on the conquest of absolute power by a united proletariat. Through a new interpretation of the laws of historical progress, it inspired them with apocalyptic hopes no less powerful than those which had formerly inspired the middle-class revolution. The result, in spite of the ultimate disappointment of these hopes, was to make the urban proletariat a self-confident and effective factor in the evolution of modern politics.

9

The Theory and Practice of Modern Liberalism

With the awakening of the urban proletariat, the stage was set for the development of modern liberalism. Liberalism, in its contemporary meaning, is belief in the ideals and methods of constitutional democracy. Government, according to the liberal conception, is legitimate only when it rests on a general will formed by the free negotiation of conflicting points of view. This calls, on the part of all major segments of the population, for willingness and ability to take part in the processes of parliamentary government. Revolutionary socialism, by arousing a third great class to political self-consciousness, had completed the work, begun by the Enlightenment and the conservative reaction, of creating a general desire for participation in politics. What now remained was to convert that desire into an equally general acceptance of the principles of liberal negotiation. Apocalyptic class doctrines, with their exclusive emphasis on the needs and experience of a particular social group, were incompatible with those principles. To break down the intransigence of earlier theories, and to unite their respective followers in an effective general will, was the problem of modern liberalism.

At its inception, modern liberalism was a product not of theoretical considerations but of practical experience. Parliamentary institutions, adopted in the first instance as an unwelcome but inevitable compromise between the claims of the Enlightenment and of the conservative reaction, provided the framework for fruitful experiments in the art of reconciling class interests. Although enlightened progressives and conservative traditionalists might continue to regard their respective doctrines as a final answer to the needs of humanity, the inability of either group to gain exclusive control made it necessary for them to negotiate their differences. With the awakening of the urban proletariat this process of negotiation had to be extended to the rest of the secular community. Theoretical commitments could not prevent the representatives of rival social interests from adjusting their demands to the exigencies of parliamentary life. By the end of the nineteenth century, therefore, many parliaments were serving in practice as agencies for the creation and implementation of a comprehensive general will. This concrete experience, emerging in the face of powerful ideological resistances, was the foundation of modern liberal thought.

The evolution of liberal practice could not continue indefinitely, however, without the support of an appropriate liberal theory. As long as people continued to give their allegiance to absolutist doctrines, they could feel no real enthusiasm for the institutions of parliamentary government. In comparison with apocalyptic hopes, every compromise appears at best as a disappointment and at worst as a betrayal. One promising experiment in constitutionalism, in an earlier period of Western history, had already foundered on the rocks of a similar intransigence. During the later Middle Ages, when the unity of the church was in process of disintegration, some people had tried to halt the decline by using representative councils as a mechanism for the negotiation of religious differences. But even though the conciliar movement succeeded for a time in rescuing the church from disaster, it never managed to gain a secure hold over the loyalties of Christendom. Because of its traditional prestige as the infallible representative of the Holy Ghost, the papacy was able to undermine the authority of councils, and to embark on a policy of ecclesiastical intransigence which ended in the destruction of Christian unity. The Enlightenment with its belief in free markets, the reaction with its belief in conservative monarchy, and Marxism with its belief in the class-conscious proletariat, were no less intransigent than papal absolutism. As long as each social group regarded its own favorite institution as the historically designated agency of progress, there could be no question of winning allegiance to any secular counterpart of the conciliar movement. The Christian church failed to maintain unity because the councils could not persuade men that they rather than the papacy were the supreme earthly representatives of the Holy Ghost. In their emphasis on the free market, the conservative monarchy or the class-conscious proletariat as representatives of a natural harmony of interests, exclusive class ideologies offered a similar challenge to parliamentary democracy. It likewise was doomed to failure unless it could convince people that parliamentary institutions, rather than the institutions of a particular social class, were the proper guardians of the secular interests of mankind.

Fortunately theoretical bases for an effective integration of the secular community were already in existence. Although intransigent class doctrines had a considerable appeal they were a comparatively recent development and lacked the established solidity of an ancient political tradition. Parliamentary institutions, on the other hand, enjoyed a certain traditional prestige as representatives of the total interests of society. This was true not only in England and America, where respect for constitutional processes operated from the beginning as a check on class extremism, but also in many parts of Europe. Because of their common dependence, moreover, on the traditional habits of Western thought, the prevailing class ideologies were not as divisive as they seemed. Although enlightened progressives, conservative traditionalists, and revolutionary socialists were in disagreement on many issues, there were also important points of agreement between their respective doctrines. By causing men to concentrate on these points of agreement, and by persuading them to recognize parliamentary action as the proper means of negotiating the remaining disagreements, liberal theorists had a chance to reconcile specific class doctrines in a new and more comprehensive philosophy of community action. To make use of this opportunity was the task of modern liberal thought.

One useful point of agreement between the several class doctrines was with regard to the question of the relationship between government and society. Modern liberalism, in its attempt to place the administrative apparatus of the state under the legislative and executive control of parliaments, is an expression of the Western belief that government is an administrative agency designed to implement the moral values of an independently organized society. Although the earlier ideologies differed in their views as to the proper form of social organization, all three had a similar tendency to deny the moral autonomy of

government. The philosophy of the Enlightenment, with
its moralistic fervor, was so little interested in politics that
it was prepared to accept any form of state which promised to defend the truly creative work of the free market.
The conservative reaction believed that human welfare
depended on the existence of a conservative society, and
welcomed absolute monarchy only on the condition that
it act as a defender of traditional institutions. Marxism,
with its emphasis on economic classes as the source of all
achievement, went even farther than the Enlightenment
in its indifference to purely political questions. All three
were nonpolitical doctrines, whose sole interest in politics
consisted in the desire to prevent state action from interfering with the spontaneously creative forces of society. If
parliamentarism proved, therefore, to be the best means of
accomplishing this purpose, there were no ideological
commitments to prevent anyone from adhering to the
principles of parliamentary government.

The most important point of agreement, however, was
with regard to the question of the relationship between
the individual and society. Christianity had taught that
the salvation of individual souls was the end of temporal
existence, and that the function of the church was to serve
as a means to that end. Transferred from the religious to
the secular plane, this conception of society as the servant
of the individual remained as a bond of union between
the conflicting schools of nineteenth-century thought. The
philosophy of the Enlightenment taught that the purpose
of society, organized in the form of free markets, was to
release the creative energies of individual reason by defending it against every form of public or private coercion.
Although the conservative reaction held a less exalted

view of the rational capacities of men, it recognized the empirical wisdom of individuals as the source of social achievement, and defended the traditional organization of society as a basis for individual action. Marxism defended its program of economic reorganization with a similar plea that favorable economic conditions were indispensable to the realization of individual potentialities. Each of these doctrines had a different conception of the evil which threatened the secular salvation of men. For the philosophers it was political coercion and private violence, for the conservatives it was social instability, and for the Marxists it was economic exploitation. Their views as to the proper form of social organization were correspondingly diverse. These diversities did not prevent them, however, from being in agreement on the basic function of society. According to all these doctrines society was an organization dedicated to the optimum development of individual men.

Modern liberalism is an attempt to use these two points of agreement as the basis for a new conception of politics. Like the preceding class ideologies it starts from the assumption that society should serve the needs of individuals, and that government should serve the needs of society. Where it differs from its predecessors is in its insistence on political organization as a crucial factor in the life of society. To maximize the creative potentialities of individuals is a complex problem. Freedom of negotiation, social stability and economic security, all these are no more than partial statements of the conditions necessary to the liberation of the rational capacities of men. Class ideologies, by concentrating on the needs of a part of the community, lead to a drastic oversimplification of the problem. If society is to perform its proper function as a mediator between the government and the individual, it must provide a political mechanism for the testing and reformulation of all the partial truths suggested by the experience of particular individuals and groups. Like its predecessors, modern liberalism believes in the existence of a natural harmony of interests. Under favorable conditions, the natural tendency of reason is to work for the welfare of mankind. This rational harmony does not, however, emerge spontaneously from the operation of class institutions, but as the result of a comprehensive process of political deliberation. Participation in the organized political life of society is a necessary means to the realization of human freedom. This belief is a distinguishing feature of modern liberal thought.

This conception of politics did not arise through the creation of a new school of political theory, but through the gradual modification of earlier class doctrines. As long as people had faith in their own class institutions as predestined exponents of the natural harmony of interests, they had no reason to concern themselves with the political organization of society. Nineteenth-century conditions tended, however, to undermine that faith. Class institutions proved in operation to be rather less satisfactory than parliamentary institutions as means for the satisfaction of class interests. This gradually forced people to pay attention to the theoretical as well as to the practical problems of politics. Among the theorists of every social group confidence in the adequacy of class institutions became subordinate to an increasing recognition of the need for political action. This led to various revisions of class doctrine which in their totality constitute the theory of modern liberalism.

The middle classes were the first to lose confidence in the adequacy of their original position. The philosophy of the Enlightenment had taught that the establishment of free markets would insure individual freedom. Experience soon led to the disappointment of that hope. The theory of free competition rests on the assumption that all men, in proportion to their ability and effort, will enjoy an equal opportunity for competitive success. In the early days of the commercial and industrial revolutions, when people with limited means found it relatively easy to establish businesses of their own, this assumption was reasonably realistic from the standpoint of the middle classes. But as the progress of industry led to larger accumulations of capital, men with small or middle-sized financial resources found it harder to survive in competition with wealthy rivals. Industrial and commercial monopolies came to dominate the operation of free markets. For a majority of the middle class, therefore, the apocalyptic hopes of the Enlightenment proved illusory. In practice, the free market was an obstacle to the economic self-expression of all but a limited number of its original devotees. For them no less than for the representatives of other social groups it had failed to serve as a vehicle of the natural harmony of interests.

The result was an increasing current of middle-class interest in politics. If the spontaneous operation of free markets failed to produce satisfactory conditions, the obvious thing to do was to remedy its defects by legislative action. By the middle of the nineteenth century middle-class opinion had begun to swing in that direction. Industrialists in economically backward regions, like Germany, who found that they could not compete with the well-established industries of England, rediscovered the advantages of tariff protection. Small enterprisers, threatened by the pressure of large-scale organizations, began to look to the state for antimonopolistic and other forms of remedial legislation. While continuing to regard free competition as the normal basis of society, they saw that the maintenance of genuinely competitive conditions called for positive political action. Thus the state gradually came to replace the market as the guarantor of middle-class interests.

The importance of this development in the evolution of modern liberalism is nowhere more clearly shown than in the history of the United States. American society in the nineteenth century was almost exclusively dominated by the middle classes. The progress of industrialization was so slow, and the social composition of the urban working classes so heterogeneous, that the class-conscious proletariat was relatively late in making its appearance as a factor in American politics. This country had, moreover, no groups comparable to the nobility and peasantry of Europe. The rural majority consisted of independent farmers who, in their restless search for novel opportunities, were essentially middle-class enterprisers with a middle-class point of view. It is therefore significant that the trend of nineteenth-century politics in America, as elsewhere, lay in the direction of positive state action. Through the efforts of American industrialists the United States became an early and ardent convert to the policy of tariff protection. As the power of American capitalism increased, enthusiasm for legislative regulation of the market soon extended to the small farmers and other middle-class elements of the agrarian west, who sought political protection against the power of eastern financial and industrial monopoly. This protest movement, which at one time went under the name of populism, led to government regulation of railways and banking, to government operation of many public utilities, and to other measures of socialized control. In more recent times similar elements in the community have been behind the drive for government ownership and operation of power resources. It is true that, in the absence of conservative and proletarian pressures, these developments never went so far in America as in Europe. As a product of middle-class action, however, they constitute a particularly convincing demonstration of the changes which were taking place in the middle-class conception of politics.

This tendency to interfere with the operation of free markets necessitated a substantial revision of the philosophy of the Enlightenment. During the first decades of the nineteenth century certain classical economists had become aware of the limitations of the earlier faith in the natural harmony of interests. During the period following the Napoleonic wars the political life of England was dominated by the issue of the corn laws. The growing urban population, with its interest in cheap food supplies, wanted free trade in agricultural products. To the disappointment of those who believed in the natural harmony of interests, the rural population showed no willingness to abandon tariff protection. This experience led Ricardo, a prominent economist of the time, to the conclusion that there can be no identity of economic interest between people who derive their incomes from the control of a natural monopoly, such as land, and people who earn their living by nonmonopolistic means. Marx's theory of inevitable class conflict owes much to Ricardo's analysis. But even though Ricardo recognized the difficulties of admitting monopoly within a competitive system, he did not feel that there was anything to be done about it. The idea of having the state assume control of land and other natural monopolies was too extreme for his taste. He simply concluded that conflicts were an inescapable part of the economic order. This depressing theory, which helped to give classical economics its reputation as the "gloomy science," did not lead to an immediate revision of laissez-faire doctrine. It did, however, prepare the way for middle-class acceptance of the fact that monopoly creates conflicts of interest which can only be resolved by political action.

The theorist who first carried these developments to a systematic conclusion was John Stuart Mill. The starting point of Mill's political thought was orthodox utilitarianism. As the son of James Mill, a prominent friend and associate of Bentham, he had been educated from infancy to carry on the leadership of that school. The expectation of his teachers was in large measure fulfilled. Unlike many infant prodigies, however, the younger Mill proved to be a thinker of vigor and originality. Although the training of his early years did much to influence his work, he showed a surprising ability to appreciate the weaknesses of the early liberal position. His three most celebrated political essays, *On Utilitarianism, On Liberty,* and *On Representative Government,* contain many significant departures from the philosophy of the Enlightenment. These depar-

tures form an important stage in the development of
modern liberal thought.

Although Mill continued to pay lip service to the pleas-
ure-pain principle, the central tendency of his work was
idealistic rather than hedonistic in character. This made
it possible for him to avoid many of the pitfalls of the early
utilitarian position. The doctrine of the greatest good of
the greatest number, with its subordination of the individual to social statistics, is incompatible with the Western
conception of the value of every human soul. A theory
erected on this foundation can easily lead to majority
despotism. In the philosophy of the Enlightenment, however, hedonism had been tempered with a strong vein of
ethical idealism. This vein was particularly clear in the
writings of Kant. According to Kant's ethical theory the
primary purpose of life is not happiness, but the moral
and intellectual development of individual men. Political
and social institutions are good only insofar as they encourage the widest possible exercise of moral responsibility. This principle had led Kant himself to conclude that
republicanism, with its wide diffusion of political responsibilities, is indispensable to the full expression of the
moral personality. A similar emphasis on ethical considerations brought Mill to similar conclusions. For him also,
respect for the moral personality of all men, rather than
the greatest happiness of the greatest number, was the
guiding principle of social and political action. This enabled him to reorient utilitarianism in the directon of
constitutional politics.

Mill's ethical emphasis provided the justification for a
new appreciation of the importance of social factors in
human life. Without denying the existence of altruistic

motives, the tendency of hedonism is to focus attention on the pursuit of individual pleasure. But if the main purpose of life is to secure the maximum development of all human potentialities, self-regarding action must give way to other-regarding action. Respect for the dignity and importance of every human soul led Christians to recognize the obligation of universal charity. On the secular plane, a similar consequence was implicit in the ethical theory of Mill. He was, to be sure, in agreement with earlier liberal thinkers in believing that nothing could take the place of individual initiative and responsibility as a means of developng the human personality. His essay *On Liberty* is a classic vindication of individual freedom in the intellectual and moral realm. Respect for the equal rights of other men serves, however, to place limits on the scope of permissible individual action. The philosophy of the Enlightenment had proceeded on the assumption that every man should be free to do as he pleased as long as he did not interfere by force with the equal rights of others. But murder, robbery, and other forms of violence and fraud are not the only obstacles to the development of individual potentialities. Man is a product not only of his own efforts, but also of his environment. A child brought up in the household of an impoverished drunkard has less chance of expressing his inherent qualities than does the equally talented son of a James Mill. Genuine respect for the individual involves a sense of responsibility for the equalization of social opportunities. As a person of strong utilitarian training, Mill was reluctant to see the adoption of social controls at the expense of individual responsibility. In principle, however, he was ready to admit the need for legislative and other social measures to serve as a basis for individual freedom. Subsequent middle-class theorists, like Green and Hobhouse, were able to accept a much wider range of social responsibility without departing from this principle.

Although Mill himself was cautious in recognizing the need for social action, the logic of his position forced him to make a radical departure from the political thought of the Enlightenment. Most eighteenth-century philosophers, with their belief in the primacy of individual action, had considered politics a relatively unimportant sphere of life. Because of his greater sense of social responsibility, Mill saw the matter in a different light. If the maximization of human potentialities is the ultimate secular value, and if the realization of that value depends on the maintenance through legislation of optimum social conditions, it follows that political action is an indispensable part of the moral responsibility of men. Mill's essay *On Representative Government* was an elaboration of that theme. According to the theory there propounded, participation in the work of representative government is a major phase in the education of the individual. Electoral and parliamentary debate provide a forum for the rational examination of legislative proposals. By entering that forum the individual contributes his own store of wisdom and experience to the political welfare of mankind, and acquires in return a fuller awareness of the needs of his fellow men. Although Mill himself did not believe that untrained and ill-educated people could be entrusted with the responsibilities of self-government, he felt that universal suffrage should be the ultimate goal of every liberal society. Unlike the majority of his predecessors, he saw politics not as a regrettable necessity but as an opportunity for positive achievement. The influence of his writings did much to establish constitutional democracy as an integral part of modern liberal doctrine.

This movement toward constitutional democracy was not confined to the middle classes. Toward the end of the nineteenth century a parallel movement began to appear in the ranks of the urban proletariat. Although the theory of revolutionary socialism, unlike the philosophy of the Enlightenment, had not yet been put to the test of a successful revolution, the course of events had done much to dim its apocalyptic promise. The institution of the class-conscious proletariat had proved in practice to be no more successful than the institution of the free market in living up to the expectations of its original devotees. This led to a revision of proletarian theory which brought it in closer agreement with the principles of constitutional government.

The main obstacle to the success of revolutionary socialism lay in the numerical weakness of the proletariat. Marx had rested his promise of ultimate victory on two essential propositions: a belief that the tendency of modern industrialism would be to concentrate the ownership of wealth in the hands of a constantly shrinking capitalist class; and a further belief that the majority of propertyless individuals would join the ranks of the class-conscious proletariat. The course of late nineteenth- and early twentieth-century development failed to justify either expectation. Although the trend toward large-scale organization and control continued unabated, the use of corporations, cartels, and other legal devices made it possible to concentrate economic control in the hands of a few without producing a comparable concentration in the ownership of wealth. As direct stockholders, or as investors in savings accounts and insurance policies, substantial numbers of people were able to retain a financial interest in the profits of the capitalist economy. Of those who sank to the position of salaried employees, moreover, a large proportion failed to identify their interests with those of the factory workers. Modern industry has room for a large army of salesmen, clerks, and other white-collar workers who tend, in spite of their economic insecurity, to feel socially superior to manual laborers. Thus the revolutionary hopes of Marxism, based on the expectation of a numerically preponderant proletariat, were disappointed by the development of nineteenth-century capitalism.

Doubt as to the efficacy of their class institutions led the proletariat, for reasons comparable to those previously operative in the case of the middle classes, to place new emphasis on the importance of political action. It is true that the working-class movement, in the absence of revolutionary success, was able to accomplish many of its ends by nonpolitical means. Increasing skill in the use of strikes and other forms of organized resistance gave the factory workers some control over the life of factory communities. Under the pressure of market competition, however, the only sure way of consolidating working-class gains was to embody them in legislation. In order to safeguard the high standard of living obtained in countries with a particularly effective labor organization, tariff protection was frequently needed. In order to prevent specific factories or industries from exploiting the weakness of unorganized workers to the detriment of the rest, uniform legislation on wages, hours, and other conditions of employment was desirable as a supplement to direct working-class action.

Although the proletariat were insufficiently numerous to gain an absolute majority, their electoral strength was great enough to give them a substantial measure of parliamentary power. The fact that the middle classes themselves had abandoned their faith in absolute market freedom made it relatively easy to gain a hearing for working-class demands in the matter of social legislation. By bargaining with other groups in return for electoral or parliamentary support, a politically organized proletariat was in a position to accomplish many purposes within the framework of constitutional democracy. Thus the fading of revolutionary hopes was accompanied by increasing confidence in the efficacy of parliamentary action.

In countries where the parliamentary tradition was particularly strong, political experience enabled the working classes to acquire self-consciousness without succumbing to the appeal of revolutionary socialism. This was true not only in America, where the proletariat itself was comparatively slow in developing, but also in England, the homeland of the industrial revolution. Long familiarity with the constitutional arts of negotiation and compromise had made the British middle classes comparatively conciliatory in their early relations with working-class organizations. The influence of middle-class liberals like John Stuart Mill also did something to encourage the adoption of social legislation. This led to the evolution of a labor movement which, in its ideological commitments, was never radically at variance with the principles of modern liberalism. The Fabian socialism of intellectuals like Sidney and Beatrice Webb, who advocated the attainment of working-class ends by evolutionary rather than by revolutionary means, was a characteristic expression of British proletarian thought. Although revolutionary Marxism had some influence in the formation of British socialism, it never succeeded in becoming the dominant force. The result was to make England an unusually early and successful exponent of the theory and practice of modern liberalism.

In countries where Marxism had gained a strong hold on the imagination of the proletariat, the abandonment of apocalyptic hopes was more difficult. Toward the end of the nineteenth century, however, increasing recognition of the advantages of parliamentary action led many Marxist thinkers to face the problem of revising revolutionary socialism in an evolutionary direction. The "back to Kant" movement which agitated socialist circles at this time was the expression of a widespread desire to escape from the materialistic determinism of Marx into the freer air of rationalistic self-determination. Appreciation of the value of responsible political action was particularly strong in Germany, where an unusually numerous and well-organized working class had succeeded, in spite of revolutionary Marxian commitments, in gaining legislative concessions through the exercise of electoral and parliamentary power. German socialists accordingly played a leading part in the revisionist movement. Thus Eduard Bernstein, in his book on *Evolutionary Socialism*, directly challenged the revolutionary presuppositions of the Marxian interpretation of history. By demonstrating that the actual development of modern capitalism had failed to follow along the lines of Marx's economic analysis, he tried to convince his fellow Marxists that patient political action within the framework of constitutional government was the necessary means for the attainment of working-class ends. Although the efforts of evolutionary socialists did not wholly succeed in breaking the hold of revolutionary Marxism, they did much to reconcile the working-class movement with the principles of constitutional democracy.

During the course of the nineteenth century a similar reconciliation was also taking place among the conservatives. In the days when liberal constitutionalism had been little more than a device to prevent governments from interfering with the operation of free markets, agrarian traditionalists had had no choice but to place themselves in the hands of absolute monarchs. The evolution of modern constitutionalism made parliaments increasingly attractive, however, as a vehicle of conservative action. The electoral power of the agricultural classes in most European countries was sufficient to enable conservative party organizations to exercise substantial parliamentary influence. Now that the middle classes and the proletariat were willing to recognize the propriety of using positive state action as a basis for the defense of their own interests, there was no theoretical reason why they should reject agricultural protectionism and other legislative measures for the defense of traditional interests. By negotiation and compromise with other groups conservative politicians were in a position to secure a reasonable measure of consideration for the needs of a conservative agrarian society. Conservative devotion to the institution of absolute monarchy had always been rather grudging and superficial in comparison with the loyalties accorded in other circles to proletarian or market institutions. When the opportunity for parliamentary action presented itself, most conservatives were prepared to forget their previous ideological commitments. This made it relatively easy for them to adapt themselves to the theory and practice of modern liberalism.

One of the most significant features of this conservative development was the change which took place in the policy of many Christian churches. The philosophy of the Enlightenment, insofar as it tended to encourage individual selfishness at the expense of social responsibility, had been incompatible with the teachings of Christian morality. Its doctrinaire progressivism also made it the natural enemy of institutions which, like the established churches, had deep traditional roots. During the early nineteenth century, therefore, the maintenance of absolute monarchy impressed most European churchmen as the only possible basis for the defense of Christian interests. But this open alliance between Christianity and conservatism, though temporarily convenient, soon proved to be a disaster. By alienating the middle-class and proletarian enemies of absolute monarchy it contributed to the partial or complete de-Christianization of a large part of the Western world. When this fact became obvious, many churchmen lost their faith in conservative institutions. Christian socialists of various faiths began exploring the possibility of reconverting the masses by organizing Christian trade unions and other working-class associations. Their purpose was to make the principles of Christian morality an active force in contemporary society. Under existing conditions liberal constitutionalism was the best available means to that end. Although sincere Christians could not submit to compromise in matters of faith, there was no reason why they should not enter the arena of competitive politics and negotiate with other groups on questions relative to the organization of secular society. By using their electoral power to force concessions, they could do more to safeguard the position of the church than by clinging to an outworn alliance with absolute kingship. Christianity had always taught that any form of government is legitimate as long as it is willing to maintain the external conditions indispensable to the performance of the religious mission of the church. Because of its compromising spirit, modern liberalism was more willing than earlier class doctrines to make allowance for the religious needs of men. Toward the end of the nineteenth century, therefore, increasing numbers of churchmen had ceased to look upon constitutional democracy as an enemy. The pontificate of Leo XIII saw the beginning of a policy whereby Catholics were permitted and even encouraged to participate in democratic politics. Politically conservative Protestant churches followed a similar line of development. In this way many of the former supporters of absolute monarchy were reconciled to the processes of parliamentary government.

Something more than parliamentarism was needed, however, to insure the success of modern liberalism. If rival social groups were to abandon their apocalyptic hopes in favor of parliamentary action, it could only be on the assumption that all would have an effective voice in the determination of national policy. Although the organization of modern legislatures tended to encourage the process of reconciliation between opposing points of view, it provided no absolute guarantee against the oppression of minority interests. In medieval parliaments, where the representatives of social classes were organized in separate estates, each was in a position to defend itself by vetoing the decisions of the others. In modern parliaments, on the

other hand, majority rule has been the prevailing principle. It is true that bicameralism has occasionally served to
mitigate the effects of majoritarianism. Insofar as particular sectional or class interests, as in the case of the British
House of Lords or the French and American senates, have
succeeded in gaining control over a particular chamber,
they sometimes have been able to force concessions from
popular majorities. But unlike medieval parliaments,
which served merely as adjuncts to an independent royal
administration, modern legislatures bear primary responsibility for the formulation and execution of state policy.
To form a stable majority in support of any positive program is so difficult in itself that it has been undesirable to
complicate the process by giving separately organized interest groups the right of absolute veto. In the absence of
such a right, however, there is always the danger that
statesmen will concentrate on the organization of majorities at the expense of minority interests. If any substantial
minority finds that its requirements are neglected by the
parliamentary process it will look for other ways of achieving its ends. Intransigent majorities, no less than intransigent minorities, are incompatible with the formation of a
comprehensive general will. To guarantee the rights of
minorities against parliamentary majorities has therefore
been one of the crucial problems of modern liberalism.

Constitutional limitations on parliamentary action provided a partial solution to the problem. Even in the days
when royal absolutism was at its height, the Western
world had never entirely abandoned the belief that government is subject to law. When parliaments replaced
kings as the primary agencies for the control of government, this manifestation of Western legalism received a

new lease of life. The idea that popular legislatures were not supreme, but derived their authority from written or unwritten constitutions, quickly established itself as a principle of modern liberalism. This made it possible to provide legal safeguards against many potential violations of minority interests. If all groups were to take a share in the formation of public opinion, it was necessary that majorities should not use their control of the state apparatus to inhibit the propaganda and organizational efforts of minority parties. Elaborate constitutional guarantees for the defense of civil liberties helped to satisfy that need. If minorities were to give their allegiance to parliamentary processes it was necessary that majority governments should refrain from using their power to violate the basic convictions of any considerable part of the community. Constitutional limitation on legislation infringing religious freedom, private property, the rights of organized labor, and other particularly cherished interests tended to keep parliamentary action within generally acceptable bounds. Federalism, by guaranteeing certain areas of local autonomy, also provided a means of safeguarding minority interests which happened to coincide with recognizable geographical areas. In many different ways the concept of the constituent power was capable of mitigating the anti-liberal dangers of majoritarian democracy.

The effectiveness of constitutionalism itself depended, however, on the development of a new system of political morality. Centuries of royal or parliamentary absolutism had accustomed the Western world to the concept of sovereignty. This concept asserts that every state must have a single determinate authority vested with absolute legislative powers. Modern constitutions ascribe this sovereign authority to the amending power. In some countries, like England, the amending power can be exercised by a simple parliamentary majority. Other countries, like the United States, have amending provisions which call for larger and more complexly organized majorities. In either case, the constitution itself offers no guarantee against sovereign interference with the rights of any group too weak to influence the process of constitutional amendment. Liberal constitutionalism is possible under these circumstances only on the condition that a decisive proportion of the community, recognizing the moral value of free discussion and compromise, refrains from using its sovereign powers in such a way as to impair vital minority interests. Thus the establishment of modern liberalism called for the creation of a moral consensus with regard to the inalienable rights of individual and group action.

Unfortunately the traditional concept of sovereignty stood as an obstacle to recognition of the rights of organized minorities. Through the work of earlier natural-law theorists, much had been done to familiarize people with the idea that individuals have certain inalienable rights which they are justified in asserting against the pretensions of the sovereign state. The idea of ascribing comparable rights to organized minority groups was incompatible, however, with the current presuppositions of juristic thought. According to the theory of corporations which had prevailed ever since the rise of the modern state, the legal existence and specific rights of organized groups depend on the discretion of the sovereign. The classic legal doctrine, inherited from the days of Roman absolutism, asserted that the association was simply a fictitious person (*persona ficta*) created from time to time by the sovereign state to satisfy its convenience. To speak of an artificial creation as having rights against its own creator is absurd. Thus the *persona ficta* theory of corporations was incompatible with any thoroughgoing attempt to secure recognition for the rights of minority organizations.

This tradition of hostility to group action was shared by the original exponents of modern constitutionalism. The idea that the existence of particular wills is fatal to the general will was one of the leading principles of Rousseau's political thought. In this respect his theory was a typical expression of the early liberal position. It is characteristic that the French Revolution, in a systematic crusade against independent associations, initiated drastic legislation against local and vocational groups. Subsequent attempts to ban trade unions and other forms of working-class organization demonstrate the persistence of this attitude. Even political parties, now recognized as an indispensable agency of constitutional politics, impressed the earlier theorists, from Rousseau to *The Federalist*, as a dangerous abuse. Regarding the emergence of "factions" as a sign of the decay of republican virtue, responsible statesmen did everything in their power to inhibit the growth of party organizations. When George Washington included both Hamilton and Jefferson in his cabinet he did so in the conscious hope that it would prevent these political rivals from indulging in party politics. According to the original conception of the general will, a healthy society is one in which there are no associations to stand between the individual and the state. This conception long continued to inhibit the development of liberal thought.

In spite of all theoretical objections, however, the nineteenth century was actually characterized by a vigorous

development of group life. In a world of increasing political and economic centralization most individuals were
powerless to gain their ends without joining together in
associations. The conservative reaction and revolutionary
socialism, with their emphasis on traditional or proletarian
agencies of social solidarity, were a reflection of the inadequacy of a society based on the atomic individualism of
the Enlightenment. Under the conditions of parliamentary government, the growth of party politics likewise
served to demonstrate the unrealistic quality of early constitutional thought. People discovered that the only way
to get what they wanted was to form political parties. The
need for party organization in carrying on the work of any
large representative assembly, and in giving central direction to a mass electorate, was so obvious that it could not
fail to gain universal recognition. In spite of Washington's
efforts, American presidential elections quickly fell into a
clear-cut party pattern. The political evolution of other
Western countries followed along comparable lines. Practical experience everywhere demonstrated that the freedom of individuals was to a large extent a function of the
freedom enjoyed by political and other associations.

Because of the persistence of established ways of
thought, recognition of the importance of group life was
slow in penetrating the theory of modern liberalism. During the late nineteenth and early twentieth centuries,
however, the attention of liberal theorists turned increasingly in this direction. Dissatisfaction with the absolutist
conception of sovereignty gave rise to an influential group
of political thinkers best known to the English-speaking
world under the name of political pluralists. The common
purpose of this group was to challenge the proposition that

associations are an artificial creation of the state. This belief in the spontaneous reality of group life arose in various
ways. Thus the German jurist Otto von Gierke arrived at
his conclusions through a study of early German law.
Since the freedom of associational life was greater in medieval times than in the period following the emergence
of modern sovereign states, the result of this study was
to throw new light on the potentialities of independent
group action. Others, like the English churchman Figgis,
reached similar conclusions as a result of their interest in
preventing churches and other religious associations from
succumbing to the claims of the modern nation state. The
experience of such people as the English socialists Cole
and Laski, who came to accept the importance of group
life largely through contact with the needs of trade unionism, was also typical of the movement. From one direction
or another, many people reached the conclusion that the
association is a more vital thing than the *persona ficta* theory would admit. This led them in various ways to assert
that groups, like individuals, are endowed with an inherent right to existence and self-expression. Recognition of
that right became for them one of the basic principles of
constitutional government.

Emphasis on the inalienable rights of associations gave
rise, however, to serious problems with regard to the maintenance of public order. The ultimate tendency of any
thoroughgoing philosophy of natural rights is to justify the
right of revolution. In the history of early liberalism, belief
in the inalienable rights of individuals had led to revolutionary conclusions. According to the philosophy of the
Enlightenment, individuals had a moral obligation to
obey governments only insofar as the activities of those

governments served to maximize the area of individual freedom. The English, American, and French revolutions all found justification in the belief that the preceding political authorities, by failing to perform their duty toward the individual, had forfeited their claim to obedience. Impressed by the importance of revolutionary action as a check on political abuses, Thomas Jefferson even went so far as to assert that the maintenance of freedom in America would depend on the occurrence of at least one American revolution in the course of each generation. With the development of political pluralism, this revolutionary element in the liberal tradition received a new lease of life. Although groups, on the same basis as individuals, might recognize the duty of submitting to regulation in the interest of general freedom, belief in the existence of inalienable group rights tended to encourage disobedience to any government, parliamentary or otherwise, which seemed to neglect those rights. The early liberal fear of factions found support in the fact, repeatedly exemplified in this history of ancient and medieval republics, that organized groups are more effective than isolated individuals as a source of revolutionary action. Under these circumstances it would have been hard to deny that new possibilities of disorder were implicit in the philosophy of political pluralism.

This difficulty made it necessary for the theorists of modern liberalism to reconsider the place of order in the hierarchy of political values. Sixteenth- and seventeenth-century absolutists, who were largely responsible for the modern concept of sovereignty, had considered the value of order to be so great that they had been willing to sacrifice other values, including individual and social justice,

in its name. Liberalism had been from the beginning a reaction against this point of view. The philosophers of the
Enlightenment and the revolutionary socialists had believed in the justice of their respective patterns of social reorganization so thoroughly that they had accepted revolutionary disorder as a permissible means to the attainment
of their ends. Even the conservatives, with all their respect
for political authority, had considered it proper to apply
counterrevolutionary force against states which neglected
the traditional interests of society. In the writings of Kant,
the theory that conflict is an indispensable stimulus to the
realization of the idea of justice had already found expression. Working from individualistic premises, Jefferson had
welcomed the prospect of recurrent revolutionary disorder
as a guarantee against unjust corruptions of the American
constitutional process. If the theory of modern liberalism
was to provide any comparable guarantee against the
abuses of democratic majoritarianism it needed to emphasize the primacy of justice over order, not only in the relationship between states and individuals but also in the relationship between states and associations.

The theorist who went farthest in this direction was
Pierre Joseph Proudhon. Although he described himself as
an anarchist, Proudhon recognized the need for coercive
state authority. His preoccupation with justice was so complete, however, that he found it impossible to accept the
absolutist implications of the traditional concept of sovereignty. His theory of antinomies was an attempt to overcome these implications. Like Hegel and Marx he regarded conflict as the instrument of historical progress.
Where he differed from them was in believing that the
goal of history was not to eliminate opposing forces in a

final synthesis, but to perpetuate and increase the dynamic
tension between conflicting principles. For Proudhon the
metaphysical nature of the universe rests on the operation
of polar opposites, known as antinomies. In manipulating
the antinomy of dark and light the good photographer
does not try to cover his plate with a uniform gray, but
uses contrasting values as the basis for a complex composition. Historical progress likewise, according to Proudhon,
consists in the establishment of an increasingly complex
balance between opposing values. In the social realm this
principle expresses itself in the emergence of individuals
and groups with increasingly specialized interests and
functions. The purpose of history is not to merge these differences in a gray uniformity but to manipulate them in
such a way that each will be able to make its maximum
contribution to the life of an increasingly complex society.
Justice, which teaches men to modify their own claims in
terms of the corresponding rights of others, is the principle
which enables rational men to achieve unity through di-
versity. The function of the state is to serve the ends of justice by maintaining a rational balance between perpetually opposing forces. But even though the state may use
coercive power for this purpose it should not, as the traditional theory of sovereignty asserted, enjoy an absolute
monopoly of power. The natural tendency of all men, including statesmen, is to emphasize their own needs and
experience at the expense of others. Only the experience of
conflict, by demonstrating the impossibility of imposing
the irrational will of one group on another, can inspire
men to the painful effort of seeking a rational basis for the
adjustment of their conflicting claims. If the state, therefore, is to serve the interests of justice, it must never be so

strong as to be able to impose its will absolutely on other social groups. Actual or potential disorder is the motive for a just balancing of interests. Since justice is the substance of human progress, it follows that the desire for order must always be subordinated to the desire for justice.

Although Proudhon was never a widely influential thinker his writings admirably illustrate the tendencies which have come to prevail in the theory and practice of modern liberalism. The purpose of constitutional democracy has been to seek social justice not through the concentration but through the dispersion of political power. Recognizing the potential value of all forms of human experience it has encouraged individuals and private associations to assume the widest possible responsibility for the regulation of their own affairs. For the accomplishment of purposes unattainable on a basis of voluntary negotiation between individuals and groups it has recognized the need for coercive state action. By placing the state apparatus under the control of constituent or legislative majorities it has sought, however, to limit that action to measures fully acceptable to the bulk of the community, and has recognized a substantial right of resistance on the part of those whose wishes have been overruled. In cases where the existence of society itself is not immediately threatened the liberal conscience has demanded full freedom of criticism and propaganda for discontented minorities, and even tolerates a certain amount of forcible resistance to the authority of the state. If any considerable part of the community feels so strongly about the supposed violation of its rights that it is willing to take the risks of illegal action the normal tendency of liberal societies is to seek readjustment not by the indefinite continuance of coercive measures, but by the renegotiation of grievances. The fact that increasing violation of the eighteenth amendment led to the repeal of prohibition rather than to the multiplication of police forces is typical of the liberal attitude toward intransigent minorities. The reluctance of constitutional democracies to outlaw strikes is a more generally significant illustration of that attitude. Even in the case of revolutionary violence, the custom of granting the right of asylum and other forms of preferential treatment to political offenders is an indication of the liberal inclination to minimize coercion as an instrument of social integration. Although few liberal theorists have been willing to go as far as Proudhon in modifying the concept of sovereignty, the actual tendency of modern liberalism has been to subordinate sovereign pretensions in the interest of an conscientious effort to achieve social justice by negotiating and reconciling the claims of opposing social forces. Like Proudhon, modern liberals have been willing to subordinate the value of social order to the value of rational justice.

By the late nineteenth and early twentieth centuries constitutional democracy had become the generally accepted norm of Western politics. The result was to place the legalistic traditions of the West on a newly effective basis. Although the expansion of public services during this period led to a constant increase in the size and importance of state bureaucracies, the principles of modern liberalism were strong enough to hold this development within the framework of a rigorous rule of law. The men of the Middle Ages had relied on the power of the Holy Ghost, operating through the institutions of the church, to confine the state to the execution of laws compatible with

the religious interests of humanity. Relying on the power
of rational negotiation, operating through the institutions
of constitutional democracy, to safeguard the secular interests of humanity, modern liberals succeeded even more
notably in reducing bureaucracy to a position of legal subordination. Parliaments and cabinets responsive to the
general will assumed the overall direction of legislative
and administrative policy. Backed by the moral force of
public opinion, they held civil and military hierarchies to
the execution of laws generally acceptable to the secular
community. Once again the principle of Western dualism
had emerged to guarantee the maintenance of the legalistic traditions of Western civilization.

10

The Problem
of Nationalism

With the establishment of constitutional democracy, modern liberalism went a long way toward uniting the secular community in an effective general will. Unfortunately the rise of constitutionalism was accompanied by another development which did much to vitiate the significance of that achievement. The success of the medieval church was largely due to the fact that, in its capacity as an international organization, it had been in a position to mobilize the moral consensus of the entire Western world against the abuses of particular governments. Since modern technology has called for ever larger units of social integration, the need for a comprehensive international community has tended to increase rather than to diminish with the passage of time. During the course of the nineteenth century, however, the moral unity of the Western world actually suffered a progressive deterioration. The rise of nationalism, which took place at this time, served in large measure to inhibit the growth of a secular community intensively or extensively comparable with the religious community of the medieval church. Modern liberalism, by associating itself with the idea of nationalism, became increasingly incapable of providing the moral basis for a comprehensive integration of the Western world. The result was a serious and possibly fatal impairment of its capacity to solve the problems of modern politics.

In view of its original theoretical commitments, liberalism ought to have been opposed to the development of nationalism. In spite of their many differences, the philosophy of the Enlightenment, the conservative reaction and revolutionary socialism all had their roots in the internationalist tradition of Western politics. During the many centuries which had followed the collapse of the Roman Empire, the ideal of unity had never ceased to haunt the memory of the Western world. The institutions of church and empire had helped to keep that ideal alive during the Middle Ages. Even after the triumph of the principle of territorial sovereignty, international law and balance of power diplomacy continued to implement the conception of an international community whose moral rights took precedence over the will of any particular sovereign. During the late eighteenth and early nineteenth centuries this internationalist tradition was still strong enough to exert a powerful influence on the development of political thought. The philosophy of the Enlightenment and revolutionary socialism were both cosmopolitan doctrines, offering a universal message for the secular salvation of mankind. Although the conservative reaction was less vigorous in its humanitarianism, its traditionalism likewise took the form of a universal ideal. All three doctrines addressed their appeal to the general welfare of humanity rather than to the interests of any particular state or nation. Thus the theoretical foundations of modern liberalism all tended to encourage a vigorous reaffirmation of the moral unity of the Western world.

During the earlier stages of its career liberalism did in

fact operate in the direction of international solidarity. The philosophy of the Enlightenment, the conservative reaction, and revolutionary socialism, by arousing men of all countries to a consciousness of common interests, gave rise to international movements which succeeded for a time in transcending rival political loyalties. The French Revolution at first enjoyed the support not only of the French middle classes but also of the corresponding social strata in other countries. Prior to their disillusionment with Napoleonic imperialism, enlightened Germans, for example, generally welcomed the invading French armies as deliverers, and coöperated with them against their reactionary fellow nationals. The revolutions of 1848 likewise derived much of their strength from the existence of what might be described, on the analogy of Marxist terminology, as an informal but effective middle-class international, which stood ready to exert moral and physical pressure on behalf of the aspirations of like-minded men in every part of the Western world. A similar tendency to cross national lines was characteristic of the conservative reaction. The Holy Alliance, whereby the various absolute monarchs of Europe pledged themselves to take united action against any challenge to the principle of legitimacy, was a formal embodiment of the conservative sense of international solidarity. Revolutionary socialism, with its first and second internationals, was even more consciously devoted to the principle of international coöperation. Like the supporters of the medieval church, the leaders of these movements believed that the general interests of humanity took precedence over all lesser forms of loyalty. This was the spirit which prevailed at the inception of modern liberalism.

This spirit never really succeeded, however, in gaining a decisive hold on the popular imagination. Even though the leaders of liberalism might recognize the universal implications of their position, their concept of humanity remained too purely intellectual to arouse the emotional loyalties of ordinary men. For people of limited knowledge or capacity, immediate realities are apt to take precedence over remote considerations. In order to become conscious of their membership in any comprehensive form of human association they must see the value of that association in terms of direct personal experience. Rousseau, with his emphasis on civic ceremonies as a factor in the creation and maintenance of the general will, was aware of the fact that social loyalties depend on the existence of concrete symbols and institutions intimately associated with the events of daily life. This observation is even more clearly valid in the case of ecumenical associations than in the case of those parochial city states which Rousseau himself was considering. During the Middle Ages the religious community of the Western world had found nourishment not only in the intellectually satisfying rationalizations of a universal theology, but also in the emotionally compelling rites and institutions of a universal church. Secular humanitarianism, on the other hand, was an intellectual movement which failed on the whole to embody itself in effective institutions. The attempts of occasional enthusiasts, like Robespierre and Comte, to organize a universal cult of Reason and Humanity were uniformly discouraging. Although the Holy Alliance and the socialist internationals gave some institutional reality to the conception of Western unity, they were too remote from everyday life to inspire great popular enthusiasm. The idea of humanity

remained an intellectual abstraction, unrelated to the concrete experiences of ordinary men. During the earlier
stages of liberal development, when responsibility for the
conduct of affairs rested in the hands of a limited ruling
class, liberal humanitarianism was a relatively powerful
force. Its influence on the masses was too shallow, however, to enable it to survive as a decisive factor in an increasingly democratic world.

The institution which actually succeeded in becoming
the center of popular loyalties was the modern sovereign
state. Centuries of royal absolutism had done much to inculcate the notion that devotion to a territorial sovereign
was the highest form of secular duty. The symbols and
ceremonies associated with a semidivine kingship were the
most impressive secular parallels to the rites of the medieval church. Even under constitutional monarchies and
republics much of the traditional pomp of sovereignty remained to captivate the popular imagination. The French
tricolor, like the Christian cross, was an omnipresent symbol capable of stirring the emotions of visual-minded men.
Like the church, with its elaborate apparatus of parochial
and charitable institutions, the modern state, with its per-
vasive military and bureaucratic organs, was capable of
affecting the lives of ordinary citizens in a very real fashion. Through the operation of universal military service
men of varied regional and class backgrounds met in the
common fellowship of army life, and acquired a direct interest in the glories and misfortunes of the state. Through
contact with the expanding service functions of civil bureaucracies they learned to look upon the state as a primary factor in the welfare of individual citizens. Modern
liberalism, with its emphasis on political action, encour-

aged this development. Although theorists might proclaim
the welfare of humanity as the proper goal of secular endeavor, territorial sovereignty was the instrument actually
used for the accomplishment of most secular purposes. To
a greater extent than any other institution the state was
able to embody secular aspirations in a concretely visible
form. For ordinary men it tended, therefore, to become the
primary center of modern political loyalty.

Even in the earlier stages of liberal development the
idea of territorial sovereignty was rather more important
than the idea of humanity as a factor in the political awakening of the masses. The spirit of patriotism which animated the American and French revolutions was largely a
matter of loyalty to the values and institutions of a specific
territorial state. Although the North-American colonists
had never enjoyed the privilege of political independence,
their struggles with the home country had led many of
them to believe that nothing short of independent statehood would satisfy their needs. The dream of controlling
their destinies through sovereign institutions inspired the
American patriots to wage a protracted war of liberation
against British and Tory resistance. In the case of the
French Revolution, devotion to the cause of the French
state played a similar part in the awakening of mass enthusiasm. Although the revolutionary movement impressed
many intellectuals, both at home and abroad, as a humanitarian crusade, it never succeeded in capturing the imagination of the masses until it had assumed the guise of a
patriotic struggle for the defense and glorification of the
French state. When foreign military pressure threatened
to destroy the independence of revolutionary France,
Frenchmen rose in a wave of patriotic enthusiasm. The

ensuing *levée en masse* enabled them to snatch victory from disaster, and to embark upon an ambitious career of imperialistic expansion. The French masses, although forced to bear the main burdens of Napoleonic warfare, found compensation in the glory of a regime which had raised their country to the summit of its power. Like the American revolutionists, they were willing to make sacrifices in return for the privilege of belonging to an independent state strong enough to control its own destinies. In both cases loyalty to the values and institutions of territorial sovereignty was the primary inspiration for popular participation in politics.

These initial examples served as the model for subsequent developments in other parts of the Western world. When other peoples aroused themselves to a mood of political self-consciousness, their aspirations likewise took the form of a demand for independent statehood. On the continent of Europe this followed in many cases from the experience of Napoleonic imperialism. The ruthless exactions of the Napoleonic system taught the enlightened classes of other countries that they had been mistaken in regarding the French invaders as instruments of universal liberation. To free themselves from the power of the French state became their highest aspiration. In order to break the deadly sequence of Napoleonic victories it was necessary for other peoples to increase their military and bureaucratic resources. This meant that rival territorial states would have to achieve a degree of patriotic enthusiasm and efficiency comparable to that of France. Toward the end of the Napoleonic period, therefore, leaders everywhere began to concentrate on the problem of increasing the power of their own territorial sovereigns. Through pa-

tient and skillful reformatory efforts Stein and his associates succeeded in raising Prussia to a high pitch of patriotic fervor and accomplishment. Similar movements,
of varying effectiveness, took place in other continental
states. The patriotic energy thus generated led to the overthrow of the Napoleonic system. This experience did more
than anything else to convince the politically conscious
elements of Europe that devotion to a powerful territorial
state was indispensable to freedom.

In the case of France, patriotism served to strengthen
the institutions of a previously existing state. In most regions, however, patriotic motives came in conflict with the
established units of political allegiance. Patriotism demanded, on the one hand, that the country in question
should be large and powerful enough to maintain effective
control over its own destinies. Since many states were too
small to accomplish this purpose, patriots frequently
found themselves in the position of having to advocate the
merger of several existing sovereignties in a more comprehensive form of sovereign association. The fear that the
thirteen American colonies, in their capacity as sovereign
states, would be too weak to resist the military and economic pressures of European imperialism made it necessary for American patriots to insist on the adoption of a
federal constitution. The incapacity of most of the smaller
states of Italy and Germany to counteract the threat of
French aggression led patriots in those regions likewise to
abandon the existing units of allegiance and concentrate
on the problem of political unification. But patriotism demanded, on the other hand, that all the inhabitants of any
given state should share a common spirit of patriotic devotion. Since many states were too large and heteroge-

neous to inspire common loyalties, patriots often found themselves in the position of advocating the creation not of larger but of smaller forms of sovereign association. The secession of the American colonies was partly due to the fact that increasing cleavages of economic and other interests had made it impossible for most Americans to retain a sense of common participation in the life of the British empire. The dissolution of the Austrian empire was likewise due to the existence of ethnic and other cleavages which prevented the inhabitants of its several regions from developing an effective general will. Under the conditions of constitutional democracy no state could hope to function efficiently without the willing support of its citizens. In most cases, therefore, the patriotic desire for statehood involved revolutionary political changes. Although patriotism called for an intense spirit of devotion to the institutions of a sovereign state, most of the existing units of sovereignty were either too large or too small to satisfy its requirements.

The result was to make the nation rather than the state the primary object of modern political loyalty. The nation may be defined as a social group which, for one reason or another, is conscious of the need for independent statehood. The causes underlying the emergence of particular forms of national consciousness were various, and frequently obscure. Long-established traditions of loyalty to a common sovereign authority often played a major role in this development. Even though many peoples, like the Poles and the various nations of the Balkan peninsula, had long since lost their political independence, memory of the real or mythical glories of long-extinguished kingdoms remained as an inspiration to common political action. In some cases, like Switzerland with its French, German, and Italian cantons, and France with its German-speaking Alsace-Lorrainers and its Celtic-speaking Bretons, the power of established political traditions was strong enough to preserve a common national consciousness among men of widely different linguistic and cultural backgrounds. Under the conditions of constitutional democracy, however, divergencies of language generally proved to be an insuperable obstacle to the communication of national sentiments. Thus the general tendency of modern nationalism has been to follow linguistic lines. Religious and other cultural differences have occasionally served, on the other hand, as in the cases of England and Ireland or of Serbia and Croatia, to prevent the emergence of common nationalism between the members of a single linguistic community. Through the operation of various forces most Western peoples came in the course of the nineteenth century to regard themselves as members of a particular nation, and to look upon the sovereign independence of that nation as the highest goal of political life. Loyalty to the state became increasingly subordinate to the claims of national groups. The problem of nationalism had emerged as one of the crucial problems of modern politics.

This movement had an immediate effect on the development of modern liberalism. Although the philosophy of the Enlightenment and the conservative reaction were both cosmopolitan movements, their respective supporters soon discovered that their best hope of success was to ally themselves with the emerging forces of nationalism. Revolutionary socialism, which began as a reaffirmation of the cosmopolitan tradition, was likewise forced in the course of time to make concessions to the nationalist spirit. During the eighteenth and nineteenth centuries the desire for national self-determination was so strong that exponents of class ideologies could survive only by adapting the power of nationalism to their own ends. This called for a drastic revision of doctrine in all the leading schools of modern political thought.

Of the principal class ideologies, conservatism on the whole was the one best equipped to meet the demands of the nationalist movement. This was due to the fact that both were opposed to the rationalistic individualism of the Enlightenment. As the defenders of a specific social group, the nation, nationalists were even more clearly disposed than conservatives to sacrifice individual values in the interests of society. To a large extent, moreover, their concept of society coincided with the premises of conservative traditionalism. Devotion to historic memories and institutions played an important part in the evolution of national self-consciousness. The preservation and development of national traditions was therefore a primary object of the nationalist movement. By reviving long-neglected languages and literatures, by commemorating ancient victories and other historic achievements, and by inculcating respect for native folkways and institutions, the nationalists of various countries hoped to arouse their respective peoples to a vivid sense of participation in the life of a particular nation. Unlike the philosophers of the Enlightenment, they recognized the value of tradition. This gave them an obvious point of contact with the conservative reaction.

The possibility of a conservative-nationalist alliance also found support in the fact that both movements were favorable to the growth of militarism. The philosophers of the

Enlightenment, confident in the harmonizing powers of human reason, had looked forward to the day when the evils of warfare would disappear in a peaceful and mutually advantageous community of universal free trade. From the standpoint of the conservative aristocracy, whose traditional way of life had been closely associated with the performance of military functions, this prospect was unappealing. It was also incompatible with the requirements of modern nationalism. Some of the most exciting national memories have to do with battles gloriously lost or won. Because of their emphasis on sovereign independence, moreover, nationalists have a natural interest in developing the military and bureaucratic resources of their respective states. During the Napoleonic wars many of the older French nobility, in their capacity as military and bureaucratic experts, were invited to return from exile and assume responsible positions in the administration of the Napoleonic state. Subsequent wars of national liberation or aggrandizement brought similar opportunities to the traditional ruling classes of other countries. In time of war or of preparation for war professional military men are at a premium. Common interest in the maintenance of a militarily powerful state was the factor which served above all else to encourage the collaboration of nationalist and conservative forces.

Under these circumstances it is not surprising to find that conservatives tended from the outset to take great interest in the development of nationalist thought. Opposition to the cosmopolitan tendencies of the Enlightenment was a recurrent theme in the writings of most of the earlier conservative theorists. This aspect of the conservative reaction is perhaps most clearly visible in the works of Joseph de Maistre. Many of his arguments against the abstract rationalism of the Enlightenment rest on the proposition that the eighteenth-century philosophers, by assuming the rational uniformity of human nature, were guilty of neglecting the differences of national character which distinguish the men of various nations. Man is not an abstract entity but the product of a specific environment, speaking the language and sharing the preconceptions of a particular historic society. Although there was nothing in the logic of the traditionalist position to indicate that one form of traditional association was more important than any other, Maistre tacitly assumed that the nation was the decisive factor in the formation of human character. Peoples with distinctive characteristics require distinctive forms of political and social organization. Maistre therefore believed that every nation should be free to follow its own traditional lines of political development. Republics should cling to their republican institutions, while monarchies should remain faithful to the dynasties which had shaped them from their birth. By attempting to force the whole human race within a uniform cosmopolitan framework the philosophers of the Enlightenment were violating the essential nature of man. For Maistre, conservative traditionalism appeared as a condition precedent to the expression of national character. This mixture of conservative and nationalist motives was typical of the more influential exponents of early conservative thought.

The incorporation of nationalism within the structure of conservative thought led to a thoroughgoing revision of the traditional conception of kingship. The principle of dynastic legitimacy, which had dominated the theory of monarchy, was incompatible with the principle of national

self-determination. Kings ruled by hereditary right, and
asserted their claims to territories of the most diverse national composition in accordance with the accidents of hereditary succession. Royalty, with its practice of interdy-
nastic marriages, was the most cosmopolitan of all social
classes. But even though most kings were at least partly
foreigners, frequently incapable of speaking the language
of their own countries, their work of political unification
had in many cases helped to lay the foundations of national self-consciousness. When peoples of countries like
France or Spain began to take pride in their national past
they tended to associate themselves with the martial and
other exploits of French or Spanish kings. This gave the
conservatives an excellent chance to lend nationalist color-
ing to the concept of legitimacy. In the political writings of
Chateaubriand the idea that hereditary kings were natural representatives of the national tradition had already
begun to assume the position of an unassailable conservative dogma. French royalists in particular made much of
the fact that Napoleon, whose family name they regularly
spelled in the original Italian form of Buonaparte, was a
man of foreign origin, while the Bourbons were the de-
scendants of a family that had lived and ruled in France
for nearly a thousand years. At the time of the revolution
Louis XVI and his Austrian wife had outraged national
opinion by intriguing with foreign powers. When his
brother Louis XVIII returned to the throne, the new king
was careful to appeal to national sentiment by proclaiming, as his first public statement upon crossing the border,
"One more Frenchman is returning to France." In the
light of this skillful propaganda stroke it is hard to believe
that the Bourbons had learned nothing and forgotten

nothing in their years of exile. As intelligent conservatives they at least had learned the value of associating monarchy with the rising nationalist movement.

In many respects, the conservative attempt to nationalize monarchy was quite successful. The survival of hereditary kingship as the prevailing form of government in nineteenth- and early twentieth-century Europe was due to the fact that kings, though increasingly divested of actual power, were able to acquire a respected place as symbols of national unity. It is true that in countries like Switzerland, where monarchy had had no place in earlier national history, the rise of nationalist sentiment was able to take place without the aid of kings. Since many of the most exciting national memories of France were associated with the ideas of republic and empire, French royalism likewise remained comparatively weak. But in countries where the tradition of monarchy was well-established the effect of nationalism was to give it a new lease of life. The steady rise of royalist sentiment in England during the nineteenth and twentieth centuries is a typical case in point. Loyalty to the nation generally tended to find concrete embodiment in loyalty to a particular royal family. The concepts of king and nation became so closely associated, indeed, that newly liberated peoples, like the Greeks and Rumanians, in the absence of any historic dynasty of their own, normally found it desirable to invite a foreign prince to fill a newly created throne. This curious violation of national sentiments, in a period of rising nationalism, is a tribute to the persistence of monarchist ideas in nineteenth-century thought.

If the conservatives had been able to identify themselves completely with the cause of national monarchy they

might well have succeeded in becoming the dominant
force in Western politics. The underlying assumptions of
nationalism and conservatism were so discordant, however, that the two movements were ultimately bound to
come into conflict. For the conservatives, monarchy was
valuable only insofar as it could be made to serve the
interests of a static society based on hereditary class distinctions. The tendencies of nationalism, on the other
hand, were socially dynamic. Nationalists derived their
enthusiasm not only from memories of the past, but also
from the hope of future greatness. Their love of tradition,
unlike that of the conservatives, was subordinate to the
desire for a powerful national state. While accepting the
claims of truly national monarchies, they were prepared
to rebel against any dynasty, however legitimate, which
stood in the way of national self-determination. While
recognizing the social value of established traditions, they
were unwilling to allow traditional considerations to inhibit their attempts to maximize the power of their respective nations. Their insistence that all citizens, and not
merely the hereditary ruling class, should assume active
responsibility for the welfare of the nation was also dis-
quieting from the conservative point of view. As the
dynamic implications of nationalism became clear, conservatives found it impossible to remain in sympathy with
the more extreme manifestations of the nationalist spirit.
This was particularly true in Central Europe, where
national aspirations stood in hopeless opposition to the
claims of dynastic legitimacy. In their attempts to bolster
the institutions of traditional kingship in that area conservative organizations like the Holy Alliance were forced
to adopt a policy of direct opposition to nationalism. This

deprived the conservatives of many of the advantages which Maistre and other early theorists had hoped to derive from the movement.

The result of these developments was to afford middle-class liberals an excellent opportunity to assume positions of national leadership. The cosmopolitan commitments of the Enlightenment did not prevent them from making the most of that opportunity. Tactical considerations alone would have been enough to impel them in that direction. The strongest centers of the Enlightenment lay in Western Europe, where the existing state system corresponded reasonably well with national boundaries. The stronghold of the conservative reaction was Central Europe, where the idea of national self-determination could be realized, if at all, only at the cost of drastic political readjustments. The immediate tendency of nationalism, in other words, was to consolidate the existing political structure of relatively enlightened countries like France and England, and to disrupt the existing political structure of reactionary countries like Germany and Austria. For purely tactical reasons, therefore, supporters of the middle-class Enlightenment had every reason to encourage the growth of nationalism.

For people brought up, however, in an atmosphere of rationalistic individualism, the acceptance of nationalist premises called for a number of difficult readjustments. It is true that some of the implications of nationalism were more readily acceptable to them than to their conservative rivals. Nationalist interest in the technical rationalization of political and social life, though stimulated by motives quite different from those of eighteenth-century humanitarianism, coincided reasonably well with the reformatory rationalism of the Enlightenment. The administrative and social reforms of a Napoleon or of a Baron Stein, for example, were generally more pleasing to middle-class progressives than to conservative reactionaries. The democratic implications of nationalism, while running counter to the aristocratic element in early liberalism, were also easy to reconcile with the later middle-class point of view. In its essential principles, however, the nationalist movement had less in common with the philosophy of the Enlightenment than with the conservative reaction. The demand that all other interests be sacrificed in the interests of the nation rested on the assumption that society is prior to the individual. The philosophy of the Enlightenment rested on the contrary assumption. To make room for nationalist considerations without destroying the individualist bases of middle-class liberalism was a difficult problem. The attempt to solve this problem constitutes one of the most important phases of nineteenth-century thought.

The line ultimately adopted by the theorists of liberal nationalism was to justify national self-determination in terms of individual self-expression. The writings of John Stuart Mill, in this respect as in so many others, are characteristic of the trend of later liberal thought. While agreeing with the philosophers of the Enlightenment that the object of politics was to maximize the effectiveness of individual action, he was more willing than his predecessors to recognize the importance of political and social factors in the development of the individual. This made it possible for him to incorporate a substantial element of nationalism in his political theory. According to his version of the problem of liberalism, participation in the responsibilities of political life is an essential part in the life of every fully developed individual. Mass participation in politics can only be effective, however, in relatively homogeneous societies. The possession of common traditions, linguistic and otherwise, does much to facilitate the exchange of political ideas, and to encourage the growth of a general sense of political responsibility. Under modern conditions the nation is the largest social unit capable of meeting these requirements. Participation in the political life of a nation is therefore indispensable to the personal development of every individual. The educational value of political action remains incomplete, however, unless it is fully responsible. The only political unit of modern times which enjoys complete independence, and thus bears complete responsibility for its actions, is the sovereign state. From this it follows that the requirements of individual self-expression can only be met within the framework of a nation state. As long as the individual lacks the experience of participating in the activities of an independent nation, his opportunities for self-education will be imperfect. Thus, without abandoning the individualistic premises of his predecessors, Mill was able to advocate national self-determination as one of the objectives of modern liberalism.

By its wholehearted acceptance of the nationalist position, middle-class liberalism won a decisive advantage over the conservative reaction. During the early nineteenth century, when the supporters of absolute monarchy were committed to the antinationalist policies of the Holy Alliance, ardent nationalists generally found that their best hope of success lay in association with the cause of liberal constitutionalism. Middle-class liberals recipro-

cated by devoting much of their energy and enthusiasm to
the cause of national self-determination. At the beginning
of the century the coöperative efforts of Britain and America, at that time the two leading exponents of constitutional government, led to the promulgation of the Monroe
doctrine, which enabled the peoples of Latin America to
assume control over their own destinies without interference from the Holy Alliance. The liberation of Greece, the
first of many successful wars for national independence on
the continent of Europe, owed much to the moral support
of liberal intellectuals like Byron and to the military and
diplomatic support of Britain. The revolutions of 1830 and
1848, which finally broke the power of the Holy Alliance,
were even more striking manifestations of the power of
liberal nationalism. It is true that the attempt to create
national states under liberal auspices was not uniformly
successful. The unification of Germany, for example, was
accomplished not by the liberal nationalists of 1848 but
by the statesmanship of Bismarck backed by the military
might of the conservative Prussian monarchy. This circumstance does much to explain the weakness of liberalism as a factor in later German politics. In most countries,
however, middle-class liberals were able to assume a
leading position in the nationalist movement. The unification of Italy, which took the form of a liberal crusade
against the forces of the conservative reaction, was a characteristic episode in the history of modern nationalism.
Dynasties which, like the house of Savoy, aspired to a
position of national leadership generally found it advisable to emphasize their devotion to constitutional
principles. By the middle of the nineteenth century, nationalism and constitutionalism had become inextricably

associated in the popular imagination. Since nationalism remained one of the dominant factors of nineteenth- and early twentieth-century politics, this association helped to insure the triumph of liberal institutions.

Although liberal nationalism in its earlier phases took the form of an anticonservative movement, its ultimate effect was to encourage the reconciliation of class interests. If parliamentary government succeeded for a time in becoming the dominant form of Western politics it was largely due to the fact that common devotion to the national welfare made it easy for divergent classes to find a common basis for the negotiation of their differences. Nationalist commitments compelled middle-class liberals, on the one hand, to modify their rationalist individualism with a strong infusion of social traditionalism. The acceptance of constitutional monarchy as the normal form of nineteenth-century government, and the continuation of hereditary aristocracy as an integral part of nineteenth-century society, are an indication of the conservatizing tendencies of liberal nationalism. The failure of the Holy Alliance made it necessary for the agrarian classes, on the other hand, to make their peace with nationalism, adjusting their earlier traditionalism to the dynamic implications of the nationalist point of view. The aristocracy, which still continued to exert much of its old influence in the civil and above all in the military bureaucracies of Europe, had a natural interest in promoting the more bellicose forms of national sentiment. The peasantry, with their age-old hunger for land, were unusually susceptible to the nationalist idea of territorial aggrandizement through military means. By the end of the nineteenth century, therefore, the conservative classes had become even more aggres-

sively nationalist than their middle-class rivals. This facilitated the problem of creating an effective general will.
Middle-class parties, by emphasizing the importance of
industrial efficiency and democratic enthusiasm as com-
ponents of military power, were able to gain conservative
support for many progressive measures. Agrarian conservatives, by emphasizing the military virtues of the
peasantry and the military advantages of agricultural
self-sufficiency, were able to gain middle-class consent to
the enactment of protective tariffs and other measures
useful to the preservation of traditional rural society.
Common interest in the power of the nation made it comparatively easy to reconcile the interests of both groups
within a framework of liberal negotiation.

The power of nationalism also helped to integrate the
proletarian movement within the structure of modern
liberalism. It is true that the theory of revolutionary socialism was aggressively antinationalist in character. Regarding nationalism as a bourgeois trick for the enslavement of
the proletariat, orthodox Marxists did everything in their
power to undermine national loyalties and to create a
sense of international solidarity among the working
classes. By the second half of the nineteenth century, however, the spirit of nationalism had grown too strong to be
overcome by any rival ideology. Although socialist leaders
tried to make internationalism a concrete reality, their
internationals remained weak and bloodless organizations
constantly threatened by factional cleavages, cleavages
which showed a suspicious tendency to follow national
lines. National parliaments were so much more effective
than international congresses in gaining concrete benefits
that leaders who wanted to keep their hold over the work-

ing classes of their respective countries had no choice but to enter the parliamentary arena and to participate in the negotiations and compromises of parliamentary politics. Finding that their standard of living depended more on national than on international action, workingmen tended to associate their welfare with the welfare of the nation. This development was comparatively slow in finding theoretical expression. Even the revisionists, who went farthest in their acceptance of liberal parliamentarism, continued to preach the cause of international solidarity and to oppose the more militant expressions of nationalist thought. By the end of the nineteenth century, however, the proletarian movement had in practice, if not in theory, gone a long way toward adopting the nationalist point of view. Common interest in the welfare of the nation made it increasingly possible for socialist parties to find a common basis for agreement with the parliamentary representatives of other classes. This facilitated the task of winning proletarian adherence to the processes of parliamentary government.

The scope of this development became apparent at the outbreak of World War I. Prior to that time socialists had believed that the international solidarity of the working classes would cause them to rise up in revolutionary protest against any major outbreak of international warfare. When war actually came, however, both the leaders and the followers of orthodox Marxism, with a few notable exceptions, promptly rallied to the defense of their respective fatherlands. In spite of their theoretical commitments even the most orthodox Marxists generally found that their sense of solidarity lay with their fellow nationals rather than with the international proletariat. Socialist delegations in the various national parliaments voted by overwhelming majorities to support the war effort, joining with middle-class and conservative parties in the passage of army credits and other war measures. Once again, nationalism had demonstrated its efficacy as a stimulus to party coöperation within the framework of constitutional government.

During the years immediately following World War I, the liberal-nationalist alliance reached its highest point of achievement. The peacemakers of Versailles, in their capacity as representatives of world liberalism, accepted the principle of national self-determination as the basis of their plans for postwar reconstruction. On the ruins of the Eastern and Central European empires, they erected a constellation of new or drastically remodeled states designed as far as possible to bring the political map of Europe in line with national aspirations. This remarkable extension of nationalism was accompanied, moreover, by an equally remarkable extension of liberalism. Under the influence of the victorious Western powers, constitutional democracy, republican or monarchical, became the standard pattern of government not only for the newly liberated nations but also for the defeated powers. Although many of the constitutional regimes thus established proved ephemeral, the immediate result was to lend new prestige to the principles of liberal politics. One hundred years earlier, at the congress of Vienna, liberalism and nationalism had both succumbed to the forces of conservative legitimacy. At the Versailles conference, the verdict of history was reversed. By its wholehearted acceptance of the nationalist position, liberalism had won an apparently secure position as the dominant principle of modern politics.

The inherent contradictions of the liberal-nationalist position made it extremely difficult, however, to erect a durable political order on this basis. The problem of liberalism was to create a general will by processes of free negotiation. Respect for the diversities of individual and group opinion was the foundation of liberal politics. The problem of nationalism, on the other hand, was to maximize the security of the nation. Individual and group interests, insofar as they conflicted with the requirements of security, were morally reprehensible from the nationalist point of view. In other words, liberalism called for a pluralist organization of society, while the tendency of nationalism lay in the direction of uncompromising monism. The resulting conflict did much to reduce the effectiveness of modern liberalism.

During the late nineteenth and early twentieth centuries the unfortunate consequences of the liberal-nationalist alliance were already beginning to make themselves felt in the conduct of constitutional government. The task of parliamentary statesmanship, according to the theory of modern liberalism, was to create the widest possible area of political agreement by methods of parliamentary negotiation. As long as the liberal movement retained its vitality, liberal statesmen were eager to conform with these requirements. As an alternative, however, to the rigorous and time-consuming methods of conciliation and compromise, an appeal to the unifying force of nationalism had many practical advantages. When responsible statesmen were faced with the necessity of securing the enactment of an unpopular budget, or with the problem of settling a disruptive strike, there was a strong temptation for them to reinforce their negotiations with a plea for national unity. By stigmatizing the opposition as unpatriotic or treasonable it was possible to mobilize the pressure of national opinion against those parliamentary and other groups whose interests they had failed to reconcile with the policy of the government. International dangers, real or fictitious, lent particular weight to the nationalist argument. In the crises of late nineteenth- and early twentieth-century politics liberal statesmen showed an increasing tendency to solve their difficulties by the deliberate manipulation of national sentiments. To the extent that they fell into the habit of resorting to such means, they were abandoning their proper function of negotiation in favor of coercion. Thus the power of nationalism, while contributing to the apparent effectiveness of parliamentary government, did much to undermine the foundations of the constitutional process.

Fundamentally even more damaging was the influence of nationalism on the liberal conception of individual rights and duties. The structure of constitutional politics depends in the last analysis on an uncompromising belief in the dignity and importance of individual men. The idea that any form of social justice might override the requirements of individual justice was incompatible with the liberal position. In an age of increasing nationalism, however, the liberal concept of justice was constantly in danger of being lost to view.

This danger found early and vivid illustration in the Dreyfus case, which shook the conscience of the Western world at the beginning of the twentieth century. When responsible inquiries revealed the probability that the military tribunals of France, in sentencing a Jewish army officer for complicity in an espionage scandal, had committed a grave miscarriage of justice, the normal liberal reaction would have been to proceed as rapidly as possible to a reinvestigation of the objective merits of the case. The attempt to do so was long thwarted, however, by nationalist resistance. For many Frenchmen the question of the guilt or innocence of Dreyfus was less important than the question of maintaining the prestige and discipline of the French army. Believing that the national unity of France would suffer from the revelation of widespread official corruption, many anti-Dreyfusards felt no compunction about sacrificing the life and reputation of a single inconspicuous individual in the interests of the nation. Among the adherents of Dreyfus, moreover, there were many who sought rather to strike an opportune blow at the church, the conservatives, and other political enemies than to serve the interests of individual justice. Although the liberal spirit, in this particular instance, proved strong enough to meet the challenge, the severity of the struggle and the bitterness of its aftermath were portents ominous for the future of modern liberalism.

The most immediately disastrous consequences of liberal nationalism lay, however, in the field of international relations. According to the theory propounded by many exponents of the doctrine, acceptance of the principle of national self-determination ought to have resulted in the establishment of an international order based on the liberal principle of free negotiation. The writings of the Italian patriot Mazzini are characteristic of this particular strand of modern liberal thought. Although Mazzini yielded to no one in his devotion to the national ideal, he was sufficiently in harmony with the cosmopolitan tradition to place the welfare of humanity above the welfare of any particular nation. His justification of nationalism rested on the proposition that nation states, somewhat after the fashion of individual producers in a free market, would have a natural interest in working for the establishment of a peaceful and progressive society of nations. No nation state, so the argument runs, would willingly subject itself to the moral and practical difficulties of incorporating nationally unassimilable peoples within the body politic. As soon, therefore, as any nation succeeded in reaching the goal of national self-determination, its sole desire would be to live at peace with all its neighbors. Devoting itself in friendly rivalry to the cause of human progress, each people would contribute its own particular gifts and aptitudes to the enrichment of mankind. For the more effective accomplishment of common purposes, they would also make arrangements for coöperative action. Mazzini himself believed that the period of national liberation would culminate in the establishment of a universal federation dedicated to the common interests of humanity. During the nineteenth and early twentieth centuries many liberal nationalists shared Mazzini's confidence that national self-determination would prove a steppingstone to "the Parliament of Man, the Federation of the World." The disappointment of these hopes constitutes one of the most tragic chapters in modern history.

It is true that the liberal nationalist idea was not entirely fruitless. In many parts of the Western world, the principle of national self-determination did in fact serve as a stimulus to international coöperation. Under the con-

ditions of constitutional democracy the difficulty of coping
with dissatisfied national minorities was so great that liberal governments were often willing to satisfy the national
claims of their subjects on a basis of mutual consent. The
secession of Belgium from Holland and of Norway from
Denmark were notable examples of nationalist movements
which succeeded, under the influence of modern liberalism, in accomplishing their ends without leaving a disruptive aftermath of international bad feeling. The gradual
evolution of the English-speaking parts of the British
empire into a free association of independent dominion
governments was an even more striking vindication of liberal nationalist principles. Although the establishment of
peaceful relations between England and Ireland, and the
stabilization of the international boundary between the
United States and Canada, were less peacefully achieved,
the end-results were also encouraging to the liberal point
of view. In all these cases mutual recognition of the principle of national self-determination led to a successful
pacification of international relations. Through institutions like the Hague Conventions and the League of Nations the liberal world also made serious attempts to insti-
tutionalize its cosmopolitan aspirations in the form of a
coöperative world order. All this did much to justify the
hopes of liberal nationalist thought.

In many parts of Europe, however, the principle of
national self-determination failed to provide a peaceful
solution to the problem of international relations. Cleavages of national sentiment often failed to coincide with
any conceivable delimitation of international boundaries.
Areas of mixed population, like Alsace-Lorraine or Istria,
remained as a perpetual bone of contention between

neighboring nations. This was especially true in Central and Eastern Europe, where the accidents of history had left an inextricable mixture of ethnic and cultural strains. Nationally indisputable areas in that region were the exception rather than the rule. The over-all effect of liberal nationalism was, therefore, to plague the international community with a host of irreconcilable conflicts. In their desire to create a comprehensive nation state, most nationalists found themselves in the position of having to advance territorial claims against one or more of their neighbors. In the face of such claims the only way to maintain the territorial integrity of states was to suppress national minorities. Attempts to Germanize Poles or to Polonize Germans became the order of the day. The power of nationalism was so strong, however, that these attempts were unsuccessful. The sufferings which followed from the forcible suppression of national languages and sentiments served merely to harden the determination of nation states to press every conceivable irredentist claim on behalf of their fellow nationals. The result was a progressive deterioration of international relations within the Western world.

The theory of liberal nationalism failed, moreover, to cope with the competitive implications inherent in the idea of national sovereignty. Instead of trying, after the fashion of the Swiss Confederation, to guarantee the enjoyment of linguistic and cultural rights within a framework of multi-national constitutionalism, modern nationalists had relied on the power of sovereign governments for the defense of national interests. This forced them, in the name of national security, to strive to enhance the competitive position of their own particular nations.

Struggles for the control of strategically and economically important territories arose, therefore, to complicate the issue of national self-determination. Even in the case of nations which, like France and England, had no irredentist claims against one another, commercial and colonial rivalries remained as a source of friction. As long as national independence depended on the power of the sovereign state no nationalist could afford to neglect any opportunity, economic or strategic, to increase the relative military potential of his own particular nation. It is true that, for countries like Holland and Denmark, which depended on the patronage of powerful neighbors rather than on their own resources for the defense of national interests, and for countries like the United States and Canada, which happened to occupy an unusually strong position for defense, the temptations of aggressive nationalism were relatively slight. Most nations found, however, that their security depended on maintaining the largest possible margin of superiority over the power of other nations. The international anarchy of the twentieth century, with its disastrous series of wars and crises, is the product of this particular form of international organization.

In the light of these developments the theory of liberal nationalism deserves to be reckoned as the most costly failure in the history of liberal thought. One of the tasks of modern liberalism, in its attempt to provide a secular basis for the maintenance of Western civilization, was to restore the traditional moral unity of the Western world. The cosmopolitan aspirations of Mazzini and other liberal nationalists showed that they were conscious of that need. By adopting the principle of national self-determination, however, the liberal movement incapacitated itself for the performance of its historic function. With regard both to the national and to the international organization of society, the unlaid ghost of national sovereignty stood as a perpetual threat to the accomplishment of genuinely liberal purposes. The discovery of a more effective solution to the problem of nationalism remains, therefore, as one of the most important pieces of unfinished business on the agenda of modern liberalism.

11

The Problem
of Dictatorship

Although nationalism threatened, it did not immediately shatter the unity of Western civilization. This more fateful role was reserved for another movement, the rise of totalitarian dictatorship. Unlike nationalism, dictatorship is a direct and explicit challenge to the principles of modern liberalism. Down to the period of World War I the principal effect of nationalism was to impede the formation of a liberal international order. National intransigence made it difficult to constitutionalize the life of the international community, but left the parliamentary institutions of sovereign states substantially intact. Totalitarian dictatorship has carried the assault on constitutional democracy even to this last stronghold. Disregarding the processes of parliamentary negotiation, communist and fascist elites now claim the right to subordinate society to the rule of absolute party states. In the interests of party power they find it desirable to make deep inroads on the principle of freedom under law. Although the totalitarian philosophy marks a radical departure from the legalistic and dualistic traditions of the West, it has been able to win massive support in many Western countries. To analyze the sources of its strength is one of the more urgent tasks of contemporary liberal thought.

The rise of totalitarianism, like the rise of nationalism, is a reflection of inherent weaknesses in the theory and practice of modern liberalism. Wishful thinking has blinded many liberals to this elementary truth. Since dictatorship is a departure from the legalistic and dualistic traditions of Western civilization, it is tempting to regard it as a wholly alien force. Whenever a particular country adopts this form of government, constitutional theorists are apt to minimize the matter by showing that the country in question was never really assimilated to the traditions of the Western world. To dismiss the exploits of Russian communism in terms of Asiatic influences has been relatively easy. In the case of Germany, everything from Lutheran theology and Prussian militarism to Kantian idealism has been used to show that National Socialism was simply one more episode in a perennial German war of resistance to the Westernizing influence of Rome. The fact that Rome itself fell to dictatorship rather earlier than Berlin is discouraging to this hypothesis, but special circumstances can also be found to explain the defection of Italy, of all countries, from the Western family of nations. Such attempts to investigate the historic background of specific dictatorships have not been wholly fruitless. Like other major episodes in the development of Western civilization, the totalitarian movement has varied from country to country in response to local conditions. Particular circumstances do not suffice, however, to explain the general problem. Totalitarian thought is too widespread to be dismissed as an alien or accidental deviation from the traditions of the West. Its sources lie at the very roots of Western civilization.

The intrinsically Western character of the movement is indicated by the fact that most of the pioneer work in developing the theory and practice of modern totalitarianism was done not by the opponents but by the exponents of modern liberalism. Although the government of colonial empires is rarely mentioned in this connection, colonialism actually gave the Western world its first great opportunity for dictatorial experiments. The colonial expansion of the West has been a centuries-long development. By the time of World War I it had virtually succeeded in encompassing the earth. Since the more successful colonial powers were also the most vigorous constitutional democracies, this might have been expected to insure the universal victory of liberalism. Instead it marked the beginning of a dangerous and perhaps fatal split in the political thought of the West. Governments which, in their domestic affairs, were firm believers in the value of constitutional democracy, found it natural in the field of colonial administration to employ the methods of political absolutism. Colonial administrators, faced by the necessity of maintaining minority rule over a subject population, were unable to preserve the concept of freedom under law in its European vigor. Colonial experience encouraged the notion that some people only are capable of self-government, and that others ought for their own good to submit to the discretionary rule of enlightened minorities. This idea coincides exactly with the theory of modern dictatorship. The fact that such ideas have been able to win general acceptance among the supporters of constitutional democracy is proof that dictatorial theories are not entirely alien to the Western mind. By investigating the origins of colonialism it is possible to throw considerable light on the bases of totalitarian thought.

The theory of colonialism goes back to the crusading

tradition of the West. The ancient Greeks, with their emphasis on the distinction between Greek and barbarian, and the ancient Hebrews, with their insistence on the distinction between Jew and gentile, were both uncommonly exclusive peoples, looking down on the rest of mankind from a height of uncompromising superiority. Although the Christian doctrine of the common destiny and responsibility of all human souls did something to modify this exclusiveness, devotion to the worship of a jealous God encouraged the Christians to adopt a similar point of view. Believing that their own gospel was the only basis for the salvation of mankind they could hardly escape the conclusion that the pagan world was inferior to Christendom. It is true that pagans enjoyed certain rights under natural law, and might even exert legitimate authority over Christians. The fact remained, however, that the Christian commonwealth, ruling under the spiritual direction of the one true church, was the social instrument particularly chosen by God for the all-important purpose of redeeming the human race. Although peaceful persuasion might be in theory the proper means of extending and maintaining the influence of the church, belief in the absolute value of Christianity made it difficult to resist the temptation to extend the frontiers of the Christian commonwealth by force of arms. During the Middle Ages this sense of religious superiority helped to justify the great crusades against the Mohammedans of the Near East, and the less spectacular but more enduringly successful crusades of the Teutonic Knights against the pagan Slavs. The conquest of the Americas in the sixteenth and seventeenth centuries was also in large measure an expression of the crusading tradition. It is true that the

Christian propriety of these early colonial experiments was not allowed to go unchallenged. The Spanish Dominican Victoria, for example, argued that the paganism of the American natives did not justify imperialist aggression, and that peaceful missionary work was the proper means of bringing them within the Christian commonwealth. Protests against the crusading tradition remained, however, comparatively rare. As bearers of the Christian message, most Europeans felt that they had not merely the right, but also the duty to conquer and enlighten the pagan world. The white man's burden first appeared in the form of the Christian cross.

Theoretically, the purpose of crusading imperialism was not to perpetuate but to eliminate the difference between Christian and non-Christian peoples. Christianity taught that the gift of salvation was available on equal terms to all the races of mankind. This made it necessary to look on colonial rule as a more or less temporary phenomenon. Although pagans and heretics might properly be conquered and subjected to the educational discipline of the one true church, the ultimate objective of that discipline was to transform the conquered people into full-fledged members of the Christian commonwealth. As soon as any given group of pagans had been thoroughly Christianized there was no longer any justification for discriminating between them and other members of the universal church. Thus the crusading tradition, while encouraging aggression against pagans, provided no basis for the assertion of permanent imperial authority on behalf of the Western world.

In the earlier stages of colonial expansion the universal character of the Christian faith served in fact, as well as

in theory, to give Western imperialism a somewhat tran-
sitory character. The Slavic peoples conquered by the
Teutonic Knights, instead of remaining in a position of
lasting inferiority to their conquerors, were finally accepted as equal members of Western Christendom. A
similar line of development was characteristic of the
empires established in the sixteenth and seventeenth centuries by the crusading efforts of countries like Spain and
Portugal. Although many of the conquistadors were primarily interested in booty, the influence of the Catholic
church was strong enough to lend a genuinely missionary
color to the enterprise. Serious efforts were made to
Christianize the natives, thus qualifying them for a position of equality with their European masters. It is true
that the period of educational tutelage tended to prolong
itself indefinitely, and that the leading positions in church
and state long continued in European hands. The concept
of Christian brotherhood was sufficiently compelling,
however, to prevent the emergence of any absolute line of
demarcation between the imperial and colonial peoples.
The result was a policy of racial and cultural assimilation
which secured the incorporation of the various countries
of Latin America, still largely native by blood, within the
Western family of nations.

   In the course of the seventeenth and eighteenth centuries, however, leadership in the colonial field shifted
from the Catholic to the Protestant powers of Europe.
Since Protestantism, particularly in its Calvinist form, was
less universalistic than Catholicism, this produced a significant change in the character of Western imperialism.
To the Calvinists the redeeming grace of God was not
offered on equal terms to all men, but was granted by

election to particularly chosen saints. This conception of the nature and operation of grace gave new meaning to the crusading impulse of Western Christianity. Although it was mandatory upon the saints to conquer sinners, subjecting them to the sober discipline of the Calvinist commonwealth, the motive for crusading action was not to save sinners from their inevitable damnation but rather to exalt the glory of God by triumphing over His earthly enemies. This point of view, when applied to the relationship between European and non-European peoples, led not to an inclusive and educational but to an exclusive and repressive theory of colonial responsibilities. It is true that the Calvinists, as Christians, had in theory to recognize that individuals from all races might belong to the company of the elect. The missionary activities of men like Eliot, the apostle to the Indians, show that this theory was not entirely neglected. In practice, however, the Calvinists tended to take a gloomy view of native chances for salvation. Considering that their austere principles had led them to the conclusion that most of their European contemporaries were damned, it is not surprising that their contact with the alien customs of other peoples should have left them with an impression of hopeless depravity. Nurtured on the Old Testament, with its Judaic concepts of racial exclusivism, Protestant colonists easily fell into the habit of regarding themselves as a chosen people beset by the forces of evil. To hold themselves aloof from contamination, and to keep the natives in a state of permanent subjection to the chosen people, became the essence of their colonial policy. Instead of assimilating the Indians, as in Latin America, the English-speaking settlers of North America subjected them to rigorous segregation and control. Thus the Calvinist doctrine of grace by election encouraged the practice of racist imperialism.

Although religious motives never entirely disappeared as a factor in Western colonialism, their relative importance declined with the growth of secularization in the eighteenth and nineteenth centuries. This involved no substantial change, however, in the attitude of the Western world toward non-Western peoples. The crusading impulse, like so many other aspects of the Christian tradition, itself became secularized, and in this form continued to operate as one of the constituent elements of modern liberalism. Progress, like the Christian God, was a jealous and demanding deity. Humanitarian liberals, no less than their Christian predecessors, believed that they were the possessors of a way of life indispensable to the welfare of the human race. In their earliest contacts with advanced non-European peoples, most European travelers had been of the opinion that, from the standpoint of material culture, their hosts were rather more accomplished than they. Even as late as the eighteenth century, Voltaire and other reformers felt no hesitation in invoking the real or imaginary superiorities of Asiatic nations as a rebuke to the unenlightened condition of the West. By the middle of the nineteenth century, however, the advance of Western science and technology had reversed this earlier relationship. Measured by the standards of contemporary liberalism, even the most accomplished non-European peoples seemed hopelessly benighted. The superiority of the Western world no longer rested exclusively on its possession of the Christian gospel. Democracy, industrialism, scientific medicine, and a host of other secular blessings lay within its gift. To bring these blessings to the rest of the world was a clear humanitarian duty. Although the white man's burden had ceased to be cruciform, it still continued to impose crusading obligations. If, in the depths of their ignorance, backward peoples persisted in resisting the march of progress, it was proper to conquer and enlighten them by force. The increasing military superiority of the West made it possible to apply this remedy on a universal scale. In the secular form of nineteenth-century colonialism, the crusading impulse of Western civilization achieved its final purpose of encompassing the globe.

Like their Christian predecessors, the exponents of secular colonialism represented two sharply contrasting schools of thought, which may for convenience be described as the liberal and as the racist theories of colonial responsibility. The philosophy of the Enlightenment, with its universal optimism, was closer to the Catholic than to the Calvinist conception of human nature. Believing in the potential rationality of all human beings, it explained all deviations from the standards of enlightened conduct as a consequence of ignorance. Since ignorance could be overcome by education, universal brotherhood was the ultimate destiny of man. This conception, like the Catholic theory of grace, made it necessary to think of colonialism as a temporary expedient rather than as a permanent way of life. According to the theory of orthodox liberalism, the purpose of colonial administration was to teach liberal principles to unenlightened peoples, thus preparing the way for their ultimate incorporation in the Western family of nations. In practice, however, the difficulty of imposing Western standards of rationality upon non-Western peoples was so great as to encourage the emergence of less optimistic views. Colonial administrators, after many disillusioning experiences, often came to the conclusion that there was a deep and insuperable gulf between the chosen people of the West and the lesser races of mankind. "East is East, and West is West, and never the twain shall meet." The racist conception, like the Calvinist doctrine of grace by special election, envisaged the white man's burden as a permanent rather than as a temporary responsibility. Although the West had a duty to bring the rest of the world as many as possible of the advantages of progressive civilization, there could be no hope, by education or otherwise, of overcoming the inherent inferiority of non-European peoples. To serve and obey the white man was the permanent destiny of "lesser breeds without the Law." This theory of permanent colonial subordination was diametrically opposed to the liberal theory of temporary subordination, and led to radically different conclusions in the field of colonial policy. Since both had influential supporters in all the major countries of the West, this gave rise to innumerable confusions and inconsistencies. The conflict between the liberal and the racist schools of thought did much to undermine the prestige of Western colonialism, and prepared the way for the dissolution of colonial empires in the course of the twentieth century.

It is true that, as agencies for the rapid diffusion of the externals of Western civilization, both the liberal and the racist theories were quite effective. Although they might differ as to the ultimate potentialities of non-European peoples, both were agreed as to the immediate necessity of subjecting them to autocratic discipline. Since modern industrialism, whatever its ultimate advantages, has never been widely popular at its inception, agreement on this point was a matter of considerable importance. Even in the Western world, where the new system of production originated, coercion by a politically and economically predominant middle-class minority had been necessary in the first instance to force the Enlightenment upon a reluctant population. The impact of Western industrialism on the thought and institutions of other regions was even more disruptive, and aroused correspondingly greater forces of resistance. If it had been necessary to consult the wishes of the inhabitants of those regions, the spread of modern technology would have been comparatively slow. The theory of Western colonialism made it possible to avoid such consultation. The rise of constitutional democracy, which forced the statesmen of European nations to temper their innovating zeal by consideration for the opinions of their fellow countrymen, had no immediate effect upon the course of colonial administration. Resistance to the march of progress, whether due to temporary ignorance or to permanent inferiority, was an evil to be overcome by the benevolent but uncompromising rule of enlightened administrators. At a time, therefore, when home governments were learning to respect the dictates of public opinion, and to abide by the requirements of an increasingly rigorous rule of law, colonial policy remained virtually unaffected by democratic or legalistic considerations. Without consulting the wishes of local populations, colonial administrators proceeded with ruthless celerity to force backward parts of the world to conform with the requirements of Western civilization. The rapid diffusion of modern technology stands as an enduring tribute to the efficacy of that policy.

The ultimate effect of this procedure, however, was to

produce a dangerous cleavage between the political experience of European and of non-European peoples. For the Western world the late nineteenth century was a time of rapid evolution toward constitutional democracy. According to the liberal theory of colonial responsibilities, education in the ways of parliamentary government should at the same time have been made available to all colonial subjects. A number of more or less successful attempts were actually made in this direction. Unfortunately the requirements of educational tutelage, which called for the continued technological advancement of backward areas, were incompatible with the transfer of complete authority to governments which, if fully responsive to local opinion, would probably have adopted policies unacceptable from the standpoint of Western liberalism. The racist concept of colonial responsibilities, which dominated the attitude of many Europeans, reinforced liberal reluctance to submit colonial administrations to legal or democratic restraints. For all its value, therefore, as a means of disseminating scientific hygiene, industrial efficiency and other material achievements of Western civilization, colonialism was relatively ineffective as an agency for the training of subject peoples in the theory and practice of modern liberalism. Liberal colonialism, while giving some experience with the forms of parliamentary government, tended to produce native elites who, following in the footsteps of their European mentors, felt that their superiority to illiterate fellow nationals gave them the right to disregard the wishes of all those who happened for the time being to be less enlightened than they. Racist colonialism, by arousing outraged natives to a compensating sense of racial antagonism, was even less compatible with the inculcation of democratic

principles. When increasing political maturity led, therefore, to the liberation of colonial peoples, the political development of those peoples seldom followed along the lines
of liberal democracy. Through the influence even of the
most liberal-minded colonial administrations, a large majority of the peoples of the world had been taught to believe that the temporary or permanent rule of enlightened
minorities was the indispensable instrument of progress.
Thus the effect of Western colonialism was to place modern technological resources in the hands of men whose political thought and institutions remained at variance with
the principles of modern liberalism.

If the impact of the crusading tradition had been
limited to the colonial sphere its effect on Western liberalism, though ultimately disastrous, would not have been
quickly felt. Although the colonial world includes most of
the actual population and potential resources of the globe,
the technological advantages of the West still give it a decisive preponderance of power. The attitudes which found
their earliest expression in the formation of colonial empires were, however, equally capable of influencing behavior within the Western world itself. During the Middle
Ages the crusading energies of Christendom were directed
not only against foreign pagans but also against Albigen-
sians and other domestic enemies of the faith. The apocalyptic faith of medieval Christians made it difficult for
them, in spite of their theoretical commitment to the proposition that persuasion rather than coercion is the proper
means of spreading the Gospel, to tolerate error anywhere.
In modern times this conflict between the persuasive and
the coercive traditions of Christianity has been carried
over from the spiritual to the secular realm. Although mod-

ern liberalism, with its emphasis on government by consent, is in line with the preaching aspect of the Christian tradition, it has never wholly overcome the crusading influence. Absolute confidence in the rightness of Western civilization led to the establishment of colonial empires in distant parts of the earth. The same crusading spirit, applied within the Western world itself, manifested itself in the totalitarian movement.

In the late nineteenth century constitutional democracy, for all its apparent vigor, was still a recent and precarious development in the history of the West. As secular offshoots of the Christian tradition, the philosophy of the Enlightenment, the conservative reaction, and proletarian socialism appeared at their inception as apocalyptic faiths. Believing that they alone held the keys to the secular Kingdom of Heaven, the earliest supporters of each of these doctrines were unwilling to make any compromise with opposing points of view. Although the necessity for and the practical advantages of parliamentary negotiation gradually won most of them over to the more or less grudging acceptance of constitutional democracy, there was a substantial minority in every camp which looked on this surrender as a betrayal. People whose bargaining position under conditions of parliamentary negotiation was comparatively weak were particularly apt to maintain the apocalyptic faith in its original purity, and to search for means of imposing their will on the rest of the population. Their attitude toward benighted fellow-nationals was similar to and flowed from the same ideological sources as the attitude of colonial administrators toward benighted non-Europeans. This is the origin of the dictatorial challenge to constitutional government.

The theories of modern dictatorship, like the theories of colonialism, form two clearly contrasted groups. Communism, with its concept of temporary class dictatorship, is parallel to the liberal view of colonialism as a temporary device for the education and ultimate liberation of backward peoples. Fascism, with its concept of the permanent superiority of racial or cultural elites, is akin to the racist theory of colonial responsibility. It would be hard to say to what extent this parallelism is due to the direct influence of colonial ideals on totalitarian theorists, and to what extent it is the result of independent derivation from common sources. Conscious imitation of colonial models is evident in many important phases of fascist thought, while in the case of communism the relationship seems rather less direct. Directly or indirectly the totalitarian movement has served, however, to popularize in the Western world ideas and institutions which the exponents of modern liberalism had reserved for the benefit of non-Western peoples. In the form of a struggle between communism and fascism, the contest between liberal and racist theories of colonial responsibility has been extended to the homeland of Western civilization.

The theory of permanent race dictatorship, which ultimately found expression in fascism, made its first appearance as a minor phase of the conservative reaction. Although the influence of Christianity had been strong enough to prevent the emergence of a strict caste system in Europe, the idea of blood legitimacy had played an important part in the life of the older ruling classes. Through their preoccupation with questions of family pedigree, to say nothing of their sporting interest in the breeding of dogs and horses, royal and aristocratic families were familiar with the notion that blood will tell. Superior breeding was one of the bases for their long-acknowledged right to rule the common herd. When the French Revolution challenged this right they felt that the natural order of things had been wantonly violated. Conservative statesmen, even when they yielded to practical necessities by entering the arena of democratic politics, were seldom able to work up real enthusiasm for a political system which forced men of the best families to court rather than to command the allegiance of their natural inferiors. Many aristocrats, refusing to make concessions, remained aloof from the concerns of constitutional democracy. Thus the idea of blood legitimacy helped to estrange the traditional ruling classes from modern liberalism, and made them receptive to political doctrines based on the concept of race superiority.

The earlier theorists of the conservative reaction, still strongly under the influence of the Christian tradition, made comparatively little use of racist arguments in defending their position. Divine election and prescriptive traditionalism were the bases on which they generally tried to justify their claims. By the middle of the nineteenth century, however, conservatism had produced one fullfledged race theorist in the person of Count de Gobineau. One of the scientific by-products of colonial expansion had been the development of serious interest in the science of linguistics. Increasing familiarity with the peoples of the Near and Middle East had led to the discovery that many of the languages spoken in that area belonged to the same linguistic family as did the major languages of Europe. The wide dispersion of Indo-European languages suggested that all might be descended from one language originally spoken by a single group of northern barbarians,

hypothetically dubbed the Aryan race, which by widespread conquests in prehistoric times had succeeded in
imposing itself as a ruling group upon the greater part of
the Eurasian continent. On the assumption that the various civilizations of that language area were all due to their
influence, it followed that the Aryans must have been a peculiarly gifted race, infinitely superior to the southern peoples who had come beneath their civilizing rule. During
the nineteenth century the main effect of the theory of
Nordic superiority was to lend aid and comfort to the racist theory of Western, and therefore presumably Nordic,
colonialism. In the hands of Gobineau, however, it became
an argument for the conservative reaction in Europe itself.
Most of the royal and aristocratic families of the West were
actually or reputedly descended from barbarian tribes
which had come down from the north during the Dark
Ages to pick up the pieces of the Roman Empire. Through
constant intermarriage they had kept their northern blood
comparatively pure. Since northern blood was inherently
superior to southern blood, and was alone capable of producing individuals gifted enough to carry on the work of
civilization, deposition of the traditional ruling classes
would involve nothing less than the final destruction of
world culture. In the interests of humanity itself, therefore, it was desirable for the aristocracy to maintain its racial purity, and to adopt an intransigent attitude toward
any political system which tried to subordinate them to
their racial inferiors. Although Gobineau's theory was not
widely influential in his own time, it was indicative of the
way in which conservative racism could be used to combat
the liberal position.

In the second half of the nineteenth century a certain

leaning toward racist intransigence also appeared in the ranks of the upper middle class. When this group began fighting against the restrictions of the *ancien régime,* its political philosophy had been strongly equalitarian. The triumph of laissez-faire soon led, however, to the creation of an industrial and commercial aristocracy. This aristocracy of wealth became largely hereditary in practice, and in many cases succeeded, by intermarriage or otherwise, in assimilating itself to the older aristocracy of blood. When the rise of social democracy challenged the position of the upper middle class its reaction was much the same as that of the earlier ruling classes to the middle-class revolution. The philosophy of the Enlightenment, while insisting upon the necessity of equal rights for all, had taught that the greatest rewards of competition under a system of equal rights would go to men of the highest ability. After two or three generations of uninterrupted success the more prosperous middle-class families found it easy to believe that their own particular abilities, like Norman blood, were hereditary, and that they themselves were the naturally selected leaders of the human race. Social legislation, which impaired their position for the benefit of the less successful, was an outrage against the natural order of things, to be resisted by every possible means. Since constitutional democracy meant social legislation, it became increasingly unacceptable to the more intransigent members of the upper middle classes. This disposed them to look with favor on racist doctrines which, by demonstrating their own superiority to the common herd, would justify them in opposing the democratic pressures of parliamentary government.

The man who most successfully filled the need for such

a doctrine was the English philosopher Herbert Spencer. Since there was no historic tradition to justify the assumption that successful businessmen were more Nordic than their compatriots, it would have been unprofitable for Spencer to follow Gobineau in exalting the virtues of the Aryan race. The Darwinian theory of evolution by natural selection provided him, however, with an alternative scientific basis for the racist point of view. The Darwinian hypothesis taught that evolution from the lower to the higher forms of animal life was the product of a universal war for survival. Under the stress of competition inferior individuals and races disappeared, while their successful rivals survived to propagate their kind. On the assumption that laissez-faire economics, in spite of its systematic elimination of murder, theft, and other competitive practices, resembled nature in its capacity to select superior and to reject inferior racial strains, Spencer was able to show that successful businessmen were not only richer but also genetically superior to their less-successful compatriots. By their greater abilities men acquired an economic competence which enabled them to beget and rear offspring who would tend to inherit the desirable characteristics of their parents. People of inferior abilities suffered economic penalties which subjected their less-desirable offspring to greatly increased chances of death by disease and starvation. To interfere with this process of natural selection, even by acts of private benevolence, was dangerous. To upset it by social legislation would be disastrous to the progress of the human race. Absolute and uncompromising resistance to the claims of social democracy was therefore both the right and the duty of the upper middle classes.

Although the theories of men like Gobineau and Spencer helped to stiffen upper-class resistance to modern liberalism, they did not result immediately in the creation of vigorous antiliberal movements. The rise of modern totalitarianism, both in its fascist and in its communist forms, stemmed from the intransigence of a quite different social group, the Bohemian intellectuals. We have already had occasion to say something of the conditions which induced many nineteenth-century artists and intellectuals to reject the ideals and premises of contemporary bourgeois society. As long as they were content to retire into a Bohemian environment of their own choosing their disaffection had little direct influence on the course of politics. Just as in the case of Rousseau, however, their sense of exclusion from the existing order of society gave rise not only to a desire for withdrawal, but also to a recurrent yearning for revolutionary action. Though generally lacking in that sense of blood legitimacy which proved so stimulating to the upper classes, they also enjoyed a definite sense of superiority to the ordinary run of men. The romantic cult of the genius, which considered superior artistic and literary abilities as justification for the most thoroughgoing disregard of normal standards and conventions, confirmed them in the conviction that the rest of the world existed simply as raw material for the nourishment of their own creative personalities. Since constitutional democracy was too equalitarian to fit in with this conception, politically active Bohemians were usually happiest in antidemocratic movements. Their desire for self-expression through untrammeled political leadership made them the most effective precursors of modern totalitarianism. Their influence was the main force behind the development of com-

munist and fascist ideologies. In the person of men like
Lenin, Mussolini, and Hitler they also provided totalitarian movements with a substantial proportion of their leadership. By subordinating the inferior Philistines to totalitarian governments, the inhabitants of Bohemia were able
to satisfy their long-neglected claims to social superiority.
Theirs were the efforts which served most effectively to undermine the position of modern liberalism.

From the beginning the political thought of the Bohemian world tended to gravitate toward the concept of
charismatic leadership. This is the feature which distin-
guishes it most sharply from the antiliberal theories of the
aristocratic and upper-middle classes. Although the members of these latter groups considered themselves superior
to the common herd, their attitude toward fellow aristocrats or industrialists was rather equalitarian. Noble blood
and economic success were shared in roughly similar degree by so many people that it was hardly possible for any
individual to claim outstanding superiority to other members of his own class. The romantic cult of genius, on the
other hand, was radically inequalitarian. Although talented Bohemians might be superior, as a class, to the general run of Philistines, they were prepared to admit their
inferiority to men of outstanding personal gifts. Influential
literary and artistic figures regularly acquired a coterie of
admiring partisans, who devoted themselves with fanatical
enthusiasm to the task of exalting and serving the unique
personality of their own beloved master. In the franti-
cally competitive world of Bohemia, where reputations
rose and fell with spectacular rapidity, attachment to a
prestigious leader was the condition of survival. Endless
warfare between the partisans of rival men of genius was

the essence of Bohemian politics. When men trained in this environment became interested in wider forms of political action their conception of politics remained unchanged. Life for them was a matter of discovering and rendering loyal service to a really great man, compelling rival Bohemians and apathetic Philistines to recognize his genius. To a greater extent, therefore, than any other group, Bohemian intellectuals were prepared to accept the principle of charismatic leadership as the normal basis of politics.

The political implications of the romantic cult of genius found typical expression in the writings of Thomas Carlyle. No thinker of the nineteenth century was more uncompromisingly hostile to the legalistic and dualistic principles of Western civilization. According to Carlyle's theory of history, all historic achievement is a product of the activities of individuals great enough to see through the hollow pretensions of outworn legal conventions, and energetic enough to impose their creative vision on the apathetic and ignoble masses of men. Less gifted people enjoy a share of greatness only insofar as they submit to the guidance of heroes and participate, to the extent of their capacities, in the historic work of creation. For Carlyle, a Scotchman of strongly Calvinist antecedents, life was not made for the pursuit of pleasure, but for austere and unremitting labor. Since great men alone have the intellectual and moral vigor to force men out of their normal laziness into a life of strenuous endeavor, they alone have the right to command the multitude. Constitutional democracy, which encourages swinish majorities to follow the dictates of their pleasure-loving natures, rather than to submit to the noble austerities of leadership, is irremediably corrupt. As far as Carlyle was concerned, therefore, the basic problem of nineteenth-century politics was to destroy the unnatural sham and humbug of democratic cant, and to restore the masses to a proper feeling of love and reverence for heroes who from time to time would come to shape their destinies.

The admiration of artists and intellectuals for the beauties of charismatic leadership would not in itself have been sufficient, however, to make it an important factor in the history of modern politics. In a world increasingly accustomed to democratic principles of legitimacy the ideas of so inconsiderable a minority could not hope to triumph without a substantial measure of popular support. Under the conditions which prevailed prior to World War I this support was not readily forthcoming. By participating in the processes of parliamentary negotiation most people found that they could make tolerable progress toward their political objectives. This made them reluctant to abandon the practice of modern liberalism and throw themselves on the mercies of any absolute and uncontrollable form of political leadership.

The nature of parliamentary government was such, however, that its benefits tended to be rather unequally distributed. Government by negotiation favors those whose bargaining position happens to be strong. In a world of competing pressure groups those who organize effectively prosper at the expense of less well-organized sections of the community. Manufacturers' associations and trade unions can generally get the ear of democratic statesmen, while unorganized members of the working and, above all, of the lower middle classes remain in a state of relative neglect. Whenever, as in times of drastic economic stress, this neglect causes particular hardships, it is natural for the less well-organized groups to become disillusioned with parliamentary government, and to look for alternative means of asserting their claims. For people unable or unwilling to make effective use of opportunities for parliamentary negotiation, the prospect of following the commands and sharing the triumphs of an uncontrollable but presumably well-intentioned leader can be made to seem quite alluring. These were the groups to which the Bohemian intellectuals turned in their attempt to gain mass support for their antiliberal conception of politics.

The first successes in this direction were won among the working classes. From the beginning the proletarian movement had derived most of its theoretical and much of its practical leadership from anti-bourgeois intellectuals. As long as the workers were relatively disorganized and lacked acceptable leaders of their own, they were glad to accept the help thus freely offered. In the course of time, however, the growth of trade unionism created a class of trusted trade-union leaders drawn directly from the ranks of the proletariat. Since collective bargaining and parliamentary negotiation were the most effective means of satisfying working-class needs, these leaders tended to become increasingly conservative, gravitating from the revolutionary to the evolutionary conception of socialism. Many intellectuals accepted this shift and, in the person of men like Bernstein and the Fabians, played an important part in the development of social democratic thought. On the whole, however, the attitude of the intellectuals remained more radical than that of the trade unionists. Reluctant to share their leadership with conservative proletarians, they tended to concentrate on the left wing of the working-class movement. To resist the conservatizing tendencies of the proletarian majority, and to convert as many as possible to the cause of revolutionary intransigence, was the central purpose of their lives. In their rivalry with trade-union leaders, Bohemian intellectuals became the center of resistance to the acceptance of social democracy on the part of the working classes.

This cleavage between intellectual and trade-union leaders made it necessary to develop new theories of proletarian politics. As long as their leadership had been generally acceptable to the working-class movement, it had been possible for the intellectuals to believe simultaneously in revolutionary action and in absolute majority rule. The political theory of Karl Marx, for example, had rested on the assumption that inevitable historical developments would end in the creation of revolutionary proletarian majorities in all the more highly industrialized countries of the world. When experience showed, however, that most working-class groups preferred evolutionary to revolutionary action, it became imperative for the theorists of socialism to choose between democracy and revolution. The evolutionary socialists decided to accept the verdict of the majority, and to pursue their hopes of radical reformation by democratic means. The radical wing, on the other hand, believed that revolution was important enough to be sought, if necessary, in defiance of the popular will. For them the function of leadership was not to mobilize and activate the desires of the proletariat itself, but to impose revolutionary action upon it. Like Carlyle, they began to see will rather than necessity as the driving force in politics. Revolutionary leadership, once the helpful midwife, now appeared as the active begetter of history.

This conception of the creative role of leadership is nowhere more clearly reflected than in the writings of the French revolutionary syndicalist, Georges Sorel. Unlike the Marxists, Sorel had no confidence in the historical inevitability of the proletarian revolution. Capitalists, in his disgusted opinion, were so cowardly and unmilitant that they would normally prefer to placate their employees with concessions rather than to risk a trial of force. Left to their own devices the workers would likewise be willing to receive these concessions as an acceptable substitute for revolutionary triumphs. The only way to bring the revolution to a head would be to place artificial obstacles in the way of worker-employer negotiation. By skillfully calculated propaganda means revolutionary leaders should try to stimulate the flagging intransigence of working-class groups. The myth of the general strike was Sorel's own solution to this propaganda problem. Although recognizing that the bourgeois state could never in fact be overthrown by strikes, revolutionary leaders ought to induce the working classes to believe that this was possible. Attempted general strikes would have the advantage of forcing the normally timid and conciliatory bourgeois authorities to take repressive measures which ought, with luck, to occasion a fair amount of bloodshed. The death even of a relatively small number of their respective friends and supporters would so embitter both the employers and the workers as to inhibit either from offering or accepting any sort of compromise. Thus revolutionary violence, though futile in itself, would gradually undermine the foundations of parliamentary negotiation. The result would be to place the proletariat in the hands of uncompromising leaders who would be vigorous and determined enough to encompass the destruction of the liberal state.

Prior to World War I opportunities for this kind of proletarian leadership were comparatively rare. It is true that in places where the trade-union movement happened to be particularly weak the ideas of men like Sorel were able to gain a certain amount of influence. In meagerly industrialized countries like Spain and Italy, where numerical and organizational weakness long prevented the proletariat from playing a major role in parliamentary government, syndicalism obtained a substantial hold on the working classes. The slow growth of trade unionism in the United States also made it possible at one time for the syndicalist I.W.W. to win a considerable following, particularly among the unorganized migrant workers. In general, however, the advantages of social democracy were sufficiently obvious to enable it to command the allegiance of the organized working classes. Although the slogans of revolutionary Marxism had not entirely lost their appeal as slogans, the increasing prosperity of economically and politically powerful trade unions made them reluctant to jeopardize their gains by indulging in revolutionary action. For intellectuals who continued to dream of imposing their revolutionary will upon the masses the future did not seem to be particularly bright.

In Czarist Russia, however, there was a more promising field for revolutionary action. Although Russia, like China and a few other non-Western states, had never been absorbed by any of the great colonial powers, its relation to the Western world was quasi-colonial in character. Ever since the time of Peter the Great the government of that country had rested in the hands of an aristocratic elite, partly native and partly Western by origin, which had attempted, after the fashion of colonial administrations in other parts of the world, to Westernize their subjects by the use of autocratic power. Their efforts led, by the late nineteenth and early twentieth centuries, to a situation uncommonly well-adapted to the purposes of revolutionary socialism. The introduction of modern industry created a class of factory workers which, under the leadership of Westernized intellectuals, was soon converted to Marxism. The Russian proletariat, however, was numerically so weak, and the Russian state, in spite of a few belated gestures in the direction of parliamentarism, was so autocratic, that there was less chance than in the highly industrialized democracies of Western Europe of achieving proletarian purposes by democratic means. The result was to produce unusual opportunities for revolutionary leadership. Although evolutionary and revolutionary socialism both found supporters among the Russian intelligentsia, the influence of the less radical group was relatively weak. When the inefficient Czarist autocracy collapsed under the stress of World War I, the social democrats tried to replace it with a constitutional government constructed on Western models. The revolutionary socialists, or Bolsheviks, believed that the Russian people were not yet ready for democracy, and that the only way of achieving progressive action would be to place absolute power in the hands of the Bolshevik party. Although the party at this time amounted to no more than a tiny minority of the population, it had been welded into a compact fighting force under the skillful leadership of Lenin. After many vicissitudes, this group succeeded in overthrowing the democratic republic, and in establishing itself as the unchallenged successor to the Czarist government. The Russian people, long accustomed to the rule of autocratic minorities, were indifferent to the social-democratic promise of liberal rights, and accepted the new regime without effective protest. Thus Russia, under the leadership of its revolutionary intellectuals, became the first exponent of modern totalitarian government.

The experience of Russian Bolshevism necessitated drastic revision of socialist theory. Unlike Sorel, the leaders of the Russian Revolution regarded themselves as orthodox Marxists, and tried to justify their action in terms of Marxian thought. The situation in which they operated called, however, for an entirely new emphasis on the importance of creative leadership. Although Marx had recognized the need for revolutionary leaders in the crisis of class conflict, his conception of the dialectic of history had implied that this crisis would not occur until a proletarian majority was in a position to take over a fully developed capitalist economy, proceeding quickly to the establishment of a classless society and to the withering away of the state. This apolitical position was at variance with the needs of the Russian Revolution. The task of the Bolshevik party, as the class-conscious vanguard of the proletariat, was to force the backward Russian people not merely to appropriate but also in large measure to create the apparatus of a modern industrial economy. For this purpose it was necessary that enlightened leaders should exercise absolute control for many years to come, using sheer will-power to compensate for the historic deficiencies of Russian capitalism. This meant subjecting the nonproletarian majority to the rule of the proletariat. It also meant subjecting the historically immature proletariat to the rule of the party. Within the party itself, moreover, recognition of the paramount role of individual leaders like Lenin and Stalin was suitable to the conditions of a country long accustomed to the personal autocracy of Czars rather than to the more abstract and impersonal claims of political parties. To justify these displays of absolutism without discarding the majoritarian tenets of orthodox Marxism was the basic problem of Bolshevik political thought.

The concept of the dictatorship of the proletariat was the solution to this problem. The term "dictatorship" itself came from the history of ancient Rome. As a special magistracy designed to safeguard the republic in times of sudden emergency, the Roman institution of dictatorship was an unusually clear example of the way in which temporary absolutism can be made to serve the long-run purposes of constitutional government. Prior to the Russian Revolution political theorists had made little effort to generalize from this experience. Although liberal colonialism, as a temporary exercise of absolute power designed to insure the ultimate adoption of constitutional democracy, might well have been characterized as a form of dictatorship, the term itself never gained currency in this connection. In describing the post-revolutionary rule of the working classes, Marx and Engels occasionally used the phrase dictatorship of the proletariat, but laid no particular emphasis upon it. The word does not appear, for example, in the *Communist Manifesto.* For the Russian Bolsheviks, however, the concept of dictatorship was extremely useful. Its connotation of untrammeled power could be used to justify all measures of lawless coercion required for the establishment and maintenance of party rule over the Russian people, and for the maintenance of autocratic discipline within the ranks of the Communist party. As a temporary form of absolutism it could be reconciled, on the other hand, with the Marxian belief in majoritarian democracy as the goal of proletarian politics. The dictatorship of the proletariat was to be a regime exercised by the class-conscious minority for the purpose of preparing the unenlightened majority for the responsibilities of life in a future classless society. Through the efforts of Bolshevik intellectuals the concept of dictatorship gained currency as one of the basic categories of modern political thought.

Although the terminology was new, the communist concept of dictatorship was simply a restatement of the theory of liberal colonialism. In its assumption that non-Europeans were more backward than Europeans, and therefore required a period of temporary tutelage as a preparation for liberalism, the earlier theory had maintained a sharp distinction between those peoples which were and those which were not capable of immediate self-government. The effect of communism was to eliminate this distinction, and to open up the whole world as a field for the quasi-colonial enterprise of communist elites. According to the communists, political and social backwardness was characteristic not merely of Russia but also of all countries subject to capitalist domination. White and colored workers alike were victims of the capitalist system. To overcome the effects of that system, and to prepare the way for an ultimate classless society, a more or less prolonged dictatorship of the proletariat would be necessary not in Russia only, but everywhere. Only the Communist party, with its scientific knowledge and its disciplined organization, could provide the means of successful proletarian dictatorship. The task of disseminating and perfecting the achievements of Western civilization, once described as the white man's burden, now appeared as the prerogative of a party made up of enlightened representatives of every race, and offering the advantages of temporary absolutism to Western as well as to non-Western peoples. In the doctrines of Russian communism, the theory of liberal colonialism emerged as a universal pattern for the government of mankind.

The concept of dictatorship, once developed, soon revolutionized the political thought of the Western world. It is true that communism itself encountered serious resistance. Although submission to the rule of a self-chosen party elite might be tolerable to the democratically inexperienced Russian masses, and appeared as an improvement on racist colonialism to many of the non-European victims of Western imperialism, it had little attraction for trade unionists accustomed to the ways of constitutional democracy. Thus the success of the Russian Revolution, while helping to strengthen the hand of revolutionary Marxists in all countries, did not persuade the majority of the Western proletariat to break its allegiance to the cause of modern liberalism. In the Western world there were other groups, however, who were more amenable to the idea of dictatorship. Because of their general incapacity for economic and political organization, the lower middle classes had long been the forgotten men of constitutional politics. World War I, with its aftermath of currency inflation and industrial depression, brought them sufferings entirely disproportionate to those endured by more effectively organized sections of the community. While wages and profits more or less kept pace with the rising cost of living, savings and other forms of lower-middle-class property were either entirely wiped out or reduced to a fraction of their former value. This demonstration of the insecurity of their position aroused many members of this class to a mood of drastic hostility to the procedures of constitutional democracy. Despairing of their prospects for successful parliamentary action, they began to dream of dictatorship as a way out of their difficulties. Although their sense of superiority to, and their fear of sinking to the level of the working classes made them generally unresponsive to the idea of proletarian dictatorship, they were prepared to follow any non-communist leader who promised to safeguard their position by dictatorial means. Discontented or ambitious intellectuals, themselves economically associated with the lower middle classes, were ready to assume the lead in adapting communist ideas to lower-middle-class purposes. Many theories, of which Italian fascism and German national socialism were the most notable, resulted from these efforts. In one or another of its forms, fascism proved more effective than communism in spreading the idea of dictatorship within the Western world.

The fascist theory of dictatorship differed in one important respect, however, from its communist prototype. Because of their continuing allegiance to Marxism, the leaders of the Russian Revolution had continued to preach equality as the ultimate social idea, and regarded dictatorship as a temporary means to the attainment of that end. The fascists, on the other hand, followed the lead of earlier conservatives in rejecting equality as an ultimate ideal. For white-collar workers long accustomed to regarding themselves as the social superiors of manual laborers, the prospect of sinking to the level of the proletariat was violently distasteful. Although the position of the upper classes was less precarious, they also feared the rise of social democracy and the threat of communism as a challenge to their privileged position. For such people the maintenance of the existing social hierarchy was a matter of supreme importance. The value of dictatorship from their standpoint lay in the possibility that it might provide a means of combatting the equalitarian tendencies of modern life. The fascists were unlike the communists, therefore, in regarding inequality not as a temporary expedient but as a permanent ideal. To justify permanent dictatorship was the basic problem of fascist political thought.

The answer to this problem was found by grafting the doctrine of race supremacy onto the idea of nationalism. Although nineteenth-century nationalists had tended to assume that their own nations were uniquely gifted, recognition of the equal rights of other nations had been, at least in theory, a part of the liberal creed. The fascists challenged this theory. According to the Italian and Spanish fascists the history of the old Roman and Spanish empires proved that the Italian and Spanish nations respectively were superior to all others, and that the natural destiny of lesser peoples was to submit to their imperial rule. The national socialists of Germany were more explicitly racist. They claimed that Germans, as men of superior Nordic blood, had a right and duty to subordinate all other nations, European as well as non-European, to the requirements of the master race. People of inferior blood, like the Jews, should be rigorously excluded from the imperial folk-community. Since constitutional democracy recognized the equal right of all citizens to participate in political life, and permitted the spread of communism and other internationalist doctrines among the working classes, it was necessary to destroy democracy and to place power in the hands of a racially and ideologically uncontaminated elite. Only by submitting to the dictatorship of a fascist party, under the direction of a charismatic leader, could the chosen peoples acquire the strength and discipline required for the accomplishment of their historic mission. The doctrine of race superiority, once limited to the relations between European and non-European peoples, was now used to justify the permanent subordination of inferior European nations to a single master race, and the equally permanent subordination of inferior to superior elements within the master race itself. Thus the theorists of modern fascism, and more especially the theorists of national socialism, finally brought the doctrines of racist colonialism to their logical conclusions.

Like communism, the fascist version of totalitarianism did not succeed in gaining universal acceptance. The extent of its appeal, however, was considerably greater than that of totalitarian Marxism. For desperate members of the lower middle classes, eager to bolster up their threatened sense of social superiority, the idea of belonging to the master race, and the possibility of joining a permanent party elite, were definitely beguiling. By destroying the Jews, whose competition was most keenly felt by small shopkeepers, professional men, and other middle-class elements, and by reducing the Marxist-indoctrinated proletariat to impotence, fascist movements promised an immediate improvement in the social and economic position of the middle classes, while the prospect of future imperial expansion, with its vista of innumerable administrative and other white-collar jobs for members of the master race, gave room for even brighter long-range ambitions. The upper classes, though somewhat disturbed by the lower-middle-class character of these movements, considered them preferable to communism and to the more equalitarian phases of constitutional democracy. In countries where political and economic pressures were not particularly severe, most middle-class people preferred to take their chances with liberal constitutionalism rather than to court the unknown risks of fascist dictatorship. During the decades following World War I, however, conditions in many parts of the Western world became so difficult that many were in a mood for radical experiments. For a large majority fascism was more attractive than communism. The result was the establishment of fascist dictatorships which succeeded, in the course of World War II, in gaining virtually complete control over the continent of Europe.

Although the fascist threat has receded for the time being, the conflict between liberal and totalitarian ideologies still remains as one of the basic factors in contemporary politics. This conflict is a measure of the weakness of modern liberal thought. Constitutional democracy rests on the belief that persuasion rather than coercion is the proper means of uniting men in an effective general will. Throughout the history of Western civilization this conception of a moral community united by peaceful persuasion has had to fight for survival against the opposing conception of coercive integration. During the Middle Ages there was perpetual tension between the idea that religious truth should spread only by preaching and example, and the idea that the truth might legitimately arm itself with the crusading sword. In the period of religious warfare the preponderance of the crusading viewpoint finally led to the collapse of medieval Christendom, and nearly destroyed the bases of Western civilization. Modern liberalism, in its attempt to reconstruct the Western world on secular foundations, has courted a repetition of the same catastrophe. The crusading energy of colonial empires has opened the world to Western technological influences, but has done little to acquaint non-Western peoples with the liberal principles of government by consent. Apocalyptic class doctrines have aroused the nations of the West to a sense of political responsibility, but have left many with habits of uncompromising intransigence incompatible with the principles of parliamentary negotiation. The resulting conflict between totalitarian and constitutional ideologies is a repetition of the age-old conflict between the crusading and the preaching traditions of medieval Christianity. If the crusading traditions prove to be the stronger, Western civilization will again be face to face with the catastrophe it so narrowly averted in the time of the wars of religion. This is the historic significance of the rise of modern dictatorship.

12

The Future
of Liberalism

In the light of the historic development of modern liberalism, it is possible to understand the nature of some of the more critical problems of contemporary politics. We have seen that constitutional democracy was an attempt to preserve the social and political traditions of medieval Christianity on a secular basis. Most of the strong and weak points of modern liberalism are related to the fact that some of those traditions lent themselves more readily than others to purposes of secularization. As a vehicle for the maintenance of legalistic and dualistic principles, constitutional democracy proved largely effective. In certain respects, however, it failed to establish secular equivalents for the ideas and institutions of the Middle Ages. The apocalyptic character of Western thought, when translated from the spiritual to the secular plane, gave rise to unrealistic and uncompromising political ideologies. These versions of the apocalyptic tradition, while useful in arousing people to an initial sense of political responsibility, impeded subsequent attempts to unite them in an effective general will. In spite, moreover, of persistent efforts to preserve the international character of secular humanitarianism, constitutional democracy never managed to create international institutions in any way comparable to those of the medieval church. The parochial bitterness of modern nationalism and the injustices of racist colonialism bear witness to the failure of modern liberalism to maintain the internal unity and to maximize the external influence of the Western world. In spite of its many achievements, therefore, the success of the liberal experiment is by no means well assured.

The difficulties of contemporary politics have led some people to conclude that the conception of secular liberalism itself is basically erroneous, and that the only way to preserve the values of Western civilization would be to restore the religious foundations on which that civilization was originally built. History shows many examples of societies which, with the waning of religious belief, have suffered progressive deterioration. When religious sanctions cease to reinforce established usages, habit may for a time suffice to guarantee a fair measure of traditional restraint. In the long run, however, this restraint is apt to grow ineffective. The unscrupulousness of Greek political life in the age of the Sophists, and the uninhibited criminality of Italian politics during the neopagan Renaissance, are typical illustrations of the way in which the decline of supernatural faith may undermine the ethical foundations of society. According to some critics of modern liberalism, the rise of secularism has plunged the Western world into another such crisis of social and ethical deterioration. Although the liberals of the nineteenth century, like the more conservative Greek Sophists and Italian humanists, wanted to reëstablish the values of Western civilization on a basis of secular rationalism, their principles were simply habits of thought held over by the force of inertia from the days of supernatural faith. Cut off from their living source, those habits were bound to become progressively weaker. Secular humanitarianism had no resources of its own to oppose to the ethically destructive power of tribal nationalism or racist imperialism. Modern totalitarianism, with its ruthless concentration on the conquest of power by every available means, was the natural outcome of the liberal effort to maintain traditional ethics without the aid of religious sanctions. In the face of such pressures, according to these critics, nothing less than a general revival of Christianity and the reëstablishment of a unified Christian church will suffice to preserve the principles of Western civilization.

If this analysis of the contemporary situation is correct, it is hard to see that there is any hope for the Western world. It is true that recent political and social difficulties have inspired many thoughtful people to a renewed interest in Christian dogma, and encouraged a number of ecumenical movements among the Christian churches. The deterioration of religious faith in the West has progressed so far, however, and divisions within the Christian community are so inveterate, that there can be little prospect, at any time in the foreseeable future, of reuniting the Western world in the form of an effective Christian commonwealth.

Even if this were possible, moreover, it would not solve the problems of the modern world community. With the growth of political consciousness on the part of non-European peoples, the Western world is rapidly losing its capacity to control the destinies of the rest of the human race. The majority of mankind owe allegiance not to Christianity but to other religions. Although Christianity in the past has succeeded in converting many comparatively primitive peoples, it has never been able to make much headway against Buddhism, Mohammedanism, and other highly developed world religions. To unite humanity in a Christian commonwealth would be even more difficult, therefore, than to unite the Western world. At a time when religious beliefs, insofar as they are socially effective, tend to divide rather than to integrate political communities, politics can only rest on a secular basis. If secularization is incompatible with the maintenance of political and social ethics, it follows that the future of the world must lie in the hands of the ethically uninhibited exponents of totalitarian government rather than with the more conservative supporters of modern liberalism.

Fortunately, the verdict of history does not unreservedly support the proposition that secular ethics are incapable of providing a basis for the maintenance of a traditional civilization. One example, at least, of successful secularization is to be found in the history of ancient China. During the centuries immediately preceding the Christian era, Chinese civilization underwent a crisis similar to that experienced at about the same time by classic Greece. Declining faith in the religious magic of earlier days had led to a radical deterioration of traditional morality. This deterioration was accompanied by an efflorescence of ruthless power politics which, in the so-called period of the contending states, reduced the Chinese world to a condition of near anarchy. The most successful contender in this period of international confusion was the Ch'in monarchy. By the uninhibited use of Machiavellian techniques this state finally succeeded in conquering all the rest, subjecting the whole of China to the will of its despotic rulers. The triumph of the Ch'in dictatorship proved, however, to be remarkably short-lived. In the earlier stages of religious disintegration conservative philosophers like Confucius and his followers had faced the problem of justifying the traditional values of Chinese civilization in terms of secular rationalism. While maintaining a deliberately agnostic position with regard to the existence and efficacy of supernatural powers, they had devoted themselves to the task of showing that the ancient traditions of social propriety were alone in conformity with the rational needs of men. Although the teachings of these philosophers did not immediately succeed in halting the ethical disintegration of the Chinese world, they proved in the long run to be more appealing than the Machiavellian practices of the Ch'in dynasty. Subsequent dynasties found it advisable to base their policies on Confucian principles, and to entrust the work of imperial administration to Confucian-trained scholars. The result was to preserve the essence of traditional Chinese morality on a basis of secular humanism. The subsequent stability of Chinese civilization bears witness to the efficacy of this experiment.

What was the reason for this success? That conservative philosophers, in a period of advancing secularization, should have tried to rationalize the ethical traditions of their culture was not in itself surprising. In the comparable crisis of classical civilization the efforts of men like Plato and Aristotle were inspired by motives similar to those which led to the rise of Confucianism. Unlike their Chinese counterparts, however, the Greek philosophers were unsuccessful in their attempts to place classical civilization on an enduring ethical basis. The greater vitality of Chinese humanism points to the existence of some essential difference between the two experiments.

The peculiar strength of Confucianism lay in its unique combination of rationalistic and of ritualistic elements. Recurring habitual action is more powerful than rational exhortation as a determinant of human conduct. The power of traditional religions rests in large measure on the various rituals which bring the force of religion to bear in a visible and concrete way upon the daily lives of men. Rationalistic philosophers, in their preoccupation with questions of rational demonstration, are apt to neglect the problem of embodying ethical insights in the form of habitual usages. Although some of the Greek philosophers, most notably Plato, were aware of the importance of the ritualistic element in human behavior, they never succeeded in incorporating their ethical doctrines in visible institutions. For the Confucians, on the other hand, ritual propriety was at all times a major consideration. Although they themselves did not fully share the religious convictions on which the court etiquette of ancient China had been based, they recognized that the ancient rituals had played an indispensable part in the formation of social habits. Believing that the decline of ritual propriety had done much to undermine the strength of traditional ethical restraints, they set to work restoring the ceremonial element to contemporary life. By adapting the ancient court etiquette in terms appropriate to the condition of ordinary men they sought to make the daily life of every Chinese family a ceremonial exemplification of the basic Confucian virtues. Minute regulations for the maintenance of formal propriety in every aspect of human intercourse inculcated respect for the traditional Chinese principles of social obligation, rendering conformity a matter not merely of rational conviction, but also of habitual second-nature. This made it possible for the secular ethics of the Confucians, in spite of the absence of religious sanctions, to persist as a political and social force for some two thousand years.

Modern liberalism is an attempt to do for the Western world what Confucianism once did in a comparable crisis of Chinese civilization. It likewise has sought to secularize the ethical convictions inherited from a preceding age of religious faith, and to incorporate those convictions in an appropriate set of social institutions. Through the procedures and rituals of constitutional democracy it has given concrete embodiment to the dualistic and legalistic aspirations of the West. Are the ethical traditions of our civilization still sufficiently vigorous to support so difficult an enterprise? Are the institutions of liberal society sufficiently compelling to convert these traditions into enduring social habits? These are the questions which arise in any assessment of the long-range prospects of Western civilization.

The great strength of liberalism lies in the fact that it, like Confucianism at the time of its inception, is able to draw upon a dwindling but substantial capital of widely accepted ethical presuppositions. The ethics of humanitarian democracy are a continuation, in secular form, of the traditional doctrines of Christian charity. Although the other-worldly preoccupations of Christianity prevented it in the Middle Ages from interfering drastically with the structure of secular society, the effect of the Christian tradition was to familiarize the Western world with the idea that all men are equal in the sight of God, and that the law of universal brotherly love is one of the two great commandments laid upon the human conscience. For people brought up in this tradition, the alleviation of human suffering and the establishment of universal peace are bound to appear as the proper ends of secular existence. Liberal humanitarianism, with its hatred of war and its emphasis on social justice, conforms closely with these inherited patterns of Western thought. In spite of the deterioration of ethical standards, associated in recent times with the rise of totalitarian government, humanitarian prejudices are still a powerful factor in politics. It is significant that even the national socialists of Germany, who went farthest in their opposition to the humanitarian tradition, found it desirable to picture themselves as the victims rather than as the initiators of military aggression, and to make the attainment of an effective social-service state one of the ostensible objects of their regime. Under the influence of Christian concepts of charity the Western world as a whole has become peculiarly sensitive to the spectacle of needless human suffering. Although nationalist, racist, and other divisive doctrines have done something to weaken the force of this sentiment, it is still strong enough to furnish a broad ethical basis for the humanitarian aspirations of modern liberalism.

Humanitarian sentiments would not in themselves suffice, however, to insure the adherence of the Western world to the principles of constitutional democracy. In its more extreme form, indeed, humanitarianism tends rather to the encouragement of absolutist than of constitutional procedures. People who feel that the welfare of humanity is the supreme end of life, and that they alone possess the knowledge necessary for the attainment of that end, are apt to believe that they themselves should exercise ab-

solute power for the benefit of their fellow men. Plato
thought that a man of transcendent wisdom, the philosopher king, would be justified in using all necessary
means, including the use of lies, to establish his benevolent
rule over the less accomplished. Because of the apocalyptic habit of thought inherited from the Christian tradition,
the Western world is unusually susceptible to this form of
absolutist appeal. During the Middle Ages the belief that
the church alone possessed the truth necessary for salvation encouraged the assertion of absolute authority on
behalf of the Roman pontiff. The philosophers of the
eighteenth-century Enlightenment, confident in the absolute adequacy of their principles for the creation of a
perfect secular society, were likewise attracted to absolutism. Belief in the unlimited power of modern science to
solve the problems of human existence leads to the feeling
that responsibility should be vested in the hands of scientifically qualified technicians. The current tendency to
equate antisocial conduct with disease, and to give psy-
chiatrists and social workers unlimited discretion in the
treatment of criminals, is indicative of the extent to which
respect for the judgment of technicians has come to
replace earlier conceptions of freedom under law. The
trained nurse, who knows exactly what is good for her
patients, and carries out her orders in brisk disregard for
their misguided wishes, is one of the typical products of
contemporary civilization. The totalitarian view of life,
which envisages the reduction of all mankind to the status
of patients under the stern but curative treatment of
scientifically qualified elites, is the logical outcome of the
ideal of the modern hospital. This at least is one possible
outgrowth of the humanitarian faith.

There is reason to believe, however, that the apocalyptic tradition, on which these developments rest, is at present losing some of its hold on the imagination of the Western world. Contemporary scientists, in comparison with their eighteenth- and nineteenth-century predecessors, are skeptical of the capacity of scientific method to discover absolute truth. Growing awareness of the hypothetical character of scientific laws makes it relatively difficult to justify on rational grounds any form of dictatorship by scientifically qualified elites. From the humanitarian point of view, moreover, the practical consequences of totalitarian government have been profoundly disappointing. Knowledge of the actual operation of communist and fascist regimes, with their concentration camps and other calculated brutalities, leaves little room for confidence in the possibility of achieving an immediate kingdom of heaven on earth by vesting absolute authority in an exclusive clique of self-styled scientific experts.

At the present time it is too early to say what the outcome of this experience will be. In the case of the philosophy of the Enlightenment, loss of confidence in the adequacy of the pseudoscientific doctrines of early liberalism led not to the disappearance of apocalyptic hopes, but to the emergence of a new apocalyptic faith in the form of dialectical materialism. Even in the nineteenth century, however, the widespread acceptance of constitutional democracy showed that many people were willing to abandon the quest for absolute certainty, and to pin their hopes for humanitarian betterment on the slow and patient processes of parliamentary negotiation. Platonic absolutism can only thrive in an atmosphere of absolute faith in the power of reason. The tendencies alike of scientific thought and of political experience are calculated to undermine the power of that faith in the contemporary world. Modern psychology, with its emphasis on the irrational drives underlying every aspect of human activity, is particularly damaging to the notion that any human being can be trusted to behave in a rational manner. Western constitutionalism first arose in the Middle Ages, when the doctrine of original sin, by limiting men's confidence in the intellectual and ethical reliability of any single individual or group, made it possible to accept negotiation as a means of solving problems which were too narrowly secular to affect the revealed truths of Christianity. Although the modern world, in the first flush of its enthusiasm for secular science, was tempted to attribute the certainty of divine revelation to the operations of human reason, it is now reverting to the more cautious rationalism of the medieval tradition. If this development continues, it will strengthen the position of modern liberalism.

Another favorable factor is the Western tradition of individual responsibility. Although this aspect of Christianity was less fully developed in Catholic than in Protestant circles, the Christian religion in all its forms has been notable for its emphasis on the importance of the individual conscience. According to the Christian faith, no form of social allegiance can exempt any man from the ultimate necessity of facing divine judgment on the basis of his own individual actions. During the Middle Ages religious conscience enjoined the duty of passive or active resistance to unjust political authority. This tradition still makes it comparatively difficult for the Western world to accept any form of politics based on the absolute surrender of political authority to particular elites. The history of modern absolutism itself bears witness to the power of this tradition. Unlike the absolutist governments of the past, which generally sought to discourage popular interest in politics, contemporary dictatorships regularly try, by plebiscites and other forms of popular action, to give their subjects a sense of personal responsibility for the conduct of government. Although these pseudodemocratic procedures, in contrast with the realities of absolute party rule, are little more than formalities, the tradition of individual responsibility is still so strong that no governments in the Western world can afford to dispense with laborious and costly efforts to justify authority by appealing to the conscience of ordinary men. The fictitious nature of this appeal is so obvious, however, that it can hardly satisfy the Western desire for responsibility. Constitutional democracy, with its genuine opportunities for popular participation in the responsibilities of government, is more in harmony with the traditions of Western politics.

The traditional foundations of modern liberalism would seem on the whole to be reasonably vigorous. It remains to enquire whether its institutional framework is sufficiently strong to maintain these traditions as an enduring force. Confucianism succeeded in preserving the traditional values of Chinese civilization by incorporating them in an all-pervasive complex of social institutions. The rituals and procedures of parliamentary negotiation are the liberal counterpart of the Confucian family system. The future of liberalism depends on the ability of these rituals and procedures to maintain liberal habits of thought and action within the Western world.

The great weakness of the liberal experiment lies in the fact that it has devoted most of its attention to the institutions of a single form of social organization, the modern sovereign state. This is the feature which most strongly differentiates it from the Confucian experiment in ancient China. Confucius and his followers believed that the smallest units of social life were the most effective instrumentalities of ethical training. They therefore concentrated on the development of family rituals, and relied on the behavior patterns thus established to permeate the imperial and other more comprehensive forms of social organization. Liberalism, on the other hand, has been mainly interested in the institutions of parliamentary government. National legislatures and, to a lesser extent, local and municipal assemblies have been at the center of most liberal efforts to reform society. Universal suffrage and the establishment of free elections for public office have been the accepted criteria of liberal progress. Although the value of these developments has been considerable, the result has been to make the parliamentary state the only fully effective institution of modern liberalism. But the state is at once too large and too small a unit for the regulation of contemporary society. Each of these contrasting inadequacies has helped in its own way to jeopardize the success of the liberal experiment.

In view of the current need for international organization, insufficient comprehensiveness is probably the most striking deficiency of the modern liberal state. In this respect, indeed, the history of liberalism is discouragingly reminiscent of the history of ancient Greece. Classical civilization, in the time of Plato and Aristotle, also faced the necessity of developing an effective international or-

der. In their attempts to preserve traditional values, however, most of the conservative philosophers saw fit to
concentrate on the improvement of the city state, and
gave little or no attention to the problem of creating wider
forms of political organization. Belated devotion to outworn institutions made it impossible for them to incorporate their ethical teachings in an effective institutional
framework, and paved the way for the triumph of Macedonian and Roman empires which, although relatively
alien to the classical tradition, were able to give the
exhausted classical world relief from the evils of international chaos. Undue preoccupation with the equally outworn institutions of the sovereign state promises to lead
modern liberalism to a similar catastrophe. Although few
people at the present time deny the necessity of international organization, the habit of associating liberalism
with national self-determination has thus far been strong
enough to prevent the liberal world from taking decisive
steps toward the satisfaction of international needs. The
history of the United Nations is a sufficient case in point.
Fascist and communist dictatorships, alien though they
may be to the traditions of Western politics, have the advantage of being willing and able to undertake the con-
struction of comprehensive imperial systems. In the modern as in the ancient world the supporters of traditional
values may well come to grief through failure to provide
an alternative solution to the problems of international
politics.

In the field of domestic as contrasted with foreign
policy the dangers of overemphasis on state institutions,
though somewhat less obvious, are perhaps even more
serious from the long-run point of view. Liberalism de-

pends on the existence of a general willingness to accept
the results, and widespread ability to use the techniques,
of free negotiation. The ancient Confucians succeeded
in making their ethical principles a matter of habitual
second-nature to the Chinese people by incorporating
them in the daily routine of family life. If modern liberalism is to be equally successful it must likewise endeavor
to give the rituals and procedures of parliamentary action
an organic place in the daily lives of men.

Preoccupation with the institutions of the sovereign
state has led many liberal theorists to neglect this aspect
of the problem of liberal politics. Acting on the assumption
that national and local parliaments are the main institutions of liberal society, they emphasize the exercise of the
electoral franchise and the control of parliamentary representatives as the primary duties of liberal citizenship.
This attitude is unfortunate both from the standpoint of
parliamentarians and from the standpoint of the general
public. The complexity of modern society is so great that
no single national assembly, and no collection of local
assemblies, can hope to perform all the work of negotiation necessary to reduce social frictions to a tolerable level.
Undue emphasis on these institutions has led, therefore,
to the imposition of impossible burdens on parliaments, to
the detriment of the prestige and efficiency of constitutional government. The operations of these bodies are,
moreover, so remote from the daily affairs of most citizens
that they fail to provide any sense of continuing participation in the life of liberal society. Voting in an occasional
election and the signing of an even more occasional letter
of petition or protest is hardly sufficient to give the ordinary citizen direct acquaintance with the processes of par-

liamentary negotiation. Vicarious participation through the reading of parliamentary proceedings, even if those proceedings were actually read, would hardly suffice to remedy this defect. Parliaments alone can never make liberalism a central part of everyday experience. More intimate forms of popular participation are needed to give the principles of liberal negotiation the force of habitual second-nature.

In recent times the development of private associations has placed the aspirations of modern liberalism on a somewhat sounder basis. Organizations for the satisfaction of a wide variety of needs have been spontaneously multiplying in all liberal societies. Chambers of commerce, cartels, trade-unions, coöperatives, and other organized groups have largely replaced the individual worker or employer as agencies of contemporary economic life. Neighborhood, parent-teacher, farmer, and other special associations are being relied upon increasingly to supplement and check the activities of governmental agencies. Since many of these organizations are concerned with matters closely related to the daily interests of their members, it is often possible for them to attract a degree of public participation impossible in the case of larger and more remote units of social life. They also give ordinary citizens a fair amount of contact with the rituals and procedures of parliamentary negotiation. Policy and personality conflicts arise even in the smallest associations. In a liberal society, the desire to iron out those conflicts by compromise leads most associations to adopt the institutions of parliamentary democracy. From national organizations down to the least pretentious social clubs, each has its constitution and by-laws, its elections, and its rules of parliamentary procedure. Under liberal influence even the institutions of family life, in their rejection of paternal despotism and their emphasis on free discussion in the determination of family policies, have tended in some measure to follow the parliamentary pattern. Although the activities of most private associations are not important in themselves, they serve to acquaint people with liberal procedures of negotiation, and to inculcate respect for that delicate balance between majority and minority rights which is essential to free government. These, rather than the institutions of national or local government, are the organizations which do most to keep the habits of liberal action alive in the Western world.

The hope of modern liberalism lies in the further development of private associations. Dictatorship appeals in the main to unorganized masses of men. People who lack effective outlets for the expression of their social energies are apt to feel lost, and to embrace any doctrine, however eccentric, which gives them sense of participation in the life of the community. The exponents of totalitarianism are well aware of this fact. As soon as a totalitarian regime is established, its first objective is to destroy or cripple every form of private association, and to channel all social activities within the carefully regimented institutions of the totalitarian state. In their attacks on a still-functioning liberal society they likewise try by infiltration to capture or destroy the effectiveness of private associations. For people accustomed to the management of their own group activities, however, the prospect of surrendering to dictation is relatively unattractive. Habitual acquaintance with the procedures of free negotiation prepares them to accept the principles of parliamentary government, and to react strongly against those who, as members either of the national community or of private associations, endeavor to sabotage those principles and procedures. Although experience of this sort is not yet sufficiently widespread to render any liberal society immune to the attractions of dictatorship, the development of private associations in many countries has gone far enough to show that this may be an effective means of consolidating modern liberalism.

Liberal weakness in the field of international organization would seem, at first glance, to be unrelated to the problem of private association. Actually there is reason to believe that the strengthening of organizational life within the various national communities of the Western world would indirectly improve the prospects of uniting those communities in a comprehensive liberal order. Nationalism in recent times has been the main obstacle to the adoption of constitutional procedures in the conduct of international relations. Like dictatorship, nationalism is largely a product of the organizational deficiencies of early liberalism. At a time when the commercial and industrial revolutions had destroyed or weakened most of the traditional institutions of Western society, and when alternative institutions had not yet had time to develop, the easiest way to find an outlet for temporarily thwarted social energies was to develop a quasi-religious sense of participation in the life of the nation state. Although the resulting habits of narrowly exclusive patriotism still persist, they are challenged by the ever-growing vitality of other forms of association. Ardent nationalists often find it shocking when private associations, as in the case of international cartels, negotiate mutually satisfactory agree-

ments without reference to the particular national interests of their respective countries. To people, however, who
are organized for the accomplishment of specific objectives, economic, religious, educational, and the like, the
concrete benefits of international coöperation are apt to
be more appealing than vague national sentiments. The
intransigent claims of extreme nationalism are relatively
alien, moreover, to the habits of a society in which most
men have learned through practical experience to appreciate the advantages of negotiation. Although the growth
of private associations can only exert a slow and indirect
influence on the conduct of international relations, it
should help to alleviate the difficulties of this particularly
crucial aspect of liberal government.

To further this growth is the most urgent task of contemporary liberalism. If people show sufficient wisdom
and energy in organizing for the attainment of group
objectives, totalitarianism will lose most of its appeal
within the Western world. If substantial numbers fail in
their daily lives to acquire the skills of free negotiation,
constitutional democracy will fail for lack of firm foundations. The conflict between dictatorship and democracy
is no mere matter of electoral battles and parliamentary
skirmishes, but an all-embracing struggle for the organization and control of social life. The outcome will depend
more on overall success in the discovery of practical solutions to concrete social problems than on any immediate
developments in the field of political thought. In the long
run, however, no movement can evoke the fullest energies
of its supporters unless it offers them an adequate theoretical justification for the things they are doing. The orthodox theory of modern liberalism is inadequate in that

it tends to inhibit rather than to encourage the organizational developments on which the future of liberalism depends. To overcome these obstacles is the basic problem of contemporary liberal thought.

Perhaps the most serious weakness of the orthodox theory is its continuing reliance on the absolutist concept of sovereignty. In practice, constitutional democracy presumes the existence of a pluralistically ordered society. While recognizing the value of central political authority, backed by coercive power, for the accomplishment of many social purposes, it subordinates the exercise of that authority to recognition of the independent claims of other social groups. The idea of creating social order by free negotiation rather than by arbitrary fiat, an idea underlying the operations of all constitutional governments, is incompatible with the conception of politics as an expression of the will of a single, irresistible sovereign. Although breakdowns in the process of negotiation may from time to time compel liberal societies to adopt dictatorial procedures for the sake of survival, these are temporary deviations from the norm of constitutional politics. Under ordinary conditions liberal governments are reluctant to impose policies which are unacceptable to any considerable segment of the population. This reluctance is so strong that it is apt to persist even in times of considerable stress. During the recent war hard-pressed government officials usually found it desirable to spend time negotiating with striking workers, rather than to coerce them by an act of sovereign will. Although Soviet purchasing agents sometimes expressed amazement that these workers were not summarily shot for treason, liberal opinion would have been unwilling to accept the propriety of so drastic a procedure. Continuing lip-service to the idea of sovereignty makes it difficult, however, to provide any clear-cut justification for the liberal as contrasted with the dictatorial position. Whenever, as in the case of labor disputes, hitches occur in the process of negotiation, it is tempting to look for an assertion of sovereign authority, and to level an accusation of weakness against liberal governments which, in spite of their theoretical claims to sovereignty, refrain from settling problems by arbitrary fiat. In the field of international relations the theory of sovereignty is even more tempting as an alternative to the labors of negotiation. Although formal acceptance of this theory has not kept liberal statesmen, especially in matters of domestic policy, from making substantial progress toward constitutional democracy, it has inhibited their efforts, and prevented the nature of their accomplishments from being appreciated. A clear break with this remnant of royal absolutism would add considerably to the prospects of modern liberalism.

A second, closely related weakness of orthodox liberal theory is the inadequacy of its recognition of the nature and functions of organized groups in the life of the liberal community. Contemporary totalitarian absolutists derive much of their power from the fact that their theory, by refusing to recognize the rights of any group not organized and directed by the party state, deprives the individual of capacity to resist the dictatorial elite. The theory of early liberalism, while devised for different ends, was hardly less unfavorable to the development of independent group action. For Locke and the philosophers of the Enlightenment, society was a collection of atomic individuals. Believing that an enlightened state was the only form of social organization necessary for the protection of individual rights, they disapproved strongly of all attempts to form trade unions and other private associations for the furtherance of group interests. Although nineteenth-century developments did much to modify liberal thought in the direction of increased respect for the importance of group action, remnants of the older tradition still remain to hinder an effective approach to the problems of contemporary group life. In a society where vital human interests depend on the activities of a wide variety of private associations, it is unrealistic to think of liberty exclusively in terms of the mutual relationships of individuals and states. Impairment of the rights of associations to which an individual belongs may be even more damaging than the impairment of his specifically individual rights. Despotic private associations may, on the other hand, be even more effective than despotic states in destroying the freedom of their members. Modern liberalism depends, therefore, not only on a careful definition of the mutual relations of individuals and states, but also on a no less careful definition of the rights and duties of private associations. Although liberal societies have made some progress toward delimiting these latter rights and duties, preoccupation with individual-state relationships has prevented them from proceeding with anything like the necessary vigor. The belated and fumbling efforts of American legislators to remedy the abuses of trade-unionism, or to eliminate antidemocratic aspects of the party primary system, are the fruit of a philosophy which long persisted in regarding the rights and duties of private associations as a matter of indifference. A more clear-cut recognition of the importance of group action would do much to strengthen the legal and theoretical foundations of constitutional government.

If the most promising lines of practical and theoretical development are followed, liberalism may succeed in providing an effective basis for the organization of the Western world. This in itself would not be enough, however, to guarantee its long-run survival. The spread of modern technology is rapidly giving rise to conditions which can only end in the creation of a single world order. Although the countries of the West, as pioneers in the use of that technology, are at present a good deal stronger than all other countries put together, this superiority cannot last indefinitely. In the long run, the greater population and resources of other areas, when combined with new technological skills, will give those areas a preponderance of economic and military power. If the influence of liberalism is confined, therefore, to the limits of the Western world, it cannot long survive the pressures of modern life. Western civilization has given potentially overwhelming technical resources to peoples whose ethical and social traditions are radically at variance with those which led to the development of modern liberalism. Unless the political thought and institutions of the West succeed in exercising a power of attraction comparable to that already exercised by Western technology, the achievements of Western civilization will have been self-defeating. The question of adapting constitutional democracy to the needs of non-European peoples should therefore be reckoned as a crucial problem of modern liberalism.

As far as the immediate future is concerned, this problem is probably insoluble. For countries inadequately equipped with the technical resources of modern civilization, the speedy introduction of that equipment is bound under present conditions to appear as a matter of life or death. The industrialization of a nonindustrial society involves so radical an interruption of established social habits that it can hardly take place by democratic means. The sacrifices entailed in any extensive program of capital investment are too extreme to appeal to those who, without enjoying the immediate benefits, must bear the principal burdens of the enterprise. Rapid modernization is therefore difficult to combine with a political system which subordinates the determination of economic and social policy to the will of a democratic electorate. In the earlier stages of Western industrialization strict limitation of the franchise made it possible for a small elite of middle-class enterprisers to introduce their innovations without considering the desires of the rest of the community. The contemporary role of dictatorial elites in Russia and other industrially backward countries is very much the same. Dictatorship, whether in its earlier colonial or in its modern totalitarian form, has proved historically to be the most effective means of imposing Western technology on non-European peoples. Beyond the limits of the Western world, the pressure for industrial modernization will probably continue to make dictatorship rather than democracy the predominant form of government for a considerable time to come.

Liberal countries are in a position, however, to mitigate and perhaps even, in some cases, to overcome these pressures. The economic rigors of modernization are most severe in societies which, like nineteenth-century Europe and contemporary Russia, are forced to withdraw capital savings from current production alone. This involves a highly unpopular sacrifice of present welfare in the interests of future consumption. To the extent, however, that it is possible to acquire capital from foreign rather than from domestic sources, the problem of present economic sacrifice does not arise. In spite of the destructive effects of two world wars, the economic progress of some democratic countries has been so remarkable that they are in a position, without impairing their own existing standard of living, to provide the rest of the world with substantial amounts of export capital. The availability of such capital will not in itself suffice to eliminate dictatorship. Entirely apart from the problems of capital accumulation, cultural resistances to the unfamiliar ways of industrialism will make it difficult to modernize many areas without some measure of dictatorial coercion. The fear of foreign domination in recently liberated colonial areas is so great, moreover, that many governments will be reluctant to make use of foreign capital resources. If well used, however, these resources could do much to mitigate the rigors of technological modernization, and to reduce the pressures which are now leading to the establishment and maintenance of many dictatorial governments.

Although the economic power of the liberal world offers useful possibilities of remedial action, no conceivable effort would suffice to prevent a major part of the human race from remaining under the influence of dictatorship for a considerable time to come. The important question is whether or not that influence is likely to be permanent. The answer depends primarily on the extent to which modern liberalism succeeds in providing an effective basis for the organization of the Western world itself. Contemporary dictatorships are engaged in introducing many features of Western civilization to a wide variety of non-Western peoples. In their emphasis on technical modernization they are reproducing many of the social and economic conditions which led, in nineteenth-century Europe, to the emergence of democratic self-government. In the case of communism, at least, they are also introducing many of the forms of democratic action, and teaching men, if only in theory, to believe that dictatorship is no more than a temporary phase in the evolution of modern politics. It is possible that the propaganda and police resources of the totalitarian state will make it possible for dictatorial elites, unlike the rulers of nineteenth-century Europe, to frustrate future movements toward genuine self-government in these areas. At the present time, however, it is too early to assume that this will be the case. Because of its leadership in the technological field, the Western world still enjoys a good deal of prestige. If liberalism succeeds in uniting the West in a strikingly effective political system, that system should be able to exert great powers of attraction upon non-European peoples. The hope of modern liberalism lies in the possibility that it may succeed by example in stimulating increasing numbers of dictatorships to evolve in the direction of constitutional democracy.

In view of the fact that the traditional background of most other peoples is markedly different from that of the West, the chance of converting them to liberalism might seem at first glance to be rather dim. In many important respects, however, democracy comes a good deal closer than dictatorship to conforming with the traditional ideas of most non-Europeans. Although other great religions have been rather less effective than Christianity in sensitizing their adherents to the necessity of alleviating human suffering, they also have encouraged ideals of human sympathy and brotherhood which can only with difficulty be reconciled with the more brutal manifestations of totalitarian coercion. The despotic empires of the ancient East differed from modern dictatorship, moreover, in their respect for the rights of traditional associations. Even under the most autocratic rulers of the past, the peoples of China and Japan, for example, were allowed a substantial degree of freedom in the management of their own affairs. This experience has given them a habit of loyalty to the family, the village, and to other organizations whose independence is incompatible with the centralizing requirements of totalitarian government. It is significant that when the Japanese militarists tried, under German influence, to impose a full-fledged totalitarian dictatorship on the Japanese people, the continuing resistance of family and other private groups made it impossible to carry out the program with anything like the thoroughness of Western totalitarianism. Constitutional democracy, with its emphasis on free negotiation between independent social groups, has much in common with the traditional pluralism of most non-European societies. When it comes, therefore, to a choice between dictatorship and democracy, there is some reason to believe that the latter will prove to be the more popular form of government for a large majority of the human race.

If a liberal world order were actually established, many of the specifically Western features of modern liberalism would undoubtedly suffer modification under the impact of alien traditions. Although it is impossible to predict the

final consequences of such an extensive intermingling of
cultures, the result might well be to strengthen rather than
to weaken the institutions of constitutional democracy.
The development of vigorous private associations, on
which the future of liberalism so largely depends, has had
in the Western world to contend against the divisive
effects of an extremely individualistic tradition. The more
fully developed group consciousness of other peoples, and
their inherited skill in the techniques of informal group
action, could serve as a useful counterbalance to the
excessive individualism of the West. The apocalyptic tradition, which makes it so difficult to satisfy Westerners
with the slow and plodding processes of parliamentary
government, is yet another aspect of Western liberalism
which might profit by contact with non-Western cultures.
People untouched by the Judaic conception of history,
with its vision of a future kingdom of heaven on earth, are
comparatively impervious to the apocalyptic promises
which have contributed so powerfully to the appeal of
totalitarian dictatorship in Europe. Although modern liberalism itself is a product of Western civilization it has
had to contend with forces of resistance inspired by other,
less favorable elements of the Western tradition. By modifying these forces of resistance the influence of other
cultures might help to remedy many of the present weaknesses of constitutional government.

In spite of the difficulties of its current situation there is
no reason to believe that modern liberalism is inevitably
doomed to extinction. Constitutional democracy, with all
its errors and deficiencies, still offers many promising lines
of future development. If liberal opportunities are wisely
and energetically pursued, both domestically and inter-

nationally, the theory and practice of liberalism should survive as a major component of the rapidly emerging world civilization of the future. There is no certainty, to be sure, that this promise will be realized. In a world living under the daily threat of military destruction the time available for liberal experimentation is dangerously short. If liberal statesmen fail in the near future to satisfy the prevailing hunger for economic and military security, the masses of mankind will turn with relief to the apparent simplicity and certainty of dictatorial solutions. To remedy the existing deficiencies of democracy in so short a time will be difficult, and may prove to be impossible. That the effort should be made, however, is a matter of the highest consequence. Liberalism offers the one last chance to preserve the characteristic achievements of Western civilization for the benefit of future generations.